PETER R. GLUCK &
RICHARD J. MEISTER

SOCIAL
CHANGES AND
INSTITUTIONAL
RESPONSES
IN URBAN
DEVELOPMENT

CITIES IN
TRANSITION

CITIES IN TRANSITION

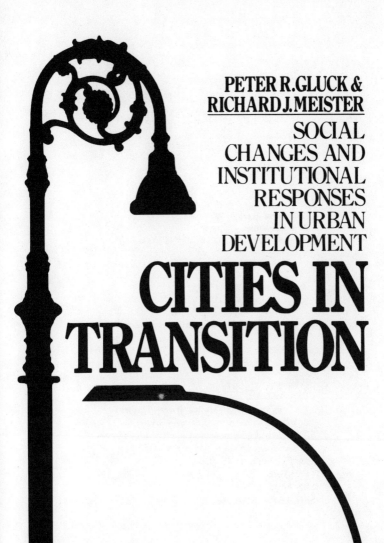

PETER R. GLUCK &
RICHARD J. MEISTER

SOCIAL
CHANGES AND
INSTITUTIONAL
RESPONSES
IN URBAN
DEVELOPMENT

CITIES IN TRANSITION

New Viewpoints
A Division of Franklin Watts
New York   London

New Viewpoints
A Division of Franklin Watts
730 Fifth Avenue
New York, New York 10019

Library of Congress Cataloging in Publication Date

Gluck, Peter R
    Cities in transition.

    Bibliography: p.
    Includes index.
    1. Cities and towns—United States—History.
    2. Urbanization—United States—History.
    3. Municipal government—United States—History.
    4. Sociology, Urban. I. Meister, Richard J.,
1938- joint author.   II. Title.
HT123.G568   301.36′0973   79-12214
ISBN 0-531-05409-8
ISBN 0-531-05623-6 pbk.

To our parents

Acknowledgments

A number of people have been extremely helpful in the preparation of this book. Our colleague in the Department of Sociology Professor Wilfred G. Marston patiently and painstakingly read and commented on an initial draft of the entire manuscript. Bill's willingness to offer timely, incisive, and constructive comments made the task of revising the initial draft more tolerable and valuable.

Our secretaries, Mrs. Betty Holloway in History and Mrs. DeAn McDaniel in Political Science, showed great patience and dependability as we worked through all the drafts of the manuscript. Then, too, our editor at New Viewpoints, Mr. Will Davison, offered advice and assistance, as well as encouragement and support, during the preparation of the manuscript.

Finally, a word of thanks goes to our families. Roberta, Jason, and Adam Gluck, and Joan, Chris, Erica, and Jon Meister; they endured many fatherless weekends as we worked to meet numerous self-imposed deadlines. Their support was essential.

To all of these people we express our gratitude and a share in the credit for the quality of this book. We, alone, bear responsibility for its liabilities and defects.

Peter R. Gluck
Richard J. Meister
University of Michigan—Flint

Acknowledgment

Contents

CITIES IN TRANSITION

CHAPTER I.

Introduction:
Understanding Urban Development

URBAN DEVELOPMENT IN PERSPECTIVE

Challenges of Urbanization

The most significant aspect of American urbanization is not the extent to which we have become an urban nation, but the fact that the process of urbanization has occurred within a relatively short time frame. When the first census was taken in 1790, 5 percent of the population was classified as urban. However, a hundred and fifty years later, the urban population accounted for 56 percent of the total population of 132 million. By the 1970s nearly three out of four Americans were classified as living within urban areas. These statistics dramatize the changes that occurred within society. Such changes generated instability and seriously weakened the existing institutions' ability to respond successfully to the resulting problems.

The purpose of this book is to examine from a historical and analytical perspective the way in which governance institutions responded to the challenges associated with rapid urban development. Our concern is less with the problems of urbanization per se and more with the role of governmental institutions in shaping those conditions. The literature on urbanization and metropolitanization is replete with analyses of and prescriptions for urban problems.[1] It is less helpful in providing an understanding of the social changes transpiring during urban development, and the role of governance institutions in meeting the challenges of growth associated with that development. Our hope is that this book will help to fill that gap by analyzing these social changes and describing the role of governance institutions in shaping responses to the

3

problems associated with it. Inasmuch as the challenges associated with urban development serve as the starting point for this analysis, it is useful to identify and examine them at this point.

The challenge facing the first urban dwellers in the United States was to establish a legal basis for cities. Governance arrangements in seventeenth-century cities reflected English precedents and the modification of these to fit the "new land" and the character of the people who immigrated to it. There were both differences and similarities among the major urban centers of the seventeenth and eighteenth centuries. The differences were reflected in the attitudes toward the indigent, the nature of urban services, types and powers of local government, extent of urban planning, degree of political participation, and the groups that held political power. This diversity was created by many of the same factors that account for the diversity of twentieth-century central cities. The manner of the founding of an urban center is an important factor in understanding its social and political characteristics. The people who first settled the community, more than those who came later, influenced the nature of local government.

The popular attitude toward government is an important factor determining the role of governance institutions in society. Take, for example, the admonition "that government is best which governs least." The doctrine made a lot of sense when the first census was taken in 1790. At that time, 95 percent of the American people lived on farms or in towns having fewer than 2500 persons. Compared to the situation in 1970, for example, when over 63 percent of the people lived in urban places and about 70 percent were residents of metropolitan areas, there was little for government to do. The men of the eighteenth century, while recognizing that governmental institutions were necessary, sought to limit and circumscribe the power of public officials by establishing a system of checks and balances at all levels. As a result, the approach to governmental organization was largely negative and preventive, i.e., government was to keep certain things from happening but not act in a positive manner vis-à-vis social conditions and change. In addition, the emphasis on and support for decentralizing political power and authority led to the establishment of autonomous, overlapping units of local government. With the passage of time these units not only remained but new ones were created to meet the challenges of growth in an increasingly urban society.

From the eighteenth until nearly the mid-nineteenth century, cities were limited in size and had virtually no mass transportation system. Land use was mixed with rich and poor living in close proximity to one another. Governance institutions played a limited role in providing services and facilities and most were provided privately, i.e., through voluntary organizations and philanthropic institutions. The opportunity for growth and development was met by men of wealth and ambition seeking a substantial return on their original investment. These men were the urban boosters. They advertised their cities as the best in the West, if not a new Athens, at least a second Philadelphia. New urban centers provided commercial services for the increasing number of farmers, merchants, and small manufacturing concerns established to provide goods for the local population. Local government, while limited in what it could do by state legislation, responded by fostering growth. Those in control of local politics, and thus governmental institutions, were the merchants, land speculators, and professional men, who had the most to gain from urban development. Services such as roads, canals, railroads, and docks were provided to assist the economy. While cities could not provide these alone, the local government, as an institution, was active in supporting state legislation or subsidies for these services.

Growth also created instability. The majority of the population, aside from the founding families and those with property, was always changing. There was a continual stream of transients passing through the city. The basic labor force was in flux. Services had to be established which not only encouraged growth but also created stability. Volunteerism was the first response to the need for stability but there were limits to what it could accomplish. Therefore, after the mid-nineteenth century urban America moved from the "private" city to the "public" city.

Complicating this were changes in the economic and political systems. By the mid-nineteenth century America had moved from a preindustrial to an industrial era and had adopted universal white male suffrage. In the latter half of the nineteenth century governance institutions were generally unsuccessful in responding to the social and economic developments and demands of the Industrial Revolution. The influx of large numbers of "deprived classes" brought demands for services and facilities that existing private institutions were unable to meet. The resulting gap between public needs and governmental responses had implications for the role of governance institutions and processes. Extragovernmental institutions developed to meet the increased demands of the growing central city population. Political machines evolved in central cities throughout the nation. They provided a variety of services to city residents in return for their votes on election day. The electoral support of selected groups was sufficient to keep machine candidates in control of governmental machinery which, in turn, enabled the machine to continue to benefit from jobs, preferential treatment from public officials, favors, etc.

The graft and corruption spawned by political machines have been thoroughly documented.[2] There is little doubt about the extent to which political bosses operated beyond the limits of the law. Though political machines served some useful and important purposes for the class, ethnic, and race groups who supported them, they also created the next major challenge in urban development. It was believed that machine-controlled local governments were not only corrupt and graft-ridden, but also inefficient and unresponsive to the needs of the city-as-a-whole. In response, the municipal reform movement was successful in altering the governmental structure and political processes of many cities. Council-manager and commission governments took the place of the mayor-council form of government, at-large election of city councils replaced ward-based election, and nonpartisan elections were held instead of partisan ones. In addition, civil service and other procedural reforms (in accounting and purchasing, for example) systematized and streamlined the conduct of the government's business and, not incidentally, took spoils out of public institutions.

The decade of the twenties was, in a number of ways, the pinnacle of the industrial city. The "professionalized" governmental institutions seemed to work quite well in a number of cities. As judged by the values of the largely white, middle-class bias of municipal reformers, "reformed" governments measured up to the expectations held of them. The decade was also one of growth, in terms of both population and bricks and mortar. Cities were prosperous; new institutions and welfare capitalism seemed to be meeting social needs.

However, the Depression, combined with the end of the era of expansion of the industrial city, ended the optimism of the twenties. It might be argued that even without the Depression major cities of the Midwest and Northeast had reached the limits of growth and development. The twenties began the age of the automobile and ended an era of annexation. Within the cities other important social changes occurred that had an impact in later years. The massive migration of rural blacks and whites, combined with the erosion of established ethnic communities and institutions, changed the character of central cities.

World War II provided a respite for the cities but the postwar period brought new challenges. These included increasing dissatisfaction of nonwhites and working classes with their representation in political and governmental institutions. Groups that had not benefited from reforms in the Progressive Era began to view city government as increasingly unresponsive. Another problem that began to make itself felt was the belief that city governments lacked direction, leadership, and clear lines of responsibility and accountability. Responses to these challenges involved yet another round of structural reform. The strong-mayor form of government became popular as a vehicle for improving the accountability and responsibility of elected officials. Also, for those cities wishing to retain professionalism in governmental administration, a chief administrative officer or city administrator was combined with the strong-mayor form of government. Many believed that this hybridized form would meet the needs of those who sought popular accountability and responsibility in government (the mayor) as well as those who wanted a professionally trained, experienced administrator responsible for the day-to-day operations (the chief administrative officer/city administrator).

The decades of the fifties and sixties marked the rapid growth of metropolitan areas and increasing urban unrest. While some central cities increased in population during the 1950s, this was more than offset by policies in housing and transportation which encouraged the development of autonomous communities lying beyond their boundaries. During the decade of the 1960s there was an increasing lack of confidence in the ability of city governments to alleviate the problems affecting the working-class and nonwhite populations. A number of responses were proposed to deal with these challenges. First, the federal government began to offer a variety of programs designed to deal with the social problems of urban development. Programs in housing, unemployment, urban renewal, and transportation were enacted and financed through categorical grants. Second, a new reform movement advocated metropolitan governmental reorganization that included structural and functional integration as well as interlocal cooperation and contracting. The metropolitan reform movement sought to reduce the inefficiency and complexity created by the presence of numerous small units of government in the same metropolitan area by integrating all governments into a single unit operating on an areawide basis. However, the advent of riots in many central cities in the mid- to late-1960s brought a demand for institutional reform in the other direction, i.e., decentralization of city governments to give local neighborhoods more control over the decision-making process as it affects the allocation of governmental dollars and activities.

The most recent challenge to confront cities, especially those in the Midwest and Northeast, has manifested itself in the 1970s. It may very properly be called the challenge of survival. It takes the form of a serious threat to the continued existence of central cities as autonomous, viable entities. After two and a half decades of federal grants-in-aid and at least two separate periods of institutional reform, cities appear to be no better off than they were at the turn of the twentieth century.

The question of whether America's central cities will deal effectively with this present challenge remains open. It is almost certain that cities will survive, but in what condition no one knows for sure. In some respects the conditions of eligibility for state and federal aid imposed on New York City radically altered the accepted and traditional notions of autonomy of local government.

The purpose of this analysis is not to predict whether and how cities will survive. Rather, it is to broaden our understanding of how cities developed and how decisions, made in the process of urban development, shaped responses to the challenge of change and most recently of survival.

INSTITUTIONAL RESPONSES IN URBAN DEVELOPMENT

The main focus of this book is the role of governance institutions in shaping responses to the problems associated with urban development. However, it needs to be understood at the outset that throughout much of American urban history responses to the problems associated with urban development were developed and initiated by social and political institutions existing outside the formal structure of government. The reason for this is that prior to the post-World War II era, cities were left more or less on their own to cope with the social problems of growth and development. There was certainly nothing approaching a coherent and comprehensive national urban policy. Moreover, programs enacted by the federal government often did as much to exacerbate as they did to alleviate the problems of urban development. For example, the "highways only" approach of federal transportation policy, beginning with the Federal Aid Road Act of 1916, did a great deal to improve interurban mobility; it also provided little assistance in dealing with the problems of intraurban mobility. In fact, the 1916 act stipulated that municipalities with populations of 2500 or more were prohibited from receiving federal benefits for highway construction. It wasn't until the Federal Highway Act of 1944 that federal policy recognized intraurban transportation needs.

State governments, for their part, did little to assist municipalities in coping with the challenges of change in urban development. In fact, some actions taken by the states limited the ability of cities to deal with their own problems. One of the notable instances of "benign neglect" by state government is in the area of legislative reapportionment. Despite the fact that by the end of the 1920s it was apparent that cities had become the centers of population and economic activity in many states, state legislatures did nothing to reapportion their representational districts to reflect changes in population, thus giving cities the increased representation in state government they deserved. As a result, many state governments remained under the control of rural and agrarian interests whose representatives seemed bent more on containing the problems of the cities than in helping to mount an effective response to them. It wasn't until the early 1960s that the United States

Supreme Court ordered the states to reapportion their legislatures, as well as the lower house of the U.S. Congress, in accordance with the principle of "one man, one vote." By then, of course, cities were already losing population to the outlying suburbs of metropolitan areas. As a result a rural-suburban coalition in state legislatures was able to shape or even dictate the states' responses to the problems of urban development. Reapportionment of state legislatures was, in a sense, too little too late.

The challenges of growth and survival have been met by cities with some admirable results. Indeed, governance institutions in the cities have at times taken a leading role in shaping and managing their own development. The nature and extent of that role is best understood by identifying and describing four patterns of behavior that characterize the relationship between challenges of development and institutional responses to them. We believe that those recurring patterns constitute a framework for understanding urban development. Hopefully, an understanding of these patterns will provide a greater measure of wisdom as we approach urban problems today.

Unifying and Diversifying Forces

The first pattern is the tension between forces which unify and diversify the urban network. Major unifying forces in the colonial urban network were the English urban traditions, including the chartering process, and the sociocultural influences of major English cities. In the eighteenth century the major unifying influence was the corporate charter which legally established commercial communities and gave them power over many economic matters. However, despite the fact that corporations represented the most popular governmental arrangement in English and colonial cities, the major colonial cities displayed considerable diversity in their governmental institutions. Such diversity among cities was also caused by different socioeconomic forces present in the colonial cities.

With the end of royal authority a second unifying influence emerged in the form of state authority. In the post-Revolutionary era cities were uniformly considered creatures of their respective states. In fact, cities were legally municipal corporations of states and received their charters from state governments. The city-state relationship was also a source of diversity, however, inasmuch as there existed considerable variation in the way states treated their municipalities. Some states, for example, made broad grants of authority to local governments while others were not nearly so generous, establishing severe limitations on the nature and exercise of power by municipal governments.

The presence of these and other unifying forces has supported a unitary conception of cities. The essence of such a conception is the belief that cities are similar in origin, development, and condition. Consequently, problems of development can be approached with a uniform and comprehensive policy. The unitary view can be very misleading, however, as reflected in one of the most recent phenomena of urban development, the growth and prosperity of newer Sunbelt cities. A substantial body of data indicates that Sunbelt cities are enjoying socioeconomic prosperity and vibrance while their counterparts in the industrialized Northeast and Midwest suffer economic decline and an outmigration of the middle class to the suburbs. The central cities in the older, industrialized states are becoming increasingly populated by ethnic and racial minorities, a large percentage of whom are poor.[3]

The importance of the unitary conception, whether it is an accurate one or not, lies in the fact that many of those who shape the policy responses to the problems of development seem to work from it. For example, when it became apparent that city governmental institutions in the late nineteenth century needed to be freed from the dominance of political machines, a municipal reform movement that was national in scope took shape. It treated the institutional shortcomings of all cities as similar and prescribed a comprehensive set of reforms, structural as well as procedural, for implementation on a nationwide basis.

We believe that a more accurate conception of cities recognizes the pluralistic nature of the urban development experience. Such a view does not reject the idea that cities have similar experiences as they grow and respond to the challenges of change and survival. Rather, it subscribes to the belief that different patterns of social change produce different institutional responses to the problems associated with urban development. It is our view that the role of governmental institutions in urban development is influenced by these different patterns of social change. This brings us to a second pattern of behavior in urban development.

Influence of Socioeconomic Forces on Governance Institutions

The role of a city's governance institutions has been shaped by social changes associated with urbanization. These changes are mediated through a city's political process. Thus, the institutional arrangements used to govern cities, and through which they respond to the challenges of development, are a reflection of the relative influence of social groups and economic interests existing at different stages of development. In consequence, responses to the problems associated with urban development reflect the interests of these groups. This premise is particularly important, for it means that the policies initiated by state or national governments must be channeled through a city's governance institutions which can reject or modify, or even initiate on their own, responses that must be acceptable to the prevailing coalition of interests.

The emergence of political machines in the late nineteenth century is an example of the operation of this pattern of behavior in urban development. The influence of working-class ethnic groups that supported political machines was mediated through the party organization and its control of city government.

Most city governments existing in the mid-nineteenth century were unprepared to meet the economic, social, and political demands created by the migration to the industrializing cities of large numbers of Europeans and rural Americans. Existing political and governmental institutions were unable to absorb these newcomers. Moreover, governmental institutions were too fragmented and lacked the effective coordination needed to provide the public services and facilities necessary to manage a large, diverse, and expanding industrial society.

The municipal reform movement of 1900 also shows the influence of socioeconomic forces on governmental structure. This predominantly middle-class, business-oriented movement prescribed changes in political and governmental institutions and processes designed to mitigate the consequences of the working-class, immigrant-orientation of political machines. A number of structural and procedural reforms, including city manager and commission government, nonpartisan and at-large elections, and civil service, were incorporated into the reform agenda to weaken political machines and their control of city governmental institutions and practices.

Metropolitan reform in the mid-twentieth century shows the influence of a middle-class-based, business-oriented concern for economy and efficiency. Here we find the tradition of "good government" advocating reorganization of governmental units in metropolitan areas to eliminate overlapping jurisdictions, reduce duplication of functions and services, and increase the economy and efficiency of local governments. The agenda of metropolitan reform sought to integrate the structure of government through annexation, city-county consolidation, or metropolitan federation. Difficulties encountered in trying to achieve an areawide governmental system led metropolitan reformers to advocate functional integration through such measures as interlocal cooperation and agreements, service contracts, and regional coordination through the use of councils of government.

The decade of the 1960s saw dissatisfaction by minorities and the urban poor contribute yet another dimension to the influence of socioeconomic interests on city governmental structure. This time, however, reformers demanded greater responsiveness by government through decentralization and community control at the neighborhood level. The result of this struggle for reform was a plethora of administrative and political changes designed to give city residents more control over government decisions and services. Arrangements seeking to achieve this objective included community control, little city halls, neighborhood service centers, and citizen participation in Community Action and Model Cities programs.

In virtually every instance demand for structural reform in city government grew out of dissatisfaction with the way in which the institutions of government were responding to the problems associated with urban development. This dissatisfaction recurs with sufficient regularity to constitute the third pattern of institutional behavior in urban development.

Failure of Governmental Institutions
to Meet the Challenges of Development

Governmental institutions in the cities have generally been unable to meet the challenges posed by urban development. This is particularly true with respect to providing increased and more varied public services and facilities.

Prior to the emergence of political machines, the nineteenth century can be described as the era of the "private city." Citizens' needs for services and assistance were met by subscription drives, private philanthropies, and charitable organizations. Even the most basic of services like police and fire protection were provided through private, volunteer efforts, as most cities did not move to establish an organized police force until well into the nineteenth century.

Municipal reformers found fragmentation and paralysis a pervasive and common feature of local government. Nowhere was this more in evidence than in Galveston, Texas. In 1900, a hurricane and a flood devastated the city, and local government was unable to take timely and effective action. As a result, city government as it existed at that time was suspended; a temporary arrangement, known as the Galveston Commission, was established to organize and supervise the relief and recovery effort. The commission was so successful that it was later installed as the form of government on a permanent basis. In a short period of time cities across the nation used the Galveston model of commission government as the basis of their own efforts at governmental reform.

The post-World War II trend toward the use of special districts is one of the more recent steps taken in metropolitan areas to deal with the failure of governmental institutions to meet the challenges of urban development. Special districts became popular for a number of reasons, not the least of which was the fact that existing geographic boundaries and governmental institutions were unable to develop appropriate responses to demands for specialized and areawide services and facilities. As a result, special districts were set up to provide for water and sewage treatment, parks and recreational facilities, transportation systems, public housing, and other public services. In all cases the services provided by special districts are governed and operated outside the existing structure of general purpose local government.

It is difficult to assess the failure of governmental institutions to meet the challenges of urban development without considering the fact that cities have enjoyed a rather special and limited role in the American federal system. This brings us to the fourth and final pattern of institutional behavior in urban development.

Subordination of Cities to a Higher Authority

Throughout their history, American cities have always been subordinate to a higher authority. In colonial times cities were subject to the authority and control of the Crown; immediately after the Revolution state government stepped in to fill the vacuum created by the departure of royal authority. In the twentieth century cities have come to rely increasingly on the federal government. Unlike the state-city relationship, however, that between cities and the federal government is more subtle and less legalistic in nature. It tends to manifest itself in the imposition of eligibility requirements and performance standards for federal grants-in-aid.

Local governments in the United States are creatures of the states and have always been so. The states set the ground rules for municipalities in laws, constitutions, and administrative regulations. Through these means the states have always been able to determine the structure and much of the procedure used by city governments, including their territorial size, service and regulatory powers, and financial authority. In point of fact, cities and other units of local government owe their very existence and legal status to their respective states.

Throughout the history of urban development states have chosen to define the powers and responsibilities of municipalities in widely varying but commonly restrictive ways. For example, most states impose strict limitations on the right of municipalities to bond for capital improvements. In addition, states frequently impose restrictions on the kinds and rates of taxes cities can levy for operating revenues. Limitations of these kinds are frequently written into state constitutions and municipal charters, a feature that makes them almost impossible to change. The permanence of such restrictions on the powers of city government most certainly impairs the ability of cities to play an active and positive role in responding to the problems of urban development.

It is sometimes suggested that home rule, advocated by municipal reformers in the early part of the twentieth century, would free American cities from the restrictive circumstances and consequences of their subordinate status vis-à-vis state authority. However, we find that variations in the way states grant or withhold home rule from cities creates widely divergent situations from one state to another. Home rule is available to all cities and villages in Oregon and Wisconsin, while in other instances, California and Colorado, home rule is available only to cities and villages that meet or exceed a minimum population standard. Some states, Washington and Pennsylvania, grant home rule powers to a limited number of cities, while other states, Arizona and Nebraska, make home rule for cities a self-executing provision of the state constitution. Texas and Wisconsin require the passage of legislation before a city can adopt a home rule charter. Whatever the variations the presence of home rule is preferable to its absence; yet home rule powers do not alter a city's basic subordinate status to state government.

State governments have on occasion imposed other, more specific limitations on the ability of cities to respond to local conditions and problems associated with urban development. It was common practice in the early twentieth century for state governments to enact legislation controlling the conditions under which cities could expand through annexation or consolidation. While some states, Oklahoma and Texas, have made it relatively easy for incorporated municipalities to annex adjacent territories, most have established conditions and requirements that render annexation extremely difficult.

It seems fair to say that the subordination of cities to state governments resulted in the existence of conditions that made a positive and active role for city government in dealing with the challenges of urban development all but impossible. Moreover, the attitude of the states toward the problems of urban development has vacillated between ambivalence and hostility.

In the absence of assistance from state governments, the federal government has moved with great dispatch to assist cities in overcoming the problems and challenges of change. Too often, however, this has resulted in the imposition of yet another subordinate relationship for city government. Since World War II there has appeared in federal-city relationships a myriad of legislative and administrative regulations and conditions associated with eligibility for federal programs. These have had the effect of making cities dependent upon the priorities and attitudes of Congress and its committees and executive branch agencies. From the vantage point of city hall, federal-city relationships have substituted (or even added) one set of masters (federal) for (or to) another.

It is our belief that the four patterns of institutional behavior in urban development provide a valuable and informative framework for understanding the role of governance institutions in responding to the challenges of change and survival associated with urbanization. To complete this framework, however, we need to examine two trends that have influenced the role of governance institutions in urban development. These are, first, the movement from scarcity to abundance in human and material resources and, second, the movement from the "private" to the public city.

The influence of abundance on those who immigrated to America has been thoroughly documented and explored by people like J. Hector St. John de Crevecoeur in the eighteenth century and David Potter in the twentieth century.[4] Both show how the abundance of resources in the United States shaped not only the American character but also popular expectations of the role of public institutions in society.

Recently Zane Miller has argued that a return to scarcity is one of the most significant features characterizing contemporary urban society.[5] He points out that the seventeenth century, dominated and defined by the assumption of scarcity, led to public policies enacted by a central authority based on the premise that both material and human resources were limited and finite. This justified a role for governance institutions that involved economic regulation and control to assure survival. After the mid-seventeenth century, however, underlying assumptions about scarcity and the concomitant need for regulation and centralized control began to change as a variety of natural and technological developments made possible an abundance of resources. Attitudes toward the role of government changed accordingly. As Miller puts it,

> Cities, though traditionally conceived as commercial corporations for regulatory purposes, had in fact functioned as dynamic factors in social, economic, and cultural development.... The emergence of the society of plenty helped shift the perception of the role of cities to mesh with their traditional and very real functions. Simply put, the reduction of the emphasis on commercial community in the definition of municipalities made it easier to see cities as stimulators rather than as regulators of economic and social development.[6]

Miller suggests that the urban scene is now experiencing a return to scarcity, not so much because resources or human capabilities have diminished but because such trends as zero population, limited economic growth, the energy crisis, and the end of the migration of blacks and whites from the rural South to the urban North have imposed limits on what can be done with existing resources. If this interpretation is correct, then attitudes toward the role of governance institutions in effecting urban development will have to undergo yet another change. Expectations of what government can do to deal with the problems associated with urban development will have to be reconciled with the return to scarcity.

The second movement, from the "private" to the public city, draws on the ideas of Jon Teaford, Bayrd Still, and Sam Bass Warner, Jr.[7] From colonial times until the nineteenth century many services provided in the cities were under private auspices. A variety of techniques were used, including subscription drives, private philanthropies, and charitable organizations. By the end of the second half of the nineteenth century, however, the influence of abundance had combined with the technological advances of the Industrial Revolution to break down prevailing attitudes about the provision of services. As a result, public sponsorship and delivery of services became increasingly common. Government at all levels, including city government, assumed an increasing role in providing residents with services, including police and fire protection, street maintenance, health and safety regulations, etc. The programs of the New Deal firmly established an active role for government in maintaining public welfare.

It is important to understand the consequences of a return to scarcity for the survival of the public city. If, indeed, scarcity of resources is again part of the urban scene, then the role of governance institutions in urban development will be circumscribed by the finite and limited availability of those resources. Assumptions about abundance that helped to create and sustain the public city will have to be modified (if not replaced) to reflect scarcity. Failure to modify public attitudes about the role of governance institutions in urban development will result in an ever-growing and deepening chasm between popular expectations and governmental performance in responding to the challenges of change and survival.

PLAN OF THE BOOK

The historical and analytic approaches used to understand the social changes and role of governance institutions in urban development are reflected in the scope and content of the chapters that follow. Chapter II, "Urban Government in the Eighteenth Century," and Chapter III, "Urban Governance in the Nineteenth Century," provide an overview of the evolution and transformation of urban government during the eighteenth and nineteenth centuries. We see the four patterns of institutional behavior take shape. Also, the two trends that shape popular attitudes toward the role of governance institutions in urban development are traced from their beginnings in the eighteenth century. It is important to understand that these patterns of behavior and attitudinal changes, while they evolved in the earliest stages of American urbanization, have affected urban development and the role of governance institutions up to the present day. Chapters II and III are largely historical in approach, therefore, providing the groundwork for subsequent analyses of governance institutions in urban development.

In chapters IV, V, and VI we examine one of the most critical periods in urban development, the Progressive Era and municipal reform movement of the late nineteenth and early twentieth centuries. Chapter IV, "Political Machines and Urban Development," analyzes the evolution of political machines as a consequence of social changes brought on by the Industrial Revolution. As part of that analysis, we attempt to provide a balanced understanding of the role played by political machines in American cities during the first quarter of the twentieth century.

Political machines were not an unmixed blessing, however, and Chapter V, "Municipal Reform and Institutional Change in the Cities," looks at the conceptions and prescriptions of municipal reformers. The excesses of political machines contributed to a ground swell of reforms in the structure and procedures of city government and politics. Following the presentation and analysis of municipal reform, Chapter VI, "Aftermath of Reform," considers the experiences of a number of cities with reformed governmental institutions. Our purpose in this chapter is not to provide a comprehensive analysis of the performance of reformed institutions, but rather to indicate that that performance did not always meet the expectations of the reformers themselves. Moreover, we see in Chapter VI that some features of city government and politics were resistant to change while others produced later reforms of their own.

Chapter VII, "Eclipse of the Central City," examines the social changes in the initial decades of the twentieth century that contributed to the emergence of suburban communities adjacent to or beyond the boundaries of cities. It is this development that is referred to as "metropolitanization." We see the seeds of metropolitanization sown in the 1920s and 1930s and harvested with considerable speed in the post-World War II period. Our focus on the role of governance institutions in urban development shifts momentarily to the federal level, whose programs are viewed in the context of encouraging settlement and incorporation of suburban communities.

The consequences of metropolitanization on the role of governance institutions in urban development are examined in chapters VIII and IX. Chapter VIII, "Metropolitan Reform and Urban Development," examines governmental organization in metropolitan areas in the mid-twentieth century and the related movement for metropolitan reform and governmental reorganization. As with the earlier effort at municipal reform, we see metropolitan reform growing out of dissatisfaction with the way in which city and suburban governmental institutions respond to the challenges of change.

While the metropolitan reform movement was attempting to reorganize government on an areawide basis, a separate reform movement, advocating decentralization and community control, was taking shape and gaining momentum in the central cities. Chapter IX, "The Community Revolution in the Central Cities," looks at social developments and federal promotion of citizen participation in urban programs. These helped to shape the demand for community control that has characterized urban development since the mid-1960s to the present.

Chapter X, "Urban Development and the Challenges of Change and Survival," pulls together the analyses of the preceding chapters. We show how the patterns of institutional behavior in urban development have continued to the present and we consider the implications of a reappearance of scarcity of resources. Much of this discussion views urban development as involving a challenge of survival rather than a challenge of change. Though we do not foresee the disappearance of cities, we must consider whether they can survive as the viable and autonomous entities they once were. The plight of New York City, where eligibility for guaranteed federal loans makes it a virtual ward of state and federal governments, raises the question of whether urban governance institutions will be able to meet the challenge of survival in urban development. Moreover, the differential experiences of two cities, Detroit and Houston, are portrayed as examples of the challenges of change and survival in urban development.

NOTES

1. See, for example, the following recently published analyses of urban problems and policies: Edward C. Banfield, *The Unheavenly City* (Boston: Little, Brown, 1970); David A. Caputo, *Urban America: The Policy Alternatives* (San Francisco: W. H. Freeman, 1976); Robert A. Dentler, ed., *Urban Problems: Perspectives and Solutions* (Chicago: Rand McNally, 1977); Anthony Downs, *Urban Problems and Prospects*, 2d ed. (Chicago: Rand McNally, 1976); Leonard J. Duhl, *The Urban Condition* (New York: Basic Books, 1963); William Gorham and Nathan Glazer, eds., *The Urban Predicament* (Washington, D.C.: The Urban Institute, 1976); Melvin R. Levin, *The Urban Prospect* (Belmont, Calif.: Wadsworth Publishing, 1977); Louis K. Loewenstein, ed., *Urban Studies: An Introductory Reader*, 2d ed. (New York: The Free Press, 1977); H. R. Mahood and Edward I. Angus, eds., *Urban Politics and Problems: A Reader* (New York: Charles Scribner's Sons, 1969); and Daniel P. Moynihan, ed., *Toward a National Urban Policy* (New York: Basic Books, 1970).

2. Lincoln Steffens, *The Shame of the Cities* (1904; reprint ed., New York: Hill and Wang, 1957), and *The Autobiography of Lincoln Steffens* (New York: Harcourt, Brace and World, 1931).

3. See William Gorham and Nathan Glazer, eds., *The Urban Predicament* (Washington, D.C.: The Urban Institute, 1976), pp. 15-22.

4. J. Hector St. John de Crèvecoeur, "What Is an American?" in *Letters from an American Farmer* (1782); and David M. Potter, *People of Plenty: Economic Abundance and the American Character* (Chicago: University of Chicago Press, 1973).

5. Zane L. Miller, "Scarcity, Abundance, and American Urban History," *Journal of Urban History* 4 (February 1978): 131-55. See also, "Urban Crisis, Urban History, and Public Policy," *Urbanism: Past and Present* I (Winter, 1975-1976): 1-6.

6. *Ibid.*, p. 137.

7. Sam Bass Warner, Jr., *The Private City: Philadelphia in Three Periods of Its Growth* (Philadelphia: University of Pennsylvania Press, 1968); Bayrd Still, "Patterns of Mid-Nineteenth Century Urbanization in the Middle West," *Mississippi Valley Historical Review* 28 (September 1941): 187-206; Jon C. Teaford, *The Municipal Revolution in America: Origins of Modern Urban Government, 1650-1825* (Chicago: University of Chicago Press, 1975).

CHAPTER II.

Urban Government in the Eighteenth Century

Introduction

This chapter and the next will provide a brief survey of the transformation of urban government during the eighteenth and nineteenth centuries. Such an overview is necessary for developing an understanding of what has happened and is happening to American cities in the twentieth century. During the seventeenth and eighteenth centuries we see the appearance of four patterns of behavior in urban development. These patterns will recur in the nineteenth and twentieth centuries. The first of these patterns, the tension between the influences which unify and those which create diversity, is seen in the governance structures established in the colonies. While the majority of urban communities were governed by political institutions similar to those found in England, three of the five largest cities established different governance institutions, reflecting the socioeconomic character of their founders. Other unifying influences were the urban traditions and experiences carried to the New World by the first few generations of urban dwellers. Yet, these traditions and experiences were modified in different ways by the environmental influences of North America. For example, the environment made urban life and institutions in Charleston, South Carolina, much different than in Philadelphia or Boston. The second pattern evident in urban development is the interplay of socioeconomic forces and governmental institutions. In the early eighteenth century these institutions provided far less regulation of economic interests in Boston than in New York and Philadelphia. At the same time the sense of civic responsibility was more developed in Boston and Philadelphia than in New York or Charleston because of socioeconomic forces. However, the challenge presented by growth generally was not met successfully by the existing governmental institutions. This led to a third pattern of behavior, the failure of these institutions to meet the needs of a growing urban society. Reformers pushed for modification of existing structures or the establishment of new ones. In Boston and New York, because the existing structures were more amenable to meeting the increasing needs of society, they underwent modification during the eighteenth century. Those of Philadelphia and Charleston were static and thus failed to meet the needs of society. However, reformers generally were not satisfied with the ability of the governance institutions of their respective cities to meet the needs of a growing urban society. As a result, in the aftermath of the Revolution they called on the state governments to intervene and end the autonomy that cities had previously enjoyed. Thus we see the fourth pattern, the subservience of cities to a higher authority.

In addition to these four patterns of behavior in urban development, the eighteenth and nineteenth centuries witnessed the appearance of two cyclical movements that continue to affect American cities. The first of these is the transition from an assumption of scarcity to an assumption of abundance in determining the structure and role of governance institutions. It was this change in assumptions that made possible, according to Jon Teaford, the municipal revolution in America. In this chapter we will trace the impact of this movement from scarcity to abundance on urban governance institutions. A second and related cyclical movement is what we might describe as the transition from the "private" city to public city. In other words, there was a change in the way society provided the services, which today we would describe as being public. We use the term "private" to refer to the providing of urban services in a voluntary manner or through subscription. When the city was seen primarily as a commercial rather than a residential community, it was assumed that most urban services would be provided privately. However, with the advent of the residential community, urban governments began to become involved in providing for the health and well-being of their citizens. While this involvement in providing services began in the eighteenth century, it is not until after the mid-nineteenth century that we see the end of what we might call the "private" city. The next chapter will examine this movement in some detail.[1]

THE URBAN SCENE IN THE EIGHTEENTH CENTURY

Urban centers played a crucial role in the process of colonizing the New World. This is true whether we speak of the English, French, Spanish, or

TABLE 1
Colonial Cities: Estimated Population and Type of Government

City	Estimated Population (Date)	Type of Government[4]
Philadelphia	28,000 (1775)[1]	Closed Corporation
New York	23,000 (1775)[1]	Open Corporation
Boston	17,000 (1775)[1]	Nonincorporated
Charleston	10,863 (1770)[1]	Nonincorporated
Newport (R.I.)	9,209 (1774)[1]	Nonincorporated
New Haven	8,295 (1771)[2]	Nonincorporated
Norwich (Conn.)	7,032 (1774)[2]	Nonincorporated
Norfolk	6,250 (1775)[3]	Closed Corporation
Baltimore	5,934 (1775)[1]	Commission Government
New London (Conn.)	5,366 (1774)[2]	Nonincorporated
Salem (Mass.)	5,337 (1776)[1]	Nonincorporated
Lancaster (Pa.)	5–6,000 (1776)[3]	Open Corporation
Hartford (Conn.)	4,881 (1774)[3]	Nonincorporated
Middletown (Conn.)	4,680 (1775)[3]	Nonincorporated
Portsmouth (Maine)	4,590 (1775)[3]	Nonincorporated
Marblehead (Mass.)	4,386 (1775)[3]	Nonincorporated
Providence (R.I.)	4,361 (1774)[3]	Nonincorporated
Albany (N.Y.)	4,000 (1776)[3]	Open Corporation
Annapolis (Md.)	3,700 (1775)[3]	Closed Corporation
Savannah (Ga.)	3,200 (1775)[3]	Open Corporation
Williamsburg (Va.)	2,000 (1775)[1]	Closed Corporation
Burlington (N.J.)	1,750 (1750)[1]	Open Corporation
Elizabeth (N.J.)	1,500 (1750)[1]	Open Corporation
New Brunswick (N.J.)	1,300 (1750)[1]	Open Corporation
Schenectady (N.Y.)	1,500 (1775)[1]	Open Corporation
Wilmington (Del.)	1,229 (1775)[1]	Open Corporation
Perth Amboy (N.J.)	1,200 (1775)[1]	Open Corporation
Newcastle (Pa.)	1,000 (1725)[1]	Closed Corporation

SOURCE: [1] Ernest S. Griffith, *History of American City Government: The Colonial Period* (New York: Oxford University Press, 1938), pp. 448–49.

[2] Actual Census, Carl Bridenbaugh, *Cities in the Wilderness* (New York: Ronald Press, 1938), pp. 6n, 143, 303n; *Cities in Revolt* (New York: Capricorn, 1955), pp. 5, 216–17.

[3] *Ibid.* Census figures compiled by Bridenbaugh from a number of sources.

[4] Griffith, pp. 194n, 448–49.

Dutch process of empire building. By the latter part of the eighteenth century more than a score of urban centers had been established by the English, some well over a century old. Beyond the English colonies were urban communities founded by the French and the Spanish. Cities like New Orleans and St. Augustine were well-established, thriving centers of trade and administration. Others, such as the trading posts of St. Louis and Detroit and the missions of Tucson and San Francisco, were just beginning to develop.[2]

On the eve of the American Revolution the urban network along the Eastern seaboard was similar to that evident today (see table 1). While the number of urban dwellers in British North America represented less than 10 percent of the total population, they have left a lasting influence on the succeeding generations. The major urban centers were typical of preindustrial cities. There was a considerable amount of mixed land use with homes and places of employment often on the same site. The city's elite tended to live in the center of the community near their places of business and the center of government. The poor were on the fringe of the city, especially along the waterfront. Despite the more visible class distinctions than we have today, one finds in the eighteenth century that the rich and the poor, the established family and the newcomer, lived in close proximity to one another because of the limitation on the size of the physical city.[3]

While the cities were compact and small, compared to today, their influence was very important. These coastal centers, while looking across the ocean for direction, were themselves influencing the developing communities of the hinterland. The rural areas and small communities close to these urban centers were very much under their social and economic influence.

In the major urban centers the members of the elite came to see themselves less as Englishmen and more as Americans. These urban dwellers had an increasing self-confidence and awareness of responsibility for having established a livable, functioning society. They had formed an urban network in America, developed workable responses to many urban problems, modified existing governance structures or created new ones, and given the early American cities a character that has survived to the present.

COLONIAL GOVERNMENTAL FORMS

While colonial cities adopted a number of different governmental forms, most were chartered, i.e., given legal status by the Crown or Parliament. In England and in the colonies these charters were viewed as unalterable contracts. Thus the city developed a unique status within the framework of British government. These municipal corporations evolved out of the economy of scarcity and were primarily concerned with establishing a viable community so that trade and industry could flourish. As a result the main concern was to regulate and promote commerce, i.e., to provide an environment that would ensure economic justice and prosperity. To bring this about the corporation subsidized and regulated the economy. The corporation was responsible for marketing facilities as well as prices charged in the market. Bounties were provided to ensure that the community had access to certain skills. Such services as public works, poor relief, and education were secondary in terms of their importance. But by the mid-eighteenth century economic regulation became less necessary as the British Empire moved toward a capitalistic economy.[4]

The officials of the corporation exercised judicial, administrative, financial, and legislative powers. Representation on the ruling council tended to be based on economic interest. The municipal corporation enjoyed a protected status within the British Empire, since it obtained its original charter from the Crown (government) and acquired additional exemptions as time passed. The council had the power to admit "freemen" into the city. This status was necessary before one could be accepted into a particular craft and in the open corporation was a prerequisite for voting.[5]

As colonies were established in the seventeenth century, many of their urban centers were chartered according to the English practice. But the charters were not granted directly by Parliament or the king but by a legally defined authority within the colony. In New York, New Jersey, Pennsylvania, and Maryland, power was held by the proprietors. In the royal colonies the right to grant charters was vested in the royal governor who ruled in the name of the Crown. By 1750 there were over a score of chartered corporations in the colonies.[6]

There were two types of chartered, municipal corporations within the colonies: the closed corporation and the open corporation. The closed corporation was ruled by a council that was self-perpetuating. When a member died or resigned, the council would select a successor. Thus the charter named the original officers, the mayor, aldermen, and others, and vested in them the right to select their own successors. Philadelphia was the largest city governed by a closed corporation. Others included Germantown and Newcastle, Pennsylvania, Williamsburg and Norfolk, Virginia, St. Marys and Annapolis, Maryland. Sixteen cities were open corporations, i.e., ruled by elected officials. Local circumstances account for the variation between open and closed corporations in colonial cities. The cities in New York were open corporations largely because of the Dutch influence which Ernest S. Griffith argued was more democratic than the English tradition. Certain New Jersey cities were chartered as open corporations because they had previously had the town meeting form of government. Thus, this open status represented an evolution of what had previously been established.[7]

A number of urban centers lacked municipal charters. Of the ten largest urban centers on the eve of the Revolution only New York, Philadelphia, and Norfolk had municipal charters. The five New England cities, as with all New England communities, were governed by the town meeting and two, Charleston and Baltimore, were governed by other forms. Charleston, according to Carl Bridenbaugh, was the worse governed city in the colonies. One reason for this was the form of government. Charleston had no charter; it was governed by the colonial assembly. The assembly, made up of the planter aristocracy, enacted legislation to keep the city operating, but had little concern for making Charleston livable. Power was delegated to the vestry of the parish and to various commissions to oversee streets, night watch, fire prevention, and the markets. Commissions were also used in England and the colonial chartered cities to deal with new problems. This occurred in Philadelphia, where the closed corporation was bypassed and control over administering the night watch was placed under a commission. Southern colonial assemblies utilized the commission form to govern small, unchartered trading centers. In Baltimore, the commission form was established to govern not a small town nor a specific aspect of service but the entire community.[8]

Variation in city governments and the differences in powers and responsibilities specified in charters make it difficult to develop a working definition of city for the colonial period. Some urban areas could not be called cities in the legal sense because they lacked a municipal charter. Others, while legally designated as cities by their charters, could not be considered as such because of a small population and an absence of economic diversity. Certain cities were very compact while others included enormous tracts of land. For example, Albany, New York, was thirteen miles long and one mile wide. Diversity, in terms of legal status, size, or governmental structure, characterizes American cities from colonial times to the present.[9]

THE COLONIAL CITY IN TRANSITION

New England Communities

Only in New England was there a break with the English urban tradition. The New England cities began as religious communities, based on the covenant ideology of Puritanism. The political structure was designed to protect the religious community and to ensure its vitality. As a result the civil covenant was based on participation and consensus. The town meeting guaranteed this. In the early years the franchise depended not on wealth or social standing but on church membership. However, Massachusetts ended this practice, as far as local elections were concerned, in 1648.[10]

During the first fifty years town meetings usually were held four times a year. There was a minimum of political conflict and few formal votes were actually taken. Consensus was the prevailing style of decision making. Voters elected "selectmen" and other officials to conduct the day-to-day affairs of local government, as well as to settle disputes. By the late seventeenth century a change had taken place in even the smallest towns. By then the town meetings, which were held as often as once a month, generated a great deal of political activity and conflict over issues. The power of the selectmen was diminished and ad hoc committees were established to respond to the new problems and concerns. The franchise requirements were tightened and the nature of the economy made it more difficult for an individual to satisfy property qualifications necessary to vote. Class lines were manifest, especially in Boston, where wealth inequality increased during the eighteenth century. By the middle of the century only 16 percent of the men of Boston were eligible to vote, with less than one-fourth of these exercising this right.[11]

Boston, the largest of the New England communities, differed from the other major colonial cities. While Philadelphia and New York aldermen were concerned with matters of commerce, only 9 percent of the bylaws enacted in Boston in 1701 dealt with economic matters, and 56 percent concerned matters of public safety, order, and peace. Boston of the eighteenth century opposed restrictions on vocational opportunity and favored economic competition. Boston, unlike other cities, had no public marketplace. Boston also was not independent of the more centralized power of the Massachusetts assembly, the General Court. Despite the cumbersome aspects of governing a large urban center with institutional arrangements appropriate for a smaller community, Bostonians more than once opposed the move to obtain a municipal charter. The basic argument against incorporation was a fear of monopoly. More specifically the arguments included a fear that the wealthy would gain power and expand the bureaucracy, thus reducing individual freedom and increasing costs. As one opponent concluded in 1714, "Don't change what is working well." The people of Boston believed that the town meeting worked and was far more effective than the governments of New York and Philadelphia. Despite this fear of rule by the wealthy, Boston certainly was not an example of participatory democracy; less than 5 percent of the adult males participated regularly in the political process.[12]

In the debate over incorporation one issue that stood out was the role of government. The British tradition of incorporating municipalities came about because of the need to regulate the price, quality, and distribution of goods in an economy of scarcity and the need to obtain for the inhabitants of the city certain rights and exemptions. By 1715 in Boston neither of these reasons had much validity. The people of Boston did not wish to establish a restricted economy but demanded a continuation of the open economic system. In Boston and elsewhere the economy of scarcity had been replaced by the economy of surplus. Then, too, it was believed that freedom would be threatened, not strengthened, by incorporation. It would not be till later in the eighteenth century before the people would accept the idea that incorporation could be an effective mechanism for responding to the increasing number of emerging social problems.

Communities in the Middle Colonies

The municipal corporations of the early eighteenth century were primarily interested in economic regulation. In Philadelphia a little over half of the ordinances passed between 1707 and 1724 concerned matters of trade. The same was true of New York City in 1707. The men who sat on the town councils were those whom the ordinances most directly affected. Two-thirds of the aldermen in New York between 1675 and 1725 were merchants and another 30 percent were artisans and innkeepers. The revenues needed to provide services and administer the urban community were generated from these economic activities. Duties on goods, fees for licenses, fees for admission as freemen, and rents from public markets and wharves provided the revenues for the municipality.[13]

By the second quarter of the eighteenth century a gradual change became evident in the governing of the city. The city became less a commercial community and more of a residential one, i.e., the municipal corporation became less concerned with economic regulation and devoted more time to providing for the health and well-being of its residents. A sign of this change was in 1727 when the corporation of Philadelphia failed to strengthen the enforcement procedures dealing with freemanship, thus moving away from the principle of exclusionary trading rights. Four years later in New York City the council dropped the seven-year provision for controlling apprentice education. Efforts at initiating the guild or craft system found in Europe were also unsuccessful in the colonial cities.[14]

In city after city the first regulations to go were laws dealing with controls over the producers. Yet almost all cities maintained price controls over food products until well after the Revolution. There were, however, signs that even this practice was giving way. In 1763, for example, some New York City butchers joined with farmers to suspend all meat sales until newly imposed restrictions on meat prices were repealed. One New Yorker wondered how long the city would be under "the peculiar curse of being fleeced . . . by the butcher." The councils of the municipal corporations had to balance the demands for an open market by the producers with the need for reasonable prices for such staples as meat, bread, and wood. In 1773 New York bakers asked that the price of bread be increased for the first time in twenty-five years. New York aldermen had to weigh requests of this type with the interests of all the people.[15]

Just as there was less interest in regulating producers, so, too, was there a growing concern with matters of public well-being. Issues that became more important during the eighteenth century concerned fire, health, street lighting, and public order. Only 8 percent of all ordinances passed in New

York City in 1707 dealt with public safety and order; by 1773 nearly one-fourth concerned these matters.[16]

Those advocating change faced the problems of overcoming existing institutions and customs and developing alternative structures. A number of municipal corporations refused to expand the scope of their responsibility. This led the colonial assemblies to establish commissions to oversee new governmental functions. This was true in the closed corporation of Philadelphia, where the conservative self-elected elite had no interest in expanding its responsibility and making it more susceptible to public pressure.[17]

With the expansion of services and the decline of traditional revenues, new sources of revenues had to be found. Early in the century when a public works project had to be undertaken, the cost of the project was met by a public lottery or a onetime tax on the users of the facility. With the demand for expanded services, the colonial assemblies gave urban centers the power to levy direct taxes, usually in the form of property taxes in the North or poll taxes in the South. By 1775 market rents, wharf fees, and freemen's charges played a secondary role in public financing, and other forms of taxation were the mainstay of the municipality.[18]

Reasons for Change

As a result of these changes the city of 1775 is more familiar to the reader than the city of 1700. One factor accounting for the change was the transition from an economy of scarcity to one of abundance. An increase in the supply of food and manufactured goods made possible an expanding economy. This, combined with rapid growth in the urban population, made it necessary to reduce the amount of regulation. Effective regulation can only occur where the economy is static. But the colonies encouraged growth; in fact, they needed growth. The colonial economy could not function if the cities were static commercial centers.

The growth of population was a second factor in bringing about the municipal revolution. The increasing number of urban dwellers eroded the control of the intimate community. The early New England towns, because of their intimacy, arrived at decisions by consensus. But as personal relationships declined because of population growth and the waning of Puritanism, citizens looked to external authority to arrive at decisions as well as to enforce the laws necessary for maintaining public order and safety. This was true in a large city like Boston and in a small town like Dedham. Moreover, the increasing density and heterogeneity of the population resulted in paid public employees rather than voluntary workers to maintain the night watch, repair the streets, collect garbage, and construct levees. The impersonal community had more difficulty than the personal one in controlling problems, such as violating the Sabbath, excessive drinking, or poverty.

The Age of Enlightenment also had much to do with the changing structure of city government. The Whiggish views of freedom were extended to all in society. No longer was there a need to establish islands of exemptions and rights. Such rights as freemanship should be universal, or at least the prerequisites for these rights should be. The closed corporation was especially vulnerable to attack. While its origins were found in the idea of freedom, it had become a means for perpetuating an entrenched ruling clique. More important than the ideal of political freedom was the idea of economic freedom. Universal economic regulation had no place in the world of Adam Smith and supporters of laissez-faire. The Enlightenment also made man aware of his ability to solve problems that he had previously accepted as insolvable. Advances in science and technology made man confident of his ability to create a more livable environment. By 1775 we can see the beginnings of a new urban order.

As we examine the changes taking place during the eighteenth century we find that acceptance of the new philosophy about the role of the government depended very largely on the socioeconomic composition of an urban community. In Boston, the "true believers" established the precedent of a well-organized society. As Boston evolved from a relatively small, compact community of religious zealots to a prosperous seaport and trading center of 18,000, it remained relatively homogeneous, continued its well-functioning institutions such as the workhouse and schools, and retained the town meeting/selectmen institutions of government. Newport, similar to Boston in many ways, differed in two important aspects. While it was not as large as Boston, it was more heterogeneous, having a large black population and a sizable Jewish community. In addition, Newport was a less regulated community, largely because the founders were religious dissenters who did not accept the idea of the covenanted community.[19]

Philadelphia, by 1776 the largest of the urban centers in North America, was more organized, had a greater sense of humanitarianism, but was less democratic than Boston. Founded in 1682, it was the last of the colonial cities to be established. It was planned from the very beginning to be the major urban center in William Penn's experiment. Quaker control and humanitarianism remained strong through the eighteenth century. However, the municipal corporation itself, closed and self-perpetuating, was unable and unwilling to expand the formal responsibilities of government.

Two urban centers, New York and Charleston, were very different from the first three. New York was in some ways more open and more democratic than any of the cities. After the Dutch were expelled in the 1660s, English corporate practices were blended with those established by the Dutch. Also New York, because of a more heterogeneous population, was a freer society. Many observers described it as the most lively of the colonial cities. Despite numerous municipal ordinances, enforcement was lax, partly because of the openness of the society. Charleston was an urban center that is most removed from our concept of a city. Its economy was based on slave labor with nearly 25 percent of the population, or 2500 people, being enslaved. Many of the elite of Charleston, being planters, spent only part of each year there, forced by custom, business, and the weather to divide their residence between plantation and the city. The small middle class was tied to the slave economy, while the lower classes were continually competing with slave labor. The government of Charleston was the colonial assembly. The assembly concerned itself very little in making Charleston a permanently livable place. There was no public education. Sanitation, fire protection, and poor relief received little attention. The few public services which were provided benefited only the small aristocracy.[20]

THE IMPACT OF THE REVOLUTION

The American Revolution dramatically changed the institutional structure of the cities. During the Revolution and in the immediate aftermath, twenty-five towns were granted new charters by the newly independent states. The states added many new provisions and deleted others. Many closed corporate structures were eliminated. The new legislative bodies of aldermen were elected by an enlarged electorate for shorter terms. A few cities extended the franchise to virtually all male inhabitants and held elections each year. Not all cities asked for new charters. In some the debate over establishing a new charter continued off and on for a number of years, with the sides being badly divided. One group welcomed the formal end of extensive regulation of the market economy and saw a new charter as an effective instrument for providing more extensive city services. Advocates of expanded public services were charged with undermining liberties by wishing to institute an aristocratic regime of bureaucrats. In Boston the Revolution revived the call for incorporation, thus allowing government to be able to respond better to the needs of the populace. As might be expected, Sam Adams led the attack against this proposal, charging that it built "up a new fabric approximating more nearly an aristocratical or monarchical government."[21]

While some saw a threat to liberty in the new charters, others charged that the existing corporate structures were a threat to liberties. They were particularly concerned with the concentration of executive, legislative, and judicial powers in a single body of municipal officers. The debates usually ended in compromise. During the years following the Revolution, new city charters were granted or old ones amended in order to reflect the concerns of both sides. The growth, heterogeneity, and economic complexity of the city demanded extension of existing services as well as the establishment of new ones. New services came to be seen not as threats to liberties but as remedies to problems which threatened the stability and order of a free society. The acceptance of the idea of positive local government came about when other changes were introduced in the context of protecting liberties. By 1810 the franchise in most cities was extended to male taxpayers. The broadened base of the electorate combined with frequent elections to reduce the dangers of a self-perpetuating aristocracy.[22]

The other area of change involved the elimination of a single governmental institution to exercise legislative, judicial, and executive powers. The political ideology of the day firmly believed that power corrupted, especially executive power, and that the only way to offset this was through the separation of powers, combined with a system of checks and balances. The executive branch of government gradually came to center in the office of mayor. Yet, the fear of a strong chief executive, like the royal governor, led some states to make the mayor a weak, appointive position. It was not until the latter part of the nineteenth century that the powers of the office of mayor were strengthened. A few cities moved from an appointed to an elected mayor early in the nineteenth century. An easier separation of power occurred with respect to the powers of the judiciary. In the 1790s the aldermen of New York City surrendered the judicial function to newly created city judges. This same practice occurred in city after city during the first quarter of the nineteenth century.[23]

In the aftermath of the Revolution, urban reformers sought structural change even if it meant the loss of local autonomy. To bring about this change they appealed to the newly established state legislatures for new or revised charters. Positive state response resulted in the erosion of the sacredness of the old corporate charters. These charters were previously viewed as unalterable and irrevocable means of guaranteeing freedom for citizens of cities. Liberals in England and the colonies had looked upon the charters as sacred compacts which could not be changed unilaterally, even by the Crown or Parliament. But after the mid-eighteenth century many charters came to be seen as perpetuating entrenched economic interests rather than as protecting freedom or being effective mechanisms for responding to the needs of the entire urban population. While colonial assemblies had refused to violate the

municipal charters, the newly established state legislatures readily intervened. This intervention initiated a long history of state involvement in the
affairs and governance of the city.[24]

This conflict and intervention is seen in Newport, Rhode Island. In 1786,
104 citizens petitioned the state to end the corporation in Newport, arguing
that it was a form of "government novel, arbitrary, and altogether unfit for
free republicans."[25] The Revolution also made change possible in Norfolk,
Virginia, which had been governed as a closed corporation since 1736. After
two years of debate the Virginia legislature in 1789 revoked this charter,
concluding that such a structure was an "impolitic and unconstitutional
mode of electing common-councilmen for the borough of Norfolk."[26]
The new charter called for extending suffrage to all citizens who could
qualify for state elections and electing a common council every three years.
This body was vested with the right of passing bylaws and taxing the people of
Norfolk.

The essence of the arguments in the legislatures was that municipal
charters were not sacred documents but rather were legislative statutes that
could be changed at the will of the legislature. One man argued that "the
corporation is in the hands of the Legislature . . . as clay in a potter's
hands."[27] Proponents of the idea that the charters were irrevocable gained a
narrow victory in Philadelphia in 1792 but found the issue raised again a year
later. However, it was not until 1796 that the Pennsylvania legislature ended
the rule of the self-perpetuating corporation in Philadelphia. After a decade of
conflict New York City's charter was also amended by the state in 1803 and
1804. These battles continued into the first part of the nineteenth century.
Generally the position that the municipal corporation was an agent responsive
and subordinate to the state tended to prevail.[28]

The role of the federal government in all of this became clear in the
Dartmouth College case in 1819. Chief Justice John Marshall declared that
incorporation was a grant of political power and thus could be modified by the
state legislature. Justice Bushrod Washington supported this, "in respect
to . . . cities . . . the legislature may, under proper limitations, change, modify,
enlarge, or restrain them."[29] What had appeared as a victory for reformers
turned into defeat in the nineteenth century. Though state authority was used
to eliminate the power of the closed corporation and to extend suffrage and
initiate other reforms, it also was an additional and new barrier, making the
city more difficult to manage. Once the state had established its power, it
would not be willing to relinquish it. Municipalities found that the end of the
closed corporation also marked the end of home rule. Throughout the
nineteenth century state legislatures saw the city as their proper preserve
despite the fact that the vast majority of legislators came not from urban areas
but from rural ones.

Summary

As we have seen in this chapter, four patterns found in the governing of today's cities developed in the English colonial cities of the eighteenth century. Understanding the development of these patterns helps to place contemporary problems of urban development and the institutional responses to them in a meaningful perspective.

The first pattern, the tension between the influences which unify and those which create diversity is certainly apparent in the eighteenth century. Major unifying influences in the colonies were the English urban traditions, both the legal instrument, the corporate charter, and the social/cultural/political influences of English society. While the majority of cities in the colonies had charters similar to cities in England, a number of major colonial cities did not. And these exceptions encouraged the heterogeneity of the urban network within America. Two other influences encouraged diversity among American cities, the environment and the character of the people who founded the urban centers. Environmental forces affected the economy of an urban center which in turn was a factor in determining who settled the area. The resulting socioeconomic conditions influenced the policy responses of an urban center, as well as the structures and institutions established to implement these responses. For example, the environment determined much of the socioeconomic structure and thus the policy responses of Charleston, South Carolina, during the eighteenth century.

A second pattern, the interplay of the social and economic forces and the ever-changing governmental structures, tells us a great deal about the capacity of an American city to respond to its challenges. It is relatively easy to trace the governmental institutions of major colonial cities to the particular circumstances of how each was established and to the character of the people who came to the city in its formative years. The humanitarianism of the Puritans and Quakers, for example, is readily visible in Boston and Philadelphia.

A third pattern evident, the failure of existing governance institutions to respond to the challenges facing the urban community, led to the demand for major structural reform. In the late eighteenth century reformers sought to replace the autonomous municipal corporation with an entity created by and subordinate to the state. This demand for reform was successful, though it created in turn new and different challenges for the nineteenth-century reformers.

This pattern was closely linked to another, the continual presence of an authority superior to the city itself. Prior to the Revolution the Crown held this position; afterward, state governments. As Carl Bridenbaugh argues, it was these cities in the wilderness, created by the British government, that became the cities in revolt, sparking the American Revolution. Once independence was secured, important decisions were reached concerning the role of the city in American society. The resulting vacuum caused by the departure of parliamentary power and the problems found in an increasingly complex urban society led to giving the states power and authority over the cities.

NOTES

1. Sam Bass Warner, Jr., *The Private City: Philadelphia in Three Periods of Its Growth* (Philadelphia: University of Pennsylvania Press, 1968), pp. xi-xii; Bayrd Still, "Patterns of Mid-Nineteenth Century Urbanization in the Middle West," *Mississippi Valley Historical Review* 28 (September 1941): 200-204; Jon C. Teaford, *The Municipal Revolution in America: Origins of Modern Urban Government, 1650-1825* (Chicago: University of Chicago Press, 1975).

2. See John Reps, *The Making of Urban America* (Princeton, N.J.: Princeton University Press, 1965).

3. Gideon Sjoberg, *The Preindustrial City* (New York: The Free Press, 1960); James A. Henretta, "Economic Development and Social Structure in Colonial Boston," *William and Mary Quarterly*, 3d ser. 22 (January 1965): 75-92; Warner, pp. 2-45; John K. Alexander, "The City of Brotherly Fear," in *Cities in American History*, eds. Kenneth T. Jackson and Stanley K. Schultz (New York: Alfred A. Knopf, 1972), pp. 79-97.

4. See Teaford; Zane Miller, "Scarcity, Abundance, and American Urban History," *Journal of Urban History* 4 (February 1978): 131-56.

5. Teaford, pp. 3-15; Ernest S. Griffith, *A History of American City Government: The Colonial Period* (New York: Oxford University Press, 1938), pp. 34-40.

6. Teaford, p. 17.

7. Griffith, pp. 162-63, 194-97.

8. *Ibid.*, pp. 73, 250-57; Carl Bridenbaugh, *Cities in the Wilderness* (New York: Ronald Press, 1938), p. 8; Judith Diamondstone, "Philadelphia's Municipal Corporation, 1701-1776," *Pennsylvania Magazine of History and Biography* 90 (April 1966): 183-201.

9. Griffith, pp. 77-78.

10. Kenneth A. Lockridge, *A New England Town: The First Hundred Years.* (New York: W. W. Norton, 1970).

11. *Ibid.;* Griffith, p. 211; Henretta, pp. 75-92.

12. Teaford, pp. 36-44, 72-73; Griffith, p. 211.

13. Teaford, pp. 13, 18, 25.

14. *Ibid.*, pp. 47, 50.

15. Griffith, pp. 144-49; quote cited in Teaford, p. 51.

16. Teaford, pp. 18 and 52.

17. *Ibid.,* p. 60.

18. Griffith, pp. 292-324.

19. Constance McLaughlin Green, *The Rise of Urban America* (New York: Harper Colophon, 1967), pp. 9-16.

20. *Ibid.,* pp. 16-27; Griffith, pp. 196-97, 242-50.

21. Teaford, pp. 64-78; quote from p. 68.

22. *Ibid.,* pp. 64-78.

23. *Ibid.,* p. 74.

24. *Ibid.,* pp. 79-80.

25. *Ibid.,* p. 80.

26. *Ibid.,* p. 81.

27. *Ibid.,* p. 82.

28. *Ibid.,* pp. 85, 88-89.

29. *Ibid.,* p. 89.

CHAPTER III.

Urban Governance
in the Nineteenth Century

Introduction

During the twenty-five years after the American Revolution important changes occurred within urban America. These changes included the extension of the franchise, the acquisition and exercise of the power to charter by state legislatures, and the systematic policy of decentralizing power. The impact of these changes, combined with rapid growth, made the nineteenth century the "dismal era" of American urban history. In the nineteenth century, America was transformed from a preindustrial to an industrial society. Accompanying this change was the related process of the creation of the industrial city. Industrialization also accelerated the movement from the "private" to the public city and with this a change in urban governance institutions. This chapter will examine the transformation of America into an industrialized, urbanized society and the resulting impact on governance institutions.

The four patterns of behavior described in the first two chapters recur in the nineteenth century. However they were not all equally important. For example, there was not much apparent tension between unifying and diversifying influences. Certain unifying influences were present, such as the common characteristics of industrial cities and the practice by the newer cities of drawing on the experience of the Eastern urban centers. Moreover, diversity also occurred, brought on by industrial specialization, environmental influences, and the addition to the urban network of cities founded by the French and Spanish. The second pattern was very important. Socioeconomic forces had a great influence in shaping the urban governance structures that were adopted and how well these structures performed. The third pattern, the failure of governmental institutions to respond effectively to the challenges brought by industrialization, led to the continued modification of existing structures, proposals for radically different ones, and the appearance of machine politics. The last pattern, the subservience of urban government to a higher authority, the state legislatures, is responsible for many of the problems faced by the older, industrial cities today.

THE TRANSFORMATION OF NINETEENTH-CENTURY AMERICA

Social Changes

The United States in 1810 was a country of 7.2 million living in seventeen states and the territories. A vast majority of the population was still located in the original thirteen states. Neither the Old Southwest nor the Old Northwest was yet heavily populated. While the cotton gin was just beginning to stimulate cotton production, the first steamboat had yet to move up the Mississippi. And the Erie Canal was still fifteen years away. Though the population was ten times what it had been eighty years before, it tended to be composed of the same mixture of nationalities and races. Except for development in a few areas of manufacturing, the economic base of the nation was essentially unchanged.

The eighty years following 1810 brought dramatic change to society. By 1890 the population was just under 63 million. Instead of seventeen states, there were forty-four states, and the center of both population and economic power was in the Old Northwest and moving westward. Americans were spread across the continent, thousands of miles apart physically, but were in closer contact to one another than at any time in the past. The railroad, the postal service, the telegraph, and the telephone lessened the barrier of distance. While communication had improved and the rooting of American nationality had taken place, immigration brought more heterogeneity to the cultural and social fabric of society. Western expansion and industrialization increased the diversity of urban forms and governments, despite the homogenization of many aspects of urban life.

This leap in population was due to a declining mortality rate, especially infant mortality, and immigration. Immigration to the United States began anew with the end of the Napoleonic Wars in 1815. The rate of immigration gradually increased until the 1840s, when events in Europe brought over three million to America in a ten-year period. By 1860 13 percent of the population was foreign-born. Following the Civil War, English, Irish, and German immigration continued but at a reduced rate. Scandinavian immigration increased, while Southern and Eastern European immigration began.

While the population of the United States increased 900 percent between 1810 and 1890, the population in cities over 8000 jumped from 357,000 to 18,284,000. This increase influenced urban development in two ways: it increased the number of cities over 8000 from 11 to 448 and it created the phenomenon of the large metropolis. The 28 great cities held 9,698,000 people.[1] Forms of governing diversified, as each new city adopted governance arrangements reflecting the legal conditions imposed by state legislatures, the character of the population and the economy, and the influence of past urban practices. The emergence of cities with populations over 100,000 strained the human and institutional resources of urban America. The expansion of the physical city, especially in the larger cities, added to the problems facing governance institutions.

Technological Changes

During the nineteenth century the United States moved from a preindustrial to an industrializing economy. The major factors in this economic expansion were agriculture and transportation. American agriculture stimulated nineteenth-century industrialization. Mechanization enabled agriculture to become more efficient; the number of man-hours necessary for producing wheat and corn dropped dramatically. The effect of mechanization was to generate greater production and a surplus population on established farms, forcing the sons of farmers either into the urban centers or westward to open new lands. A generation later the same process was repeated. The increased production provided America with her major exports: cotton, wheat, and corn. These in turn provided more capital for economic expansion.[2]

Agricultural expansion could not have occurred without improved methods of transportation. Such improvements made the farmer a businessman. The existence of cheap land meant nothing if farmers could not ship crops to market. Until 1850 most crops, except cotton, tobacco, and sugar, usually were shipped only a few miles to the nearest urban center. It was not until after the Civil War that corn and wheat joined cotton as major exports. This was made possible by increased productivity and the railroads. Railroads opened up new areas to profitable agriculture and provided cheap long-haul transportation. The railroad made possible hundreds of new urban centers, linking them to the emerging national economy, and stimulated the iron and steel industry.

Improvements in long-haul transportation introduced new environmental influences in determining the location of urban centers. The railroad enabled urban centers to develop in areas where there were no rivers, lakes, or oceans, as well as in areas removed from natural resources. Changes in transportation brought improvements in intraurban transportation. Distances within the cities were diminished by first the omnibus, then the horse-drawn streetcar, and after 1890 the electric trolley. With each improvement in transportation the influence of the city on the areas beyond increased.

Only a small proportion of the work force was classified as industrial in 1810. Most of these workers were employed in small, family-owned operations, ranging from textile mills in New England to smelting operations in Pennsylvania. More important to the economy, especially the local economy, were craftsmen. These men, the tanners, millers, blacksmiths, wagon makers, etc., provided the products needed by local urban centers and the surrounding countryside. In these operations work and residence were often combined. The class differences between employer and employee was not very great and the relationship tended to be highly personal. Employees were young relatives, apprentices, or transient journeymen. Except in the larger urban centers, most establishments included only two or three workers. Personal economic relationships characterized those found in most small urban centers up until the 1850s. As urban centers became linked with the national economy, these personal, small-scale operations changed; in the larger cities the capitalistic economy gradually created a laboring class of many workers possessing few skills.[3]

Major changes became evident after the Civil War. These continued until 1890 when we find an emerging industrial proletariat. By 1890 the American economy was characterized by growth and instability. This growth gave rise to great fortunes, the maldistribution of wealth, and generated an increased demand for material goods. At the same time the instability created labor unrest, ruthless competition, fluctuating profits and losses, and the recognition that something was indeed wrong with society and the economy. Proposals for reform, most of which affected the cities, became more frequent and appealing.

Impact of Population Growth and Technological Change

The movement from a preindustrial to an industrial society brought with it an instability which in turn created a demand for stability. The constant tension between the desire for growth and the demand for stability characterized America during this time. During the nineteenth century dramatic changes occurred in society. By 1890 the city in the United States and in other industrialized countries had emerged as a new social form. Earlier, the small city had mixed land use, with the rich and poor living in close proximity to one another. Home and work were not always separated. The major activities of commerce, industry, and governance were located in the center of the city, with the rich living nearby. These cities were "walking cities," people moving from one section to another on foot. Manufacturing tended to be done in or close to home, while commerce depended on water transportation. While cities were densely populated, only eighty-five had a population over 8000 in 1850.

By 1890 the industrial city had evolved. Both the physical and population size of the city had changed. There were 448 centers having more than 8000 people, and 28 cities with more than 100,000. The population increase was made possible by the expansion of city boundaries. As the city expanded outward, residential segregation became more evident. Place of residence became separated from place of work. Neighborhoods reflected race, ethnic, and/or class divisions. Some parts of the central cities became almost ghettoized, with one section dominated by the Irish, another by the Poles, a third by the Germans, etc. This pattern of relative residential segregation provided each group with a means to deal with accommodation and acculturation in a new and strange environment. Commercial establishments and shops catering to the needs of these ethnic populations made it unnecessary for group members to journey outside the neighborhood, except for purposes of employment. The establishment of ethnic neighborhoods also facilitated the organization and electoral tasks of the political parties.[4]

Not only was there residential and commercial specialization of space within cities, but cities began to specialize, some serving as commercial depots and many developing as specialized manufacturing centers. The nature of American industry and the availability of cheap, long-haul freight allowed for the appearance of cities that manufactured one product, such as steel, farm implements, textiles, or vehicles. After 1890 the process of consolidation in American industry turned some cities into company towns and led to the creation of cities with an ever-increasing laboring class.[5]

The changing characteristics of the city occurred over time. Changes in industrial technology and transportation were gradual. For example, Philadelphia in 1860 was a city of substantial size in population and land area with many industrial activities present. Yet Philadelphia was more like the preindustrial city of the eighteenth century than the industrial city of the twentieth century.[6] Increased residential segregation, separation of home and work, and functional specialization of land use were not found in the city until later in the nineteenth century.

URBAN RESPONSES TO THE TRANSFORMATION
OF SOCIETY

The Professionalization and Expansion of Services

The city responded to the growth of population and physical size by evolving from what might be described as the "private city" to the public city. Growth made it necessary to increase the number of services needed by an ever-growing population. In the early eighteenth century, cities provided few public services. Though this had changed by the late eighteenth century, the break with the past was not complete. As the nineteenth century progressed it became more apparent that the public services of the eighteenth century had to be expanded and new services introduced. The increasing numbers of people, the expansion of urban boundaries, and the presence of a transient population meant growing impersonalization in urban society. Not only was society unable to control antisocial behavior but it could not identify those who perpetrated such acts. Informal social controls were replaced by more formal institutions as a means of maintaining public order.[7]

Identifying social responsibility was yet another problem. In the preindustrial community voluntary agencies were responsible for many of the services provided to the urban community. It was generally assumed that responsibility for social well-being was shared by all, with the elite responsible for the greatest share of the duties. As society became larger and more impersonal, it was relatively easy to escape such duties. Even if services demanded by the community remained relatively simple, it was apparent that something had to be done to formalize the institutional arrangements for providing them. In short, public services had to be "professionalized."[8]

The expansion and professionalizing of services evolved also because of the desire to stabilize society. The role of traditional social institutions, like the family and religion, had to be supplemented by public institutions. Certain institutions were established to protect the public from disorder. Professional police forces replaced the night watch and the constabulary. Because of fears of a standing army, society did not adopt a uniformed police force until after the Civil War. By then large cities had no choice, while the smaller cities postponed such action until it was absolutely necessary. Other examples of officials involved in providing public safety were building and health inspectors. Like the police, these officials regulated and controlled the populace. More important than the institutions that directly controlled society were the institutions that provided stability in an indirect manner. Primary among these was the public school system. By the late nineteenth century compulsory education was enforced in most industrialized states. Schools were seen as socializing institutions, especially for the newcomers to the cities. The ideas of John Dewey had great influence on public education. Children of urban immigrants and migrants were to be prepared for living in an industrialized society. They were taught vocational and social skills. It was believed that this had to be accomplished in a formalized way, whereas previously in an agrarian society this was done through informalized learning. Schooling in America did not have as its prime purpose the freeing of the mind but rather the stabilizing of society.[9]

The expansion of public services also occurred because of the rising expectations of society. Technological advances generated expectations that institutions could provide expanded services in a formal, systematic fashion. The story of the development of public water supplies is an example of this. Technology made it possible for cities, especially large cities, to provide water for most residents. The threat of what would happen if water were not provided was an added incentive. Polluted water in a large city was a health hazard to everyone. Also the steam fire engine made it necessary to professionalize fire protection services.[10]

Consequences of Expansion of Public Services

The expanding number and scope of public services affected the cities in a number of ways. First, of course, was the professionalization of such services. The phenomenon was most obvious in police and fire departments. But other areas of city services were professionalized, as the increasing complexity of governmental institutions created a need for public employees who were immune to the spoils system. This, in turn, led to a demand for civil service reform, espoused first at the national level and later other levels of the public service. Professionalization also occurred in other services, particularly public education. Teaching became a career with prescribed requirements of preparation and training. Normal schools were established in the states to train and license people as teachers. Employees in areas such as public health required formal training and professional certification.

A second result was the increased cost of providing public services. This, in turn, meant an increase in taxation. New York City spent an average of $1 per person on public services in 1810 and $34 per person in 1910.[11] New sources of revenue had to be found and the public had to agree to new taxes. By the late nineteenth century the public sector had become an important element in the economy. Even the smaller cities provided hundreds of jobs and were major customers of the private sector. Increased taxation encouraged more citizens to become aware of what was going on in city hall, leading to a greater interest in politics among the growing middle class.

The misuse or abuse of the public trust was a third result of expanding services. Corruption was a major issue, especially after the Civil War. The money involved made corruption probable. The tradition of decentralizing power made it difficult to control corruption and at times encouraged it. Of increasing importance was the incidence of corruption that came with deciding who would provide and benefit from public services. Such decisions were sometimes influenced by bribes, but more often by political or personal considerations. The "public interest" failed to operate as an important consideration in such circumstances.

IMPACT OF A CHANGING SOCIETY ON AMERICAN POLITICS

Expansion of Suffrage

In 1810 the majority of states had a property qualification for the exercise of the right to vote. This was a reflection of the eighteenth-century belief that only the propertied had a right to participate in the political process because the taxes were paid by members of this class. But in America, because of the relatively widespread diffusion of land ownership, the distinction between landholder and nonlandholder became less important. This trend, combined with the thrust given to equality by the American and the French revolutions, gave rise to the belief that "wisdom in politics" was in direct proportion to the extent of popular participation. By the outbreak of the Civil War, twenty-three of thirty states had removed property and/or tax qualifications for voting in state and presidential elections. These changes in franchise requirements were reflected in urban politics. By the 1850s many of the new city charters, as well as revisions of existing ones, extended the right to vote to adult, white males. Chicago was the first major city in the Midwest to abolish property qualifications for voting and holding office. Other cities quickly followed suit. Participation in local politics was not limited to American citizens. Because of the influx of immigrants, especially after 1845, many cities extended the vote to newcomers who indicated that they would become citizens.[12]

Rotation in Office

This belief in the efficacy of democracy produced other political changes. Frequent elections were seen as one way to make government officials representative of the people. In most cities the mayor and the members of the city council were elected annually. A proposal to elect the members of the Milwaukee city council to three-year terms was viewed "as placing them beyond the reach of public opinion." "Rotation in office" was introduced as a means of breaking the monopoly of the elite over public institutions. In America it was believed that any man was capable of performing such duties. Because of this belief, as well as the general weakness of the office, the mayor at midcentury generally served only for a term or two. In Cleveland, between 1836 and 1870, only five mayors served for more than one year. In Flint, Michigan, between 1855 and 1900, only three men served as many as two one-year terms as mayors. It was believed that the office of mayor was more a duty than an honor. In general, the office was held by respected businessmen rather than individuals who had ambitions for higher political office. There also tended to be rapid turnover on the city councils. In a thirty-five-year period in Cleveland an average of only two of the twelve members of the city council were reelected.[13]

Increasing Influence of National Politics
on Local Politics

The need of grass-roots political organizations for national and state parties had, at the local level, increased corruption and the utilization of local parties for nonlocal purposes. The cities came to play a very important role in state and national politics. The concentration of large numbers of potential voters who might easily be instructed or influenced on how to vote offered many opportunities for politicians. Large cities, especially those which were growing rapidly because of the influx of immigrants and migrants, provided the best opportunities. While reformers attempted to reduce corruption by proposing longer periods for naturalization and more exacting registration laws, little headway was made in reducing this type of electoral corruption. Even when naturalization and registration procedures were established, politicians controlled the agencies which were responsible for maintaining voter lists and the judges who administered naturalization processes. Then, too, it was in the interest of both political parties to extend the vote even to the newest urban immigrants. The Irish were seen as especially susceptible to illegal electoral practices, as reflected in one election postmortem when an immigrant from Cornwall lamented, "Thee robbing Hirish, they not honly 'ave two votes heach on Helection Day, but thee buggers vote seven years hafter they 'ave been dead hand buried."[14]

CHANGES IN LOCAL GOVERNMENT

Popular Election of Public Officials

Jon Teaford in his book *The Municipal Revolution in America* believes that the municipal revolution, begun in the early eighteenth century, was over by 1825. While this is true in some areas of local government, it was not true in all. In fact, a number of changes in city government occurred between 1825 and 1850, though some of these were a continuation of trends begun earlier. Yet even these were more a result of the social, economic, and political developments of the first half of the nineteenth century than what had taken place earlier.

Between 1820 and 1850 scores of new charters were granted to cities, as well as the revisions of old ones. The New York State Constitution of 1821 introduced many important changes. For example, the practice of appointing mayors of New York City by the state was replaced with their election by the local common council. Later this was followed by yet another change, namely the popular election of the mayor. Between 1822 and 1834 Boston, St. Louis, Detroit, Philadelphia, and Baltimore also adopted the direct election of mayor. By the midcentury many cities even dropped the property qualification for voting. Though the office of mayor became the focus of political interest and activity, the authority and responsibility of the position was not substantially changed. However, by subjecting the position to popular election and making it the focus of administration in city government, the stage was set for increased responsibility of the office later in the century.[15]

Confidence in the benefits of popular election led to the electing, rather than appointing, of officials who carried on specialized functions. School and poor relief officials were now elected. In midcentury the principle of election and thus autonomy was applied to services that had been controlled previously by city councils. The 1849 charter of New York City called for the election of a dozen department heads. Three years later the Cleveland charter required the election of mayor, city marshal, civil engineer, fire engineer, treasurer, auditor, solicitor, police judge, and superintendent of markets. Later the trustees of the waterworks and street commissioners were added.[16]

Separation of Powers

A second change introduced in local government was the principle of separation of powers. Bicameralism, i.e., a two-house legislative body, came to be accepted in a number of cities because it was an evolution of earlier forms of government and an extension of the concept of separation of powers and checks and balances to local government. The 1822 Boston charter adopted a bicameral system as a logical extension of its previous experience, with the common council representing the spirit of the town meeting and the aldermen representing the selectmen. New York's charter of 1830 adopted bicameralism, "for the same reason which has dictated a similar division of power into branches, each checking and controlling the other, in our general government." Not all cities followed suit. Cleveland had both councilmen (elected by wards) and aldermen (elected at large) sitting in a single house, while Chicago (1837) and Milwaukee (1846) had only aldermen, elected by wards.[17]

There was a revival of bicameralism after midcentury in reaction to what was viewed as hasty legislation adopted by unicameral councils. Cities adopting this change included Milwaukee (adopted in 1858 and abandoned in 1874), St. Louis (1866 to 1910), Cincinnati (1870 to 1890), and New Orleans (1852 to 1870). Bicameralism was again widely discussed in the seventies and eighties. Detroit adopted it briefly (1881 to 1887) as did Cleveland (1885 to 1894). This time the chief influences were the fear of corruption in cities where there were no checks and balances and the adoption of a supposedly scientific approach to the principles of government. Out of this came a commitment to the so-called "federal plan." The most slavish imitation of the federal government was the Bullitt Charter for Philadelphia.[18]

The federal model increased the powers of the mayor. In some cases this meant greater power over appointments and dismissals but more often it was manifested in the veto. In cities where the mayor possessed the veto, it could be set aside only by a two-thirds vote of the council.

State Interference

The growth in size and population and the establishment of new cities caused an increase in the functions of local government. In the first half of the nineteenth century these functions, although expanded on, were similar to those performed by cities in the eighteenth century. For example, New York's Croton Aqueduct, which was a public project, approved in 1835, was patterned after Philadelphia's system, established in 1798. A number of cities added a small, unorganized daytime police force to supplement the night watch. Fire companies were staffed on a voluntary basis, though the cities assumed responsibilities for equipment. School boards and relief officials were also appointed, but had no clear sense of responsibility to the local council or the people. As before, expanded services required new sources of revenue. While new charters usually granted the city the right to tax, states had to pass enabling legislation to allow local authority to go beyond the rather limited powers in existing charters. In the first half of the nineteenth century it was in the area of poor relief, education, and taxation that the state intervened. It was this precedent of intervention that led in the second half century to further interventions into largely local matters. As state politics became more partisan, it was relatively easy for the party in control of the state legislature to constrain local government, especially if it was controlled by the opposing party.

After midcentury the state legislatures increased their power over local affairs. This interference occurred for a variety of reasons, either because of politics, or a reaction to corruption, or the inability of local government to meet the needs of an ever-expanding population. After 1850 some state legislatures became involved in such petty issues as granting a pension to an individual city employee, naming a street, or closing an alley. Michigan placed the Detroit police under a state commission in 1865 while New York placed New York City's fire department, health department, and saloon licensing agency under state commissions. In some cases the state saw such activity necessary to prevent corruption, but in general it reflected a desire to hold on to political power, at times for partisan political ends. For example, the Republican-controlled state government of Illinois gave the control of the Chicago police department to a state board of police. Two years later the Democrats gained control and reduced the term of the board members from six years to three, which led to the appointment of a number of Democrats. In 1865 the situation was again reversed and the state legislature extended the terms for new members to six, but such members were to be elected by the voters, not of just Chicago, but of Cook County, which was solidly Republican. To further Republican control of the municipal government in Chicago the fire department was placed under the new police board. The evidence of state interference is seen later in the century when the New York state legislature passed over four hundred laws for New York City in the decade of the 1880s.[19]

The second half of the nineteenth century witnessed attempts at defining the limits of state interference and control of local affairs. Urban reformers faced the problem of checking the interference of state legislatures without precluding the possibility of desirable special legislation.

There were two possible remedies to the growing state interference. One was the courts, the other legislation. The courts historically protected individual rights and later corporate rights from arbitrary action by the state. But this same protection was not provided for in the municipal corporation. As noted in the previous chapter many urban reformers argued in the late eighteenth century that municipal charters were not sacred and could be changed without the agreement of both parties. The state quickly filled the void created by the dissolution of the authority of the Crown and Parliament to vest charters. It was generally assumed that new charters were not self-perpetuating like the ones of the colonial era. In the early nineteenth century decisions of the Supreme Court limited the power of states over corporate charters, but such rulings did not apply to charters granted to local governments.

The issue of the extent of the rights of municipal corporations remained in dispute. State courts handed down conflicting decisions shortly after the Civil War. In Iowa, Judge John F. Dillon concluded

> Municipal corporations owe their origin to, and derive their powers and the rights wholly from the legislature. It breathes into them the breath of life, and without which they cannot exist. As it creates, so it may destroy. [Municipal corporations] are the mere tenants at the will of the legislature.[20]

This decision was countered for a time by the decision of Judge Thomas Cooley of Michigan. He declared that there was an inherent right of local self-government which must not be violated by the state legislature. Cooley's decision implied that the state could prescribe the organization and powers of cities, but should respect the rights of self-government once these prescriptions were initially established. Other state courts in Indiana, Kentucky, and Iowa used the Cooley precedent. But even these decisions dealt only with issues arising from an attempt by the legislature to deprive the city of the right to choose certain officials.[21]

Cities found little protection in the courts. By the early 1920s state sovereignty over cities was widely acknowledged, having been established by the Supreme Court, in the decision in *Hunter* v. *Pittsburgh*:

> The number, nature and duration of the powers conferred upon these corporations and the territory over which they shall be exercised rests in the absolute discretion of the States. . . . The State, therefore, at its pleasure, may modify or withdraw all such powers . . . expand or contract the territorial area, unite the whole or a part with another municipality, repeal the charter and destroy the corporation. All this may be done . . . with or without the consent of the citizens, or even against their protest.[22]

The establishment of comprehensive municipal codes was one way to relieve cities of harassment by state governments. Illinois was the first state to do this in 1872 with the Municipal Corporations Act. This act granted some protection to all cities in Illinois. Earlier, in 1851, a related type of protection began in Ohio and spread to most states. This was the classification system by which all the municipalities of a state were classified, usually by population.

Each classification had certain powers and state laws applied equally to all cities or towns within that classification. This prohibited special legislation for a specific city, except in the case of large cities. It was these cities, especially in Ohio, which felt the continued interference of the legislature. In Ohio the eleven largest cities each had its own classification. Thus the state could continually intervene, arguing it was passing general and not specific legislation. This blatant manipulation of the classification system came to an end in Ohio with a Supreme Court decision in 1902.[23] However, such manipulation is not dead even today. In Indiana, Gary was for years in the same class as Fort Wayne and Evansville. But in 1970, in order to reduce the power of Mayor Richard Hatcher, Lake Country representatives pushed through the Indiana General Assembly legislation placing Gary in a different class, one in which it was the only member. With that, new legislation was enacted greatly reducing the appointing power of all mayors in cities in this class.

In order to grant some protection to local government, without at the same time giving up rights of control, a number of approaches were adopted in the late nineteenth century. Some states maintained the right to pass special legislation but allowed the local authority the right of veto. In New York, for example, the state passed 1639 special city bills between 1912 and 1921. Nearly 1300 of these were accepted, while the others were vetoed by the mayor of New York. In the late nineteenth century special acts for Chicago had to be approved by the people in a popular referendum.[24]

A second approach, one which was urged by reformers especially after 1900, was home rule. This called for clarifying the powers of local and state governments. Local voters could decide the structure, powers, and duties of city government. Missouri adopted the principle of home rule in its state constitution of 1875. The constitution allowed large cities to elect thirteen freeholders to draft a charter which, when ratified by the people, became the charter for the city provided it was consistent with the state constitution and state laws. The California constitution of 1879 allowed for charter making by cities over 100,000; by 1892 this privilege was extended to all cities with over 3500 people. By the end of the century only two other states had adopted this principle, Washington in 1889 and Minnesota in 1896.[25]

Corruption and Reform

Despite the changes occurring in urban governance, cities of the late nineteenth century found themselves ill-equipped to deal with the problems associated with industrialization. It was impossible to meet the demands of the ever-expanding population with a governmental system organized around the decentralization of power. Growth contributed chaos, but no one was willing to sacrifice growth for stability. Corruption was one of the most evident manifestations of this chaos brought on by urban development. Three types of corruption caused the most concern among the solid middle class: immorality, bribery, and vote fraud. It was these issues that led Lord Bryce to declare that the government of cities was "the one conspicuous failure of the United States."[26] The middle class believed liquor, sex, and gambling were undermining the values of society and were the cause of poverty and the social pathology found in the city. Because of greater democracy, moral reformers found it very difficult to enact legislation to control these vices. In cities where legislation was enacted, enforcement was impossible and the legislation actually promoted even more bribery. To counter bribery the reform mayor of Chicago, Carter Harrison, in 1882 rejected the possibility of eliminating gambling but instructed his police to raid gambling houses if

> minors, drunken men or poor mechanics were allowed to play in any house, or if suppers were furnished or liquors given away or sold, or if ropers-in were employed or cards of advertizement issued, or if a house were kept open after seven Saturday evenings.[27]

This attitude toward moral reform was also present when Tom Johnson of Cleveland allowed prostitution as long as the houses were kept clean and quiet and no bribery or robbery occurred. On being charged that he had eliminated Christianity in Cleveland, he answered that he was only trying to make Christianity possible. While moral reform had few lasting successes, it was and still is a ready issue for reformers in local elections.[28]

Bribery was a more serious problem. In the nineteenth century bribery seemed to permeate the entire political and governmental system, from national to local levels. It occurred on the local level in matters ranging from a few dollars for the local constabulary to large sums for granting franchises. While the lower class, especially the immigrant, was blamed for this form of corruption, it was quite clear to many observers at the time that bribery was not a class or an ethnic issue. The lack of a business ethic in an age of economic expansion made widespread bribery prevalent. This, combined with more visible lower-class corruption, generated demands for reform. Such reforms tended to be short-lived or ineffective.

The major achievement of reformers who attempted to eliminate vote fraud was the introduction of the Australian or secret ballot. Between 1888 and 1892, thirty-two states adopted this measure. Related to this was the establishment of governmental control over the ballot. But attempts to control voter registration, as well as reduce the immigrant vote, tended only to make vote fraud more sophisticated.[29]

Reform had little lasting impact on urban society up to 1890. However, reformers in the last years of the nineteenth century did pave the way for the Progressive Era, in terms of both actual accomplishments and municipal ideology. The successful reforms were due less to structural changes and more to the pragmatic approaches to urban problems. Hazen Pingree, who might be called a "boss reformer," provided effective leadership for Detroit between 1890 and 1897. His approach was to push what worked and was possible in a given situation. Behind all his proposals was the desire to make society better for the common man. Pingree, the politician, realized that there were more votes among the forty thousand immigrants from Eastern Europe than among the "social Four Hundred." The urban reforms initiated by Pingree included a three-cent trolley fare, regulation of some utilities, and public ownership of others. As Melvin Holli showed, Pingree was responsible "for the first significant social reform administration of any large city of the time." Other cities and their mayors were influenced by Pingree's administration.[30]

The late nineteenth century was a period when serious thought and discussion were given over to the plight of the American city. James Bryce's *The American Commonwealth*, published in 1888, had an immediate impact on America. Bryce examined the American city and identified the reasons for its problems. He saw that the principal causes of the urban condition were the corruption and incompetence of local officials, partisan politics, intervention by state legislatures, and the basic defects in the structure of urban government. While Bryce's analysis was not new, he did synthesize previous thought and effectively articulated the problems. Having identified the problems, the solutions to chaos in the city became evident.[31]

The most effective national force for urban reform was the National Municipal League. The league, which was formed in 1894, developed out of a meeting in Philadelphia at which 105 prominent persons signed the resolutions passed by the first National Conference for Good City Government. By 1897 267 local good government groups had affiliated with the league. Three years later its proposal for "A Municipal Program" was published. These proposals were directed at removing three evils found in urban government. The first was economic, namely, the misuse and waste of public funds. The second was political, reflected in the inadequacy of social services necessary to make the city livable. The third was moral, involving the use of public office for the enhancing of personal needs. In general the league's proposals called for (1) increasing the power of local government, (2) limiting the power of the state, (3) placing limits on taxes and the public debt, (4) establishing a civil service, (5) adopting the nonpartisan, mayor-council form of government, and (6) granting relatively short-term franchises to utilities where public ownership was not possible.[32]

The real importance of the league's activity, as well as the increasing concern for municipal government, was the development of a unitary approach to solving urban problems. This movement toward a national urban policy, in effect, was encouraged by the successful city governments that were found in Europe, especially Great Britain. It was very common for spokesmen of reform to make the comparison between the dismal situation in the United States and the advances made in Western Europe. Horace E. Deming in 1900 wrote:

> Does the democratic-republican form of government make impossible the honest, efficient, economical, progressive conduct of municipal affairs? In Great Britain and on the continent . . . the cities are the most conspicuous examples of efficiency, economy, and progress in the field of government.[33]

Despite the signs of possible solutions to urban problems, the condition of cities and their governments worsened in the 1890s. The Depression of 1893, the strikes, especially at Homestead and Pullman, the continued process of industrial consolidation, and the increasing number of immigrants from Eastern Europe, all seemed to be drawing America away from the ideals and vision of the "good society."

Summary

The nineteenth-century urban experience continued patterns found earlier. The city became more and more involved in increasing its social services. The general social problems associated with industrialization had to be met at the local level. Unfortunately, cities were unable to respond to this challenge successfully. The primary structural reform advocated to make the city function more effectively was the adoption of the federal system of separation of powers and the checks and balances. This reform only encouraged the decentralization of power.

As the economy became more complex, as the size differential between cities increased, and as the number of new urban centers multiplied, there emerged ever more diversity in urban America. To offset this diversity, as well as to free the cities from state interference, there were calls for a national approach to municipal problems. This call was supported by the British experience. Unfortunately, the reformers met with opposition from both the cities and the state legislatures, which were intent on maintaining their influence over the cities.

NOTES

1. Adna Ferrin Weber, *The Growth of Cities in the Nineteenth Century* (New York: Macmillan, 1899; reprint ed., Ithaca, N.Y.: Cornell University Press, 1963), p. 22.

2. See Clarence H. Danhof, *Change in Agriculture: The Northern United States* (Cambridge, Mass.: Harvard University Press, 1969); Paul W. Gates, *The Farmer's Age: Agriculture, 1815-1860* (New York: Holt, Rinehart and Winston, 1960); John T. Schlebecker, *Whereby We Thrive: A History of American Farming* (Ames: Iowa University Press, 1975); Allan G. Bogue, *From Prairie to Corn Belt* (Chicago: University of Chicago Press, 1963).

3. Sam Bass Warner, Jr., *The Urban Wilderness* (New York: Harper & Row, 1972), pp. 64-84, and *The Private City: Philadelphia in Three Periods of Its Growth* (Philadelphia: University of Pennsylvania Press, 1968), pp. 63-78; see also Samuel P. Hays, *The Response to Industrialism* (Chicago: University of Chicago Press, 1957); Lewis Atherton, *Main Street on the Middle Border* (Bloomington: Indiana University Press, 1954).

4. David Ward, *Cities and Immigrants* (New York: Oxford University Press, 1971), pp. 105-21; Zane L. Miller, *Boss Cox's Cincinnati* (New York: Oxford University Press, 1968), pp. 3-55.

5. Warner, *Urban Wilderness*, pp. 85-92.

6. Warner, *Private City*, pp. 56-61.

7. Oscar Handlin, "The Modern City as a Field of Historical Study," in *The Historian and the City*, eds. Oscar Handlin and John Burchard (Cambridge, Mass.: M.I.T. Press, 1963), pp. 1-26.

8. Bayrd Still, "Patterns of Mid-Nineteenth Century Urbanization in the Middle West," *Mississippi Valley Historical Review* 28 (September 1941): 200-204.

9. For a discussion of the role of the evolution of the professionalized police force, see James F. Richardson, *The Urban Police in the United States* (Port Washington, N.Y.: Kennikat, 1974); for education, see Lawrence A. Cremin, *The Transformation of the School: Progressivism in American Education, 1876-1957* (New York: Alfred A. Knopf, 1961), and James W. Sanders, *The Education of an Urban Minority* (New York: Oxford University Press, 1976).

10. Nelson M. Blake, *Water for the Cities* (Syracuse: Syracuse University Press, 1958); Ernest S. Griffith, *A History of American City Government: The Conspicuous Failure, 1870-1900* (New York: Praeger, 1974), p. 169.

11. Delos F. Wilcox, *Great Cities in America* (New York: Macmillan, 1910), p. 67.

12. Still, p. 195.

13. *Ibid.,* pp. 195-96; quotes from p. 195.

14. Works Progress Administration (WPA) Writers' Program (William Burke), *Copper Camp* (New York, 1943), p. 49; quoted in Griffith, p. 47.

15. John A. Fairlie, "Municipal Development in the United States," in *A*

Municipal Program, ed. for National Municipal League (New York: Macmillan, 1900), pp. 11-12.

16. Thomas Harrison Reed, *Municipal Government in the United States* (New York: Century, 1926), pp. 72-73.

17. Fairlie, pp. 13-14; quote from p. 13.

18. Reed, p. 76; Ernest S. Griffith, *The Modern Development of City Government*, 2 vols. (London: Oxford University Press, 1927), I:113-14.

19. Reed, pp. 140-42; Griffith, *Conspicuous Failure*, pp. 215-18; Fairlie, p. 22.

20. *City of Clinton* v. *The Cedar Rapids and Missouri River Railroad Company*, 24 Iowa 455 (1868), quoted in Mark T. Gelfand, *A Nation of Cities: The Federal Government and Urban America, 1933-1965* (New York: Oxford University Press, 1975), p. 5.

21. Kenneth Fox, *Better City Government* (Philadelphia: Temple University Press, 1977), pp. 23-41; Reed, pp. 142-44.

22. *Hunter* v. *Pittsburgh*, 207 U.S. 161, 178, 179 (1907), quoted in Gelfand, pp. 5-6.

23. Reed, pp. 146-48.

24. *Ibid.,* pp. 148-49.

25. *Ibid.,* pp. 151-53.

26. James Bryce, *The American Commonwealth*, 2 vols. (New York: Macmillan, 1888), I:637.

27. Griffith, *Conspicuous Failure*, p. 103.

28. Eric F. Goldman, *Rendezvous with Destiny* (New York: Vintage, 1960), pp. 129-30.

29. Griffith, *Conspicuous Failure*, p. 111.

30. Melvin G. Holli, *Reform in Detroit* (New York: Oxford University Press, 1969), p. 54; quote from p. xii.

31. Bryce, I:608-13.

32. Frank Mann Stewart, *A Half Century of Municipal Reform* (Berkeley: University of California Press, 1950), pp. 15-27; Delos F. Wilcox, "An Examination of the Proposed Municipal Program," in *A Municipal Program,* pp. 225-39.

33. Horace E. Deming, "The Municipal Problem in the United States," in *A Municipal Program*, p. 36.

CHAPTER IV.

Political Machines
and Urban Development

Introduction

Urban development in the nineteenth century created demands that existing institutions of city government were unable to handle. As the gap between public needs and institutional responses widened, city residents began to look beyond the governmental system to find appropriate remedies; political machines emerged to meet the expanded and diverse needs of the central city population and the urban economy. Political machines were able to use their role in the electoral process to gain control of the city's governance institutions. This, in turn, was used to meet the needs of individuals and groups that supported machine candidates.

Because political machines played such an important part in urban development, both in terms of responding to conditions that developed during the nineteenth century and shaping conditions that were to affect cities in the twentieth century, this chapter examines the nature of political machines and their role in urban development.

DYNAMICS OF POLITICAL MACHINES

Internal Structure

The practice of machine politics, i.e., the use and manipulation of material incentives and awards to maintain a cadre of activists and an electoral coalition sufficient to control the machinery of government, enabled party leaders to control the nomination process and, in turn, the election of candidates to various public offices in city government.[1]

The political machine was able to unite what law and tradition had separated. By confining nomination to public office to party politicians, each of them dependent on the organization rather than on his own electoral constituency, parties were able to bring together the diverse threads of city government into a reasonably unified chain of command. The cooperation and coordination of most city officeholders, precluded by law and tradition through separate election, was brought about by the control of the political machine over nomination and electoral processes. Those who refused to cooperate with the organization's leaders were kept out of governmental office by being denied access to their party's nomination.

Though variations occurred from one locale to another, the structure of political machines was remarkably similar, largely because they were set up to serve similar purposes from one city to another. Robert Merton's explanation of the persistence of machine politics emphasizes the coordinating function of centralized political machines:

> The key structural function of the Boss is to organize, centralize and maintain in good working condition the "scattered fragments of power" which are at present dispersed through our political organization. By the centralized organization of political power, the Boss and his apparatus can satisfy the needs of diverse subgroups in a larger community which are not politically satisfied by legally devised and culturally approved social structures.[2]

Fred I. Greenstein's conceptualization of the political machine from a structural and functional point of view complements Merton's nicely. Greenstein identifies the machine as an organization with the following characteristics:

1. There is a disciplined party hierarchy led by a single executive or board of directors.
2. The party exercises effective control over nominations to public office and, through this, it controls the public officials of the municipality.
3. The party leadership—which quite often is of lower-class social origins—usually does not hold public office and sometimes does not even hold formal party office. At any rate, official position is not the primary source of the leadership's strength.
4. Rather, a cadre of loyal party officials and workers, as well as a core of voters, is maintained by a mixture of material rewards and nonideological psychic rewards—such as personal and ethnic recognition, camaraderie, and the like.[3]

Machine leaders and activists at the neighborhood level used this structural framework to reach out to the diverse city population and engender the support of a sufficient number of its members to put together and sustain an electoral majority. This majority was used, in turn, to establish and maintain control of the machinery of city government. Once in power, the machine organization served as brokers, or middlemen, between governmental institutions on the one hand and organization supporters (individuals and groups alike) on the other.

Incentives of Machine Politics

Much has been written about the relationship between political machines and the urban electorate, especially as regards the practice of machine politics. Generally speaking, machine politics enabled political machines to establish and consolidate control of governmental machinery by offering incentives to city residents in the areas of citizenship and voting, employment and economic opportunity, welfare services, and social recognition and mobility.

Voting and political power. Political machines played a crucial role in initiating urban newcomers into the American political system. Despite the fact that the role played by the party organization oftentimes bordered on the illegal, as well as the unethical, newcomers to the central cities, especially the European immigrants, found the political machine anxious to assist in the acquisition of citizenship and the right to vote. Machine organizations shepherded groups of immigrants through the naturalization and voter registration procedures. For society, such assistance meant that the newcomer was one step closer to acculturation and assimilation. For the machine, such activities virtually guaranteed a new element in its electoral coalition, because in acquiring the right to vote immigrants felt a sense of gratitude and debt to the machine organization and its leadership.

One key to the machine's effectiveness in meeting the needs of immigrant groups and individuals was its willingness to use control over nomination of candidates of city offices to balance the party ticket. It was common practice for machine leaders to nominate a cross section of individuals from the various ethnic groups in the organization's constituency. Over a period of time, members of an ethnic group knew that they could count on one of the major political parties to nominate one of their own to a city office. Since votes were commonly cast for the entire ticket rather than individual candidates, each of the machine's candidates benefited from the ethnic background of the others. In short, the political machine served as a vehicle for social recognition and respectability as well as political representation of urban newcomers. Since the rural migrants and European immigrant groups eventually outnumbered the "native Americans" at the polls, their support in primary and general elections was sufficient to keep the political machine in control of city government.

Social recognition and mobility. Political machines were used by European immigrants to ensure their acculturation and adjustment in the new environment of American cities. Whereas an ethnic identity was unimportant in the homeland, it was a distinguishing attribute of urban newcomers in the New World. Being Polish, Italian, or Irish in America was a badge of distinction and differentiation, and it wasn't always the case that such distinctions proved helpful in acquiring the recognition necessary for integration into the American urban culture and life-style.[4]

The existence of ethnic enclaves or neighborhoods provided one opportunity for immigrant groups to live amongst their own kind and practice the customs, traditions, and mores of the homeland. However, that did not solve the growing problem created by the cultural pluralism that characterized the cities. Each ethnic group practiced its life-style and customs in its neighborhood enclave, but relationships that cut across the groups tended toward antagonism and tension. As each group sought to establish its place in the city's social system, it tended to resent the advances of other groups. Each nationality group came to regard the social progress and mobility of others as potentially damaging to its own.

And, to compound the problem, the small group of native upper-class residents tended to look upon the newcomers, native rural migrants and European immigrants alike, with a mixture of disdain and disregard. The largely white middle class tended to view these newcomers as having no skills or contributions to make to city life and just as often failed to recognize any need the immigrants had for social respectability and upward mobility. The attitude of the white middle class was standoffish at best and elitist at worst.

Not so the political machine. There was nothing elitist or arrogant about machine leaders' attitudes toward the urban newcomers. On the contrary, the machine not only provided the newcomers to the city with a vehicle of social recognition and mobility, it welcomed them into the organization, sought their support, and served as an instrument for their participation in urban government and politics. Harold Gosnell's classic study of Chicago's political machine shows how it brought ethnic groups into the existing social and political systems:

> In the areas where there is a concentration of Negro population, both the Republican and Democratic parties had Negro committeemen. In the areas where persons of Polish descent are found, the parties kept a Zintak, a Konkowski, a Rosenkowski, a Kucharski, a Golusinski, and a Peska as committeemen; and in areas where many persons of Italian

extraction are located, the committeemen bore such names as Serritella, Pacelli, Vignola, and Porcare.[5]

The structure of the machine, reaching down as it did to the neighborhood level, provided a valuable opportunity for urban newcomers to become integrated into and represented by existing political organizations. The system of political democracy practiced in the cities at the time meant that the vote of a Rosenkowski, O'Malley, or Pacelli was worth as much as that of a Smith, Jones, or Green.

The machine did not restrict itself to recognizing the social aspirations of immigrant groups per se. It did just as much to respond to the needs of individuals as well. The chronicle of George Washington Plunkitt sheds light on the way in which the political machine responded to the needs of individuals:

> I know every man, woman and child in the Fifteenth District, except them that's been born this summer—and I know some of them, too. I know what they like and what they don't like, what they are strong at and what they are weak in, and I reach them by approachin' at th right side.
>
> For instance, here's how I gather in the young men. I hear of a young feller that's proud of his voice, thinks that he can sing fine. I ask him to come around to Washington Hall and join our Glee Club. He comes and sings, and he's a follower of Plunkitt for life. Another young feller gains a reputation as a baseball player in a vacant lot. I bring him into our baseball club. That fixes him. You'll find him workin' for my ticket at the polls next election day. Then there's the feller that likes rowin' on the river, the young feller that makes a name as a waltzer on his block, the young feller that's handy with his dukes—I rope them all in by givin' them opportunities to show themselves off. I don't trouble with political arguments. I just study human nature and act accordin'.[6]

Employment and economic opportunity. Most of the newcomers to the city, European immigrants and native-born alike, saw it as a place to go get a good job and, over a reasonable period of time, enhance their economic standing and mobility. Industrialization had only recently come to a close when expectations were raised concerning opportunities in the cities for jobs, better housing and living conditions, economic security, etc. As the demand for more and more public services increased, the need for additional manpower became more acute. The party in power in city government found itself having to fill positions in police, fire, and sanitation departments, building inspection and maintenance, and a host of other public services and functions. In addition, jobs in the private sector in business and industry proliferated and these, too, had to be filled from among the enlarged and newly enfranchised urban electorate.

Perhaps more than any other single term, patronage has been used to describe the "coin" of machine politics and of the political machine as an organization. The political machine used the increased job opportunities in city government and their control of hiring procedures and practices to recruit and retain party activists and supporters in the electorate at large. The machine's control of city government made it relatively simple to fill the ranks of municipal workers from among the groups that constituted the party's electoral majority and cadre of precinct and ward activists.

By and large the machine used the manipulation of jobs and patronage to attract and retain party activists and electoral support at the precinct levels of the organization. It was relatively simple to engender someone's support of the party organization by making clear the fact that his or her job depended upon the continued control by the machine of city government. Frank Kent in *The Great Game of Politics* details how the political machine organized the precinct and used precinct workers to get out enough votes in primary and general elections to keep the machine's candidates in public office.[7] Usually a precinct would contain about 600 voters. Allowing for independents and registrants in another party, there were usually about 250 voters *eligible* to cast ballots in the machine's primary election. Of this number, only about 125 could be expected *actually* to vote. Therefore, it would take only 65 votes to continue control over nominations by the machine in a given precinct. It was the responsibility of *each* precinct worker in the organization to produce the 65 or so votes needed to nominate the candidate of the machine. Later, in the general election, it would be the responsibility of each precinct worker in the organization to produce the votes needed to elect the candidates of the machine to various positions in city government.

To assure control of a precinct, machine activists had patronage of their own to dispense at the neighborhood level. For example, precinct workers chose election day poll watchers and designated polling places. The necessary votes in the primary election could be easily mounted by adding the votes of the precinct worker and his or her relatives to those of the poll watchers and recipients of the rental fees from polling places and their relatives. These numbers could easily reach 35 to 40. Kent goes on to explain how the necessary 65 votes would be turned out:

> There are in every precinct some of these (office holders), and they mostly hold their jobs because of the recommendation of the precinct executive (captain). There are street cleaners or lamp lighters whom he has put to work through the ward executive who has the pull at the City Hall. There are members of the Police Department or firemen whom he helped out on the force. Or there may be aspirants for jobs of one sort or another who cannot get them without the precinct executive's backing.

There are very few precincts anywhere in which there are not at least ten persons living who are under party organization obligations of one sort or another for the offices they hold. In many precincts there are a good many more. But take seven as the average, and if each one of the seven is worth his five family votes—and it is extremely rare that he is not—then the precinct executive has got his total of sixty-five votes and a little more.[8]

If the relationship between the machine organization and its workers and supporters at the precinct level seems direct and simple, it should, because that's the way it was. The organization provided workers and voters with a variety of jobs and related economic opportunities in return for which it expected to receive the votes in primary and general elections needed to keep machine-supported candidates in positions in city government. Everyone's livelihood depended on the continued control of city government by the political machine. The political machine operated as an employment agency of sorts, but it did so for free. The fee was support of the organization's candidates for office and it was paid at primary and general elections.

Welfare and relief assistance. The political machine was particularly effective in providing "relief and friendly service" assistance to individuals and groups that comprised its electoral majority in the city. In fact, it was this type of assistance to needy individuals that engendered their undying support of the organization's candidates.

The fragmentation that characterized city government created a serious gap in the ability of existing public institutions and agencies to meet the increasing number and variety of human needs. Furthermore, there were at that time few nationally sponsored programs in the area of public assistance. Consequently, when human needs began to mushroom with the rapid and unplanned growth of the central cities, the political machine responded by becoming a quasi-public "welfare bureaucracy." It dispensed public assistance services of all kinds to individuals and groups who needed them. All that was needed was a contact with the machine through a precinct or ward captain. Soon after the organization became aware of an individual's need it took direct action to meet it.

Where did political machines get the wherewithal to develop the capacity to dispense relief and welfare services? First, the machine's candidates held the overwhelming number of elective and appointed positions in city government. This enabled machine leaders, who controlled nomination to the elected positions, to control the individuals who occupied them. This, in turn, enabled the machine to overcome the fragmentation and lack of coordination between city agencies and functions that had caused, or at least contributed to, the paralysis of city government in the first place. Consequently, if a supporter of the political machine found himself or herself with a son in trouble with the police, it was a relatively simple matter to arrange for a reduced or suspended sentence if the person had already been charged with a crime and had been brought before the local courts. It is important to remember that most local public offices, including those of judge, were filled at the polls. The machine was no less interested in the filling of judgeships than in the filling of executive and legislative offices.

Second, the alliance that formed between the machine and the business-commercial community provided a rich and often endless supply of the resources, assistance, financial aid, or even goods and services like heating materials (the infamous bucket of coal) or food (the well-known turkey on Thanksgiving Day); the machine had ready and direct access to the things that would meet existing and pressing human needs. It was almost always the case that the machine organization would have allied itself with the necessary mixture of business and commercial enterprises needed to meet the growing number and variety of human needs.

George Washington Plunkitt of Tammany Hall described the way in which relief and assistance services worked to build and maintain an effective electoral majority:

> What tells in holdin' your grip on your district is to go right down among the poor families and help them in the different ways they need help. I've got a regular system for this. If there's a fire in Ninth, Tenth, or Eleventh Avenue, for example, any hour of the day or night, I'm usually there with some of my election district captains as soon as the fire engines. If a family is burned out I don't ask whether they are Republicans or Democrats, and I don't refer them to the Charity Organization Society, which would investigate their case in a month or two and decide if they were worthy of help about the time they are dead from starvation. I just get quarters for them, buy clothes for them if their clothes were burned up, and fix them up til they get things runnin' again. It's philanthropy, but it's politics, too—mighty good politics. Who can tell how many votes one of these fires bring me? The poor are the most grateful people in the world, and, let me tell you, they have more friends in their neighborhoods than the rich have in theirs.[9]

Where would George Washington Plunkitt get the things he provided to the family victimized by fire? More than likely at least one person in the machine's alliance with the business community was a landlord or realtor with access to readily available housing. Yet another was a haberdasher who supplied the necessary variety of clothing for members of the family, and, finally, still another was a "fat cat" from whom sufficient funds were available to give the victims spending money. Repayment? The only form of repayment expected from the victims of such emergencies was support of the machine's candidates on primary and general election day.

Plunkitt's effectiveness in providing this assistance was due in part to the fact that he (the machine organization) eliminated the red tape that often characterized the operation of many private philanthropies or charitable organizations. When the machine provided relief after a disaster or catastrophe, there were no forms to fill out, no lines to wait on, no investigations to make before assistance would be authorized, etc. The relief and assistance of the machine were immediate, direct, and effective. It got the job done when and where it had to be done, at and for the convenience of the citizen-client, not the organization.

The machine by no means restricted its relief and public assistance services to disasters or crises such as fires. It was often more than financial help or shelter that the typical urban family needed. A few entries in William Riordon's account of a day in the life of Plunkitt tells the story of machine services to its constituency:

2 a.m.: Aroused from sleep by the ringing of his door bell; went to the door and found a bartender, who asked him to go to the police station and bail out a saloonkeeper who had been arrested for violating the excise law. Furnished bail and returned to bed at three o'clock.

8:30 a.m.: Went to the police court to look after his constituents. Found six "drunks." Secured the discharge of four by a timely word with the judge, and paid the fines of two.

9 a.m.: Appeared in the Municipal District Court. Directed one of his district captains to act as counsel for a widow against whom dispossess proceedings had been instituted and obtained an extension of time. Paid the rent of a poor family about to be dispossessed and gave them a dollar for food.

11 a.m.: At home again. Found four men waiting for him. One had been discharged by the Metropolitan Railway Company for neglect of duty, and wanted the district leader to fix things. Another wanted a job on the road. The third sought a place on the Subway and the fourth, a plumber, was looking for work with the Consolidated Gas Company. The district leader spent nearly three hours fixing things for the four men, and succeeded in each case.[10]

Absence of ideology. Our characterization of the incentives and rewards of machine politics has failed to indicate the ideological or programmatic direction of political machines. The reason is that machines had neither a political ideology to advance nor a set of policy alternatives to present to voters. As political organizations, machines were nonideological and pragmatic and they avoided the internally divisive consequences of arguing over issues, platform statements, or general ideology. Furthermore, machine leaders knew that effective control over organizational activists and electoral supporters came not from appealing to their ideological or programmatic preferences, but rather from having access to and manipulating material and psychological incentives and rewards like jobs, preferential treatment, relief and welfare services, and ethnic group recognition.

ROLE IN URBAN DEVELOPMENT

Assessing Political Machines

It is difficult to assess the contributions of political machines to urban development without raising the complicating factor of the machines' immorality and illegality. To be sure, political machines often operated at least at the fringes if not beyond the limits of the law. The practice of selecting governmental personnel through the use of political patronage not only failed to provide public agencies with qualified workers, it often resulted in swelling the size of city government beyond what was needed to provide the appropriate mix and levels of public services. Then, too, the practice of ticket balancing to appeal to a culturally diverse electoral majority violates the notion that an individual's vote should be based on an evaluation of each candidate's qualifications and fitness for office, rather than on the ethnic or racial composition of the ticket. Finally, the idea of a single individual, or boss, exercising near-absolute control over the party organization as well as governmental structure runs directly counter to popular notions of open, democratic government based on the consent of the governed.

Latent Functions of Machines[11]

The impact of political machines on urban development can be viewed in the context of two characteristics of the central city: (1) the social structure makes it difficult, if not impossible, for morally approved structures to fulfill essential social functions, and (2) the diverse needs of various social groups are left unmet, except for the functions performed by the political machines.[12]

We have already described the fragmented nature of the governmental system existing at the time political machines initially emerged. We have also described how that system was unable to cope with the growing number and variety of demands emanating out of the changing social and economic systems of the central cities. The fragmentation of the governmental system was in large part a result of the heritage of constitutional frameworks and the general political culture.

Two ideas that helped to shape the writing of the U.S. Constitution are the protection of individual liberty and distrust of power. The framers of the national Constitution created a federal governmental system based on the principles of separation of powers and checks and balances to ensure that the liberties of individual citizens (and states) would be protected and that power, particularly executive power, would not be concentrated in the hands of a single agency of government. The resulting system of separated institutions sharing power not only characterized the constitutional framework at the national level, but at the state and local levels as well. The dispersion of power and authority served well the purpose of preventing an abuse of power by public officials. However, it also made it difficult for those same officials to take positive, forceful, and direct action. When action was needed, no one had sufficient authority to act. The political machine moved into the vacuum created by the dispersion of authority and provided the direction, coordination, and decisional authority needed for public agencies and officials to meet public needs.

Another consideration to be taken lies in the fact that, when the various parts of the dispersed system of government could be coordinated and action taken, it was often at the expense of the individual citizen. The public bureaucracy that developed out of the prevailing political traditions was officious and legalistic. It often failed to recognize the "human side" to problems that individuals brought to public agencies for solution. The political machine humanized the public bureaucracy, bringing it to a degree of personalism and concern for human welfare that it did not have of its own development. As Herbert Croly has noted, there developed:

> a much more human system of partisan government, whose chief object soon became the circumvention of government by law.... The lawlessness of the extra-official democracy was merely the counterpoise of the legalism of the official democracy. The lawyer having been permitted to subordinate democracy to the law, the Boss had to be called in to extricate the victim, which he did after a fashion and for a consideration.[13]

Another facet of the machines' impact on urban development lies in its role in providing stability and continuity of governmental leadership. The dispersion of political power through separation of powers, limited tenure in office, and election of most (if not all) public officials impeded the emergence of experienced leadership. Frequent elections and turnover of officeholders combined to increase the relative inexperience of governmental officials. The continuity and stability of governmental leadership that seemed to be precluded by the operation of legal requirements and constraints were provided from outside the system by the machine. The political machine elected its slate of candidates to governmental office with envious regularity and consistency. Individual governmental officials were almost always renominated so long as they continued to heed the desires of machine leaders.

Merton has captured the essence of this impact of the political machines' contributions to urban development by noting that, in general terms, "the functional deficiencies of the official structure generate an alternative (unofficial) structure to fulfill existing needs somewhat more effectively."[14]

The second area in which the machines' contributions to urban development can be analyzed is the functions it performed for diverse social groups in the urban community. Political machines did not fail to recognize the social and cultural diversity of urban society. Nor did they fail to recognize the influx of substantial numbers of urban newcomers, either large numbers of rural blacks or equally large numbers of European immigrants. The machine quickly realized that these individuals had specific and different needs, and it moved quickly to meet them. It avoided dealing in remote and amorphous issues of public policy and appealed, instead, in terms of concrete and immediate needs of survival.

The organization of the machine was an elaborate yet grass-roots network of personal friendships, ties, and obligations. For the machine, politics was very much a personal process in which individuals' needs were identified and met. Individuals, in turn, owed a debt to the machine, one that was paid off at the polls in primary and general elections. The machine provided a degree of personalism in urban society that was difficult to sustain in the increasing size and complexity of the urban social system, to say nothing of its ethnic diversity. Thus, the machine, through its precinct workers and ward leaders, fulfilled the important social function of humanizing and personalizing societal relations and the conduct of public business by governmental agencies.

It is particularly important to appreciate not only the fact that the political machine provided aid to the needy, but the manner in which it did so. As noted earlier, there were in fact numerous private charitable and philanthropic organizations and agencies in urban society. However, for the most part these agencies had lengthy and complicated procedures that delayed the provision of aid and, when it came, brought with it considerable unpleasantness and loss of self-respect. The machine, on the other hand, provided aid and assistance when it was needed with no questions asked. There were no eligibility rules for aid from the machine save possibly one: the recipient had to be a registered voter of the city. In fact, the machine didn't always require that each recipient of its welfare services be a registered voter. Often the machine would provide aid to friends and relatives of supporters if only to reinforce the latter's loyalty to the organization. For the needy, then, the political machine satisfied human wants and needs in a way that could not be done by the existing social institutions in the city.

The needy or underprivileged of society were not the only ones for whom political machines met pressing demands. Another group served by the machine's presence was the business community. The assistance sought by business interests, big and small alike, usually involved immediate economic gain. Special dispensations from building codes, building inspectors who failed to notice violations, preferential treatment in awarding contracts, these and a host of other benefits formed the basis of the machine's satisfaction of the business community's "needs." Merton attempts to set the propriety of these practices in proper perspective by noting:

> ... To adopt an *exclusively* moral attitude toward the "corrupt political machine" is to lose sight of the very structural conditions which generate the "evil" that is so bitterly attacked. To adopt a functional outlook is to provide not an apologia for the political machine but a more solid basis for modifying or eliminating the machine, providing specific structural arrangements are introduced either for eliminating these effective demands of the business community or, if that is the objective, of satisfying these demands through alternative means.[15]

Political machines met a third set of needs that grew out of rapid urban development, the need for channels of social mobility. The urban society and culture that rural blacks and European immigrants came into provided few conventional and legitimate social institutions and mechanisms for gaining desired social status and prestige. The occupational areas open to the urban newcomers were almost completely limited to manual labor. The existing cultural stigma then attached to manual labor and the corresponding prestige of white-collar work forced the new urban groups to seek alternative means of achieving success.

The political machine served as a mechanism of social mobility for groups that otherwise would have had few opportunities to enhance their social status. The machine welcomed urban blacks, Poles, Irish, Italians, Catholics, and Jews with an openness that was unavailable outside each group's own network of neighborhood-based organizations and family relationships. The machine, in effect, brought diverse groups together and provided not only an avenue of upward social mobility and political representation, but also an opportunity to compete on near-even terms with the dominant (largely) white social structure.

Political Machines and the Dynamics of Urban Society[16]

Our assessment of the impact of political machines on urban development can be concluded by summarizing the many functions performed by machines and relating these to the needs of the changing urban society that machines were part of. To aid in this it is useful to refer to the work of the sociologist Talcott Parsons. Almost three decades ago Parsons presented a theory of society in which he alleged that, for any social system or society to persist through time, four functions had to be performed. These are the functions of goal attainment, adaptation, integration, and latency or pattern maintenance. Furthermore, certain functions are performed primarily by given structures, as no single structure performs all functions alone, nor is any structure necessarily unifunctional.

We think it is useful to view the impact of political machines on urban development in the context of Parsons' schema. Though Parsons asserts that no single structure performs all functions alone, the breadth of functions performed by political machines would seem to substantiate the view that they had a hand in performing each of Parsons' functional requisites of society. It goes without saying that the machine organization was more integral to the performance of some functions than others.

Goal attainment, or the setting of priorities for the society, is a function most frequently performed by the polity. The polity of the city was clearly dominated by the political machine. Machines nominated the candidates who were elected to city government offices and, through its control of nominations, elections, and appointments to public office, the machine controlled the decisions made by city officials and the actions taken by city agencies. The machine was without effective competition in influencing the agenda and priorities of the city's political and governmental systems. It was the most pervasive and influential political institution existing at the time.

The function of adaptation involves mobilization of human and material resources to support the goals set for society. The machine, with its control of governmental machinery and its direct and immediate access to the private sector of the urban economy, certainly had as much if not more to do with the performance of the function of adaptation as any other institution in urban society. In some respects, in fact, the political machine was the common thread that linked the social and economic systems, where resources needed for goal attainment were concentrated, with the political and governmental systems, where resources were used to pursue the goals of the urban society.

The fact that most structures, as well as the individuals in society, tend to be multifunctional creates the need for performance of the third functional requisite, that of integration. The purpose of integration is to bring together the structures and actors in society so that order, direction, and coherence will characterize their respective activities. The political machine served as an integrating institution in urban society by bridging the gap between social, economic, and governmental institutions and imposing, if necessary, order and coherence on the activities and roles each performed. Furthermore, the central role of the political machine in the integration of these other institutions enabled it to mediate and, if necessary, control and settle conflicts between different institutions as they performed overlapping functions.

Finally, the function of latency or pattern maintenance enables the society to foster conformity to the norms of the cultural system. As this function is performed the values of society are passed to succeeding generations and sanctions may be applied for violation or nonobservance of values or norms. The political machine played less of a role in the performance of this function than any other. Traditionally, the family, school, and church were primary agents of socialization, and the political machine made no attempt to compete with or supplant these social institutions. However, the machine played a major role as an agent of *political* socialization, i.e., transmission of the dominant attitudes, values, and beliefs necessary for the polity to survive. We have already described the pivotal role played by the political machine in bringing the urban newcomers into citizenship and the electoral system. As the machine engendered a sense of loyalty to and support of the organization in particular, it also developed and reinforced each citizen's sense of legitimacy for the political system in general. Furthermore, the machine served the important need of vitiating the potentially divisive and disruptive consequences of the social pluralism in urban society.

In no way can it be said that political machines were an unmixed blessing in urban development. We have tried to show the many ways in which machines made a positive and necessary contribution to resolving the problems created by rapid and uncontrollable growth in the central cities. However, machines also caused, at least indirectly, as many problems as they helped to resolve, and in this respect created the next set of challenges in urban growth for which institutional and policy responses had to be developed. It is to this aspect of the machines' impact on urban development that we turn our attention in the next chapter.

NOTES

1. Raymond E. Wolfinger, *The Politics of Progress* (Englewood Cliffs, N.J.: Prentice-Hall, 1974), p. 99.

2. Robert E. Merton, *Social Theory and Social Structure* (New York: The Free Press, 1957), p. 73.

3. Fred I. Greenstein, "The Changing Pattern of Urban Party Politics," *The Annals of the American Academy of Political and Social Science* 353 (May 1964): 3.

4. Robert E. Park, *The Immigrant Press and Its Control* (New York: Harper, 1922), provides an excellent account of the growth of European identity in the United States.

5. Harold F. Gosnell, *Machine Politics* (Chicago: University of Chicago Press, 1938), pp. 44–45.

6. William L. Riordon, *Plunkitt of Tammany Hall* (New York: McClure, Phillips, 1905), pp. 46–48.

7. Frank R. Kent, *The Great Game of Politics* (Garden City, N.Y.: Doubleday, 1928).

8. *Ibid.,* p. 21.

9. Riordon, pp. 51-52.

10. *Ibid.,* pp. 170-72.

11. This discussion draws heavily on Merton, pp. 71-81.

12. *Ibid.,* p. 72.

13. Herbert Croly, *Progress Democracy* (New York: Macmillan, 1914), p. 254.

14. Merton, p. 73.

15. *Ibid.,* p. 76.

16. This discussion draws heavily on Talcott Parsons, *The Social System* (Glencoe, Ill.: The Free Press, 1951), esp. chap. 2.

CHAPTER V.

Municipal Reform and Institutional Change in the Cities

Introduction

In the previous chapter we discussed one aspect of political machines, namely, their contribution to urban development at a time when other social structures were either unable or unwilling to bridge the gap between residents' needs and institutional responses. Political machines made a direct and necessary contribution toward helping to resolve the problems created by rapid and unplanned growth in the central cities during the nineteenth and early twentieth centuries. They helped to bridge the structural gap in urban society between social and economic needs and interests on the one hand and governmental and political institutions on the other. Machines enabled diverse interests to become integrated into the social and political systems of the city at a time when no other institutions or structures were able or willing to serve this purpose.

However, machines were not an unmixed blessing. While they assisted in the integration of diverse interests in urban society, they also encouraged, condoned, and benefited from substantial corruption and illegal activity in government and society. Machine leaders used their access to governmental institutions and control of public officials to secure a variety of benefits for friends and party supporters, including preferential treatment in awarding public contracts and in the conduct of the public's business. Payoffs, bribes, kickbacks, and favoritism in the enforcement of laws and regulations were an integral part of the way in which government business was conducted in the city. It was commonplace for the friends and supporters of the dominant

machine to operate with virtual immunity from the law, while adversaries of
the machine were regularly subjected to strict and regular enforcement of
building codes and inspections, health inspections, zoning and land-use
regulations, etc.

Examples of the excesses of machines abound. Lincoln Steffens, in his book
Shame of the Cities,[1] discusses the corruption of St. Louis, Minneapolis,
Pittsburgh, Philadelphia, and other cities. His articles, initially published as
separate pieces in *McClure's Magazine* in 1902, were the result of his
investigative skills and muckraking reporting about political machines and
reform in selected cities. He names the bribe givers as well as takers, the
privilege seekers as well as privilege grantors, the amounts, places, and times
of payments of kickbacks and bribes to city officials. In Pittsburgh, paving
contracts worth $3.5 million went to the firm of the city's boss, while
contracts worth $33,400 went to other companies. The favored contractor
received from $1.00 to $1.80 per square yard more than the average in other
cities. In Philadelphia, newly appointed teachers paid $120 out of their first
$141 of salary to the machine that got them appointed to teach in the schools.
Steffens also examines the extent of success in early reform efforts in Chicago
and New York. In St. Louis, eighteen members of the municipal legislature
were indicted; in Minneapolis, Mayor "Doc Ames" was indicted and
convicted. But in many instances laws weren't actually broken; they were
rewritten by machine-supported governmental officials to serve the
organization's purposes. This kind of behavior was sufficiently widespread
and commonplace as to make it impossible to know the precise dimensions of
machine corruption and inefficiency.

The negative consequences of political machines posed a threat to the very
legitimacy and viability of the city's governmental and political institutions.
Political machines were seen as disrupting and destroying more than the moral
and legal fabric of urban society; they were extending their excesses into
society at large and even to the image of American society and government
abroad.

In consequence, a municipal reform movement began to take shape in the
late nineteenth century. Its main objectives included eliminating political
machines from urban society and altering the structure of governmental
institutions. These objectives were interrelated and regarded as a means for
eliminating the waste, corruption, and dishonesty in city government.

There was no single ideology or comprehensive program of municipal reform. Neither was there a single perspective shared by all reformers. For some,
reform was a reaction to the excesses of the bosses and political machines; for
others it was a way to protect the interests of the expanding middle class in the
city; for still others it grew out of a desire to realize the goals of "good

government"; a fourth impetus to municipal reform came from the inability of existing city governmental institutions to respond effectively to an unexpected local crisis or emergency.

APPROACHES TO MUNICIPAL REFORM

Conceptions of Reform

It is generally agreed that the municipal reform movement was an integral part of the Progressive Era. However, the writings of journalists like Lincoln Steffens and the efforts of civic activists like Richard S. Childs reflected the fact that there is no single ideology or perspective on municipal reform. The different conceptions of reform are also seen in the analyses of historians Richard Hofstadter and Samuel P. Hays.

Richard Childs was perhaps the most prominent and vigorous of the municipal reformers in the Progressive Era. A man of considerable wealth, social conscience, professional background, and dedication, he worked tirelessly at municipal reform.[2] Childs's initial effort at municipal reform was manifested in the establishment of the Short Ballot Organization in 1909. The SBO was created to work for the reduction of the long voting lists on the ballot, believing this to be a way to eliminate the influence of the party bosses and their political machines. His interest in institutional reform was stimulated by the Galveston experiment with commission government. Childs sought to improve upon the concept of commission government by developing institutional arrangements that would bring time-tested principles of business management and operation to the organization of governmental institutions. His efforts resulted in the design of the city-manager plan of government which was incorporated into the Model City Charter by the Childs-led National Municipal League in 1915.

Childs believed that the deficiencies of city government lay in its mechanisms rather than moral underpinnings. Thus, he wrote, "The difficulties of democracy are mechanistic, not moral, and respond to mechanistic corrections. . . . It is the mechanism that makes the difference."[3] Mechanistic solutions to institutional problems and responsiveness abound in Childs's agenda for municipal reform: short ballots, city-manager government, and nonpartisan elections, to name a few. In his book, *Civic Victories*, he postulated three universal principles for any form of government: "elective offices must be visible," "the constituency must be wieldy," and "governments must be well integrated."[4]

Lincoln Steffens was a contemporary of Childs's, though his contributions to the Progressive Era and municipal reform were more a result of journalistic efforts than civic activism. Two of his works, *The Shame of the Cities* and *The Autobiography of Lincoln Steffens*, portray the corruption of the cities as a direct result of business and commercial enterprises seeking to enhance their interest.

Steffens's basic theme is that the corruption of government and "shame of the cities" are a result of the dominance of politics by businessmen and an economic system that holds up riches, power, and acclaim as prizes to men bold and able enough to acquire them. The point is made by Steffens in the following manner:

> Who, then, were those bad business men?... Regardless of character, education, and station, the people in these businesses were in the corruption of politics and the resistance to reform. This suggested that it was these businesses, not the men in them, that were the cause of our evil....
> ... I was emphasizing the point that society really offers a prize for evil-doing: money, position, power....[5]

What Steffens was saying, in effect, was that democracy and the economic system of capitalism were morally bankrupt because they gave rise to government *by* businessmen *for* profit. In *Shame of the Cities* Steffens writes:

> There is hardly an office from United States Senator down to Alderman in any part of the country to which the business man has not been elected; yet politics remains corrupt, government pretty bad, and the selfish citizen had to hold himself in readiness like the old volunteer firemen to rush forth at any hour, in any weather, to prevent the fire; and he goes out sometimes and he puts out the fire (after the damage is done) and he goes back to the shop sighing for the business man in politics. The business man has failed in politics as he has in citizenship. Why? Because politics is business. That's what's the matter with it. That's what's the matter with everything,... But don't try to reform politics with the banker, the lawyer, and the dry-goods merchant, for these are business men and there are two great hindrances to their achievement of reform: one is that they are different from, but no better than, the politicians; the other is that politics is not "their line."[6]

Steffens's indictment of American government and capitalism focused on the cities because it was there that businessmen reaped the largest profits from their dominance of politics. From Steffens's perspective the reform agenda had to direct its efforts toward doing something about the control of city government by an alliance of the political machines and business interests.

Richard Hofstadter's conception of the underlying ideology of the Progressive Era is best captured in a well-known, lengthy passage from his work *The Age of Reform*, published in 1955.[7] For him, the politics of patronage and favoritism practiced by political machines was the result of the presence of two divergent sets of popular attitudes toward the nature and goals of politics. These attitudes are expressed in two conflicting orientations, one typical of ethnic groups, the other held by "native" Americans. The best expression of the two orientations is Hofstadter's own statement in the following passage:

> Out of the clash between the needs of the immigrants and the sentiments of the natives there emerged two thoroughly different systems of political ethics.... One, founded upon the indigenous Yankee-Protestant political traditions, and upon middle-class life, assumed and demanded the constant, disinterested activity of the citizen in public affairs.... The other system, founded upon the European backgrounds of the immigrants, ... interpreted political and civic relations chiefly in terms of personal obligations, and placed strong personal loyalties above allegiance to abstract codes of law or morals. It was chiefly upon this system of values that the political life of the immigrant, the boss, and the urban machine was based.[8]

In what has become something of a classic use of the two traditions, Edward Banfield and James Q. Wilson analyze the nature of urban politics in terms of the "fundamental cleavage between the public-regarding, Anglo-Saxon Protestant, middle-class ethos and the private-regarding, lower-class immigrant ethos."[9] The latter ethos

> is the conception of those people who identify with the ward or neighborhood rather than the city "as a whole," who look to politicians for "help" and "favors," ... and who are far less interested in the efficiency, impartiality, and honesty of local government than in its readiness to confer material benefits of one sort or another upon them.[10]

Hofstadter saw the two conflicting orientations as rooted in much more than differing views of politics. Thus, after portraying the nature of the two orientations, he goes on to say:

> In many ways the struggles of the Progressive Era were influenced by the conflict between the two codes elaborated on one side by the highly moral leaders of Protestant social reform and on the other by the bosses, political professionals, and immigrant masses. Since they stemmed from different views not only of politics but of morals and even of religion, it is hardly surprising that the conflicts of the period, often so modest in actual substance, aroused antagonisms so intense and misunderstandings so complete.[11]

Hofstadter wasn't the first who saw urban society from this perspective.

Andrew D. White, the first president of Cornell University, wrote in 1890 that the reason American cities were the "worst in Christendom" was that they were governed on the "evil theory" that "the city is a political body."

> My fundamental contention is that the city is a corporation; that as a city it has nothing whatever to do with general political interests.... The questions in a city are not political questions. They have reference to the laying out of streets (and such matters). The work of a city being the creation and control of the city property, it should logically be managed as a piece of property by those who have created it, who have a title to it, or a real substantial part in it [and not by] a crowd of illiterate peasants, freshly raked in from the Irish bogs, or Bohemian mines, or Italian robber nests....[12]

An important alternative to Hofstadter's thesis that municipal reform was inspired by the middle class is found in Samuel P. Hays's analysis of municipal reform in Des Moines and Pittsburgh.[13] Hays rejects the idea that support for reform in general and municipal reform in particular came from the old middle class, substituting instead his own thesis that the source of support for municipal reform came from the upper class that was closely allied with "big business." His basic argument is that the leading business and professional men in each city initiated and sustained support for municipal reform.

Hays asserts that the basic weakness of the middle-class interpretation of the Progressive Era is that, in the writings of men like Hofstadter, it rests primarily on ideological rather than empirical evidence. There is a difference, he says, between alleging the middle-class nature of reform on the one hand, and the fact that reformers were distinctively middle class, on the other, specifically if they differed from their opponents in their class origins. In describing the nature of the evidence used by Hofstadter and others, Hays writes:

> Such evidence, though it accurately portrays what people thought, does not accurately describe what they did. The great majority of Americans look upon themselves as "middle class" and subscribe to a middle-ground ideology, even though in practice they belong to a great variety of distinct social classes. Such ideologies are not rationalizations or deliberate attempts to deceive. They are natural phenomena of human behavior.... Available evidence indicates that the source of support for reform in municipal government did not come from the lower or middle classes, but from the upper class.[14]

What evidence does Hays employ? He examines specific dimensions of the reform movement, including the class origins of leading spokesmen, to conclude that the municipal reform movement had a decidedly upper-class bias. He cites the dominance of upper-class businessmen who supported municipal research bureaus, city-manager government, and at-large, nonpartisan elections as evidence of their influence on the municipal reform movement. Furthermore, he demonstrates that in almost all instances the opposition to reform came from the working and middle classes in the city.

For these and other advocates of municipal reform the corruption of the cities was class-based. It resulted from the dominance of city government and political institutions by working-class ethnics who had immigrated to America in the latter half of the nineteenth century. From this perspective, the cure for the ills of urban society would come from ridding city government of control by political machines and replacing it with a government of the middle class.

Approaches to Reform

Approaches to municipal reform varied from city to city. Some recounting of how reform got started in different cities will help to show how the diverse approaches to reform reflected the pluralism of the cities.[15] In some places, for example, Populism that was primarily agrarian in concern attracted an urban element. In Nebraska, Populists were responsible for some election reforms as well as specific efforts to rid the city of Omaha of its corruption. Also, a populist governor in Colorado set his sights on an effort to clean up corruption in Denver. In North Carolina, Populists and Republicans joined forces to enact stricter election laws.

In a number of instances the impulse to reform came from local crises that existing institutions were unable to respond to or control. In Galveston, Texas, for example, the commission form of government was created in the aftermath of the 1900 flood.

Charter revision was a common approach to reform, as new institutions and practices were introduced to replace existing arrangements judged morally and legally decadent. This approach was used in such diverse places as Easton, Pennsylvania, in 1887; Long Island City, New York, in 1870; Hamilton, Ohio, Indianapolis, Indiana, and Portland, Oregon, all in 1891.

Prominent business and civic leaders supported a number of efforts at municipal reform. They did this by establishing centers to conduct research in municipal affairs as a springboard for influencing governmental structure and operation. Most often these research centers were established in the large cities because business and civic reformers found government in the larger cities more difficult to alter. One of the first such endeavors was the Bureau of Municipal Research of New York City, founded in 1906 and financed largely through the efforts of Andrew Carnegie and John D. Rockefeller. A similar bureau was established in Philadelphia in 1908, financed by an investment banker. Chicago businessmen established the Bureau of Public Efficiency in 1910. Two years later, in 1912, the cities of Dayton, Ohio, and Rochester, New York, were provided with municipal research facilities to spearhead reform of city government. In each of these instances support for reform came in substantial doses from leading businessmen: John H. Patterson of the National Cash Register Co., in Dayton, Ohio, and George Eastman, of Eastman Kodak Co., in Rochester, New York.

Two reform-oriented organizations more national in scope warrant mention at this point. They are the National Civil Service League and the National Municipal League. The former campaigned for the adoption of civil service regulations at the national and state levels of government. It was largely responsible for congressional enactment in 1883 of the Pendleton Act, the first measure establishing a merit-based civil service system for federal employees. As noted earlier, the National Municipal League campaigned at the state and local levels for the adoption of city-manager government.

The varying circumstances from which municipal reform emerged made it less a comprehensive program than a multifaceted prescription of institutional and procedural change. In almost all instances the common objective remained to rid city government of corruption and inefficiency spawned and tolerated by party bosses and political machines. It is possible to identify at least three dimensions of municipal reform.

First, there were those who sought to deal directly with the political machines. They believed that the machine was the cause of all that was wrong in the cities and this led to efforts to dismantle it as an organization in city politics. Since the strength of the machine lay primarily in its organizational base in the city's neighborhoods, part of the reform agenda consisted of weakening the political machine by instituting nonpartisan elections with at-large rather than ward-based constituencies.

Second, reformers like Richard Childs held a mechanistic view of the defects of city government. They sought to improve the capacity of government to respond to the needs of the cities by designing institutional arrangements reflecting basic principles of business management. Structural reformers, as this group is called, offered commission government and city-manager government as alternatives to the weak mayor form that was popular at the time.

Finally, there were those who called for change in the way elected and appointed officials conducted the public's business. Here the concern was less with mechanisms and institutional arrangements than with procedural openness, regularity, and accountability in the day-to-day operations and performance of public institutions. Prescriptions for accomplishing these goals included changes in personnel and financial administration, accounting, and procedures governing purchases by city government of equipment, supplies, and awarding of city contracts.

REFORM OF POLITICAL INSTITUTIONS AND PROCESSES

Electoral Arrangements

Municipal reformers recognized two things about the condition of cities: first, that much of the corruption and inefficiency of city government could be traced to the control of governmental institutions by the political machine; and second, that the control of governmental institutions by the political machine was in large part a result of its ability to organize and control elections of city officials.

A couple of features of local elections made it relatively easy for political machines to exert considerable influence over elections. As we have seen in Chapter IV, a well-organized machine could control the outcome of primary elections. By judicious use of favor, patronage, and even outright manipulation of votes, precinct captains could provide the machine with the votes necessary to ensure the nomination of its slate. In general elections, the multitude of elective offices meant that ballots were long and difficult to understand. The average voter had neither the time nor the inclination to sift through the list of candidates for each office and decide which ones to support. Instead, the machine label served as a useful and reliable cue. It was a typical practice for the voter to look for the symbol of the party he or she supported and cast his or her ballot for that party's candidates. This resulted in the election of an entire slate of candidates to the city's elective offices. Appointive positions in city government were then filled with persons recommended and approved by the party's bosses, since it was this group in the organization that controlled access to elective office by controlling access to the party's nomination.

Election procedures, where they existed at all, were sloppy and easily abused. Provisions for voter registration, for example, were careless and did not attempt to enforce eligibility requirements. The conduct of elections themselves was such that the integrity of anyone's vote could not be assured. Individuals' votes were almost everywhere subject to the scrutiny of poll watchers and election officials. Indirect and sometimes explicit coercion were used to assure that votes were cast for the "right" candidates. It was a relatively common practice to avoid coercion of voters by simply buying votes. Oftentimes the number of votes cast in an election exceeded the number of registered voters in the city. Since elections were organized and conducted around geographical subdivisions of the city called wards, it was relatively easy to organize and control electoral support in each of the city's wards.

A number of proposals were offered to change the way in which local elections were organized and conducted. Some warrant more thorough examination and analysis than others. For example, to simplify the voters' task, the short ballot was introduced. To insulate the voter from the scrutiny of a party's poll watchers, the secret ballot was proposed. To reduce the confusion on election day it was suggested that municipal elections be separated from state and national ones. To provide the voter with relevant information about candidates and issues, municipal research bureaus were established. The two most widely adopted reforms designed to weaken political machines at their organizational base were nonpartisan elections and at-large or citywide constituencies for elective offices.

Nonpartisan Elections

It is almost impossible to provide a precise definition of nonpartisanship that meets legal as well as political criteria. The reason for this is that many cities' elections are formally nonpartisan, but political parties still play an important electoral role. Therefore, it is necessary to restrict a definition of nonpartisanship to the formal and legal conditions that govern the involvement of political parties as organizations in local elections. Formally speaking, a nonpartisan election is one in which candidates for office are identified on the ballot by name only; neither the affiliation nor symbol of any political party appears on the ballot. Nonpartisanship sought to undermine political machines by removing from the ballot the symbols and labels their supporters used to elect machine candidates to city office. Part of the underlying assumption of municipal reformers was that the absence of these cues (party labels and symbols) would force the city voter to consider other criteria in deciding which candidate to support. Reformers anticipated that the "other criteria" would include a candidate's qualifications for office as well as position on the substantive and relevant issues involved in the election contest. Thus, the electorate would be informed in ways that would improve the quality of officeholders and, in the long run, the performance of public institutions in general.

The appeal of nonpartisan elections should not be taken to mean that political parties have been eliminated as participants in local elections. As noted earlier, formal and legal prohibitions against the presence of party names and symbols on the ballot do not assure the elimination of political organization influence in the conduct of elections. On the contrary, many cities using nonpartisan elections find parties of one kind or another exerting varying degrees of influence on voter choices and election outcomes. In

Chicago, for example, the Democratic party remains able to elect its candidates to major city offices despite the absence of party names or symbols on the ballot. The reason for this is that the party is so well organized and established at the grass roots that it is able to overcome the effects of formal nonpartisanship in local elections. In other cities slates of candidates are supported by various groups and organizations including, in some instances, local parties. Under yet another arrangement, "slate-making" organizations or coalitions of organizations get together to encourage and assist certain candidates. This practice frequently finds business and commercial interests pooling their support and resources behind candidates they support.[16]

The legal definition of nonpartisanship can, and often does, differ considerably from its practice. However, the initial and consistent purpose of nonpartisan elections was to attack the political machine by eliminating the central and pervasive role it played in the nomination, organization, and conduct of elections to offices in city government.

At-Large Constituencies

Nonpartisan elections were one part of the assault on the organizational base of political machines. The other was the at-large system for electing city officials. Municipal reformers sought to replace ward election of city councilmen with an at-large system that gave all councilmen a citywide constituency. The underlying rationale for the election of councilmen at large was the fact that the machine was organized around neighborhood-based wards. In drawing ward boundaries for city council elections, every effort was made to establish and maintain homogeneous areas. This enabled the machine to nominate as a candidate for the city council a person who shared the same ethnic, race, or class characteristic dominant in a particular ward.

Many evils are alleged to result from election of city councilmen by wards. One of these is most certainly the parochialism of each councilman's concerns and interests. Reformers charged that ward representatives tended to be interested only in those things that affected their ward. A variation of this parochialism is that a councilman's interest in the issues was a function of his "ward perspective." In either interpretation and approach to city issues, the whole does not always equal the sum of the parts. That is, it is not always possible to arrive at a decision that's in the interests of the city as a whole simply by adding together the partial interests of the various wards. In this view, some issues need to be approached from a perspective that transcends ward boundaries and interests; others need an approach that may oppose interests that dominate in a single ward or group of wards but are weak or absent from a citywide perspective. Municipal reformers believed that the at-large election of councilmen, giving each a citywide constituency, would weaken or even eliminate the parochialism of the ward system.

Reformers believed that the ward system, promoting the parochial perspective as it did, encouraged vote trading and logrolling on the city council. They believed that decisions should be made after a thoroughgoing examination of the merits and consequences of issues before the legislative body. Considerations of special interests like those dominant in a particular ward had no place in the decision making of a city councilman. Such was not the case, however. Under the ward system, decisions made by individual councilmen were often arrived at after intense politicking behind the scenes. The winning side on a given issue often reflected majority rule based on trading of votes and favors. Councilmen often cast their votes on a particular issue because they were obligated to do so to return a favor to a colleague and not because they believed the vote being cast was in the best interests of the city considered as corporate or social entity.

Finally, municipal reformers advocated the at-large system for electing councilmen because wards were the organizational base of political machines. So long as the machines could organize voters and conduct elections at the neighborhood level in wards, they were virtually assured of being able to elect a majority of candidates to the city council. In this way the machines were assured of continued control of the city's legislature. Combined with their control over executive offices, machines were able to control the city's entire governmental structure.

Ward boundaries usually were drawn to conform to the residential concentration of ethnic, race, and class groups in different neighborhoods in the city. This facilitated both the organization of voters at the neighborhood level and the nomination of council candidates who shared the particular ethnic, race, or class characteristic dominant in the ward. The machine became known within the neighborhoods of a ward as the political organization most likely to represent the needs and interests of the dominant group. Reformers believed that at-large election of councilmen would weaken the machine in the neighborhoods and wards by requiring the nomination of candidates with a broader, more diverse background and appeal.

REFORM OF GOVERNMENTAL INSTITUTIONS

Mechanistic Theories of Institutional Arrangements

Municipal reformers also were concerned with the structure of city government. Many believed that existing institutional arrangements were themselves defective; they impaired efficiency and responsiveness in the operation of city government. As a result, one focus of reform was the "good government" movement that sought to bring economy, efficiency, and accountability to the structure of government in the cities. Since many advocates of economy and efficiency were businessmen and civic leaders, they tended to view the problems of governmental organization from a corporate perspective.

One of the most glaring defects in the structure of city government, at least from the perspective of civic reformers, was the dispersion of authority and fragmentation of responsibility that resulted from adherence to the principles of separation of powers and popular, independent election of city executive officers. It was quite common for cities to elect, in addition to the members of their legislatures, a mayor, clerk, finance director, assessor, treasurer, controller, constable, and many other executive officials. The independent and popular election of these officials inhibited the development of coherence and coordination in the operation of the executive branch of city government, inasmuch as each official had his or her own constituency to satisfy, and often the satisfaction of one official's constituency did not require cooperation and coordination between and among executive officers of city government. Municipal reformers interested in good government viewed the popular election of executive officials as detracting from the interrelated principles of responsibility and accountability, since no single executive official both possessed sufficient authority to direct the operations of city government and be held accountable by the public. Each executive would accept responsibility only for those activities within the scope of his or her responsibility and authority, and each used other city officials as a scapegoat for the failure of government to respond to the needs of the developing city and its population.

Some civic reformers recognized corruption in government as the only mechanism for overcoming the institutional paralysis that resulted from the separation of legislative and executive functions and the dispersion of authority within the executive itself. Without corruption, government would cease to function. This notion was expressed by Henry Jones Ford in 1904 in the statement that:

> The bad operation of American municipal government is due not to defect of popular character, but to defect in the organization of government. The organic defect lies in the fact that the executive and legislative departments, in addition to being separately constituted, are also disconnected, and this very disconnection has prevented in practice the degree of separation in their functions which their integrity requires, a consequence precisely what Madison predicted if separate powers are not duly connected in their operation. The remedy is

therefore to be found in establishing a proper connection between the
executive and the legislative organs of government, so as to make the
functions of administration and control coextensive. No arrangement
can secure this short of one which gives the executive department
complete legislative initiative, and at the same time secures to the
legislative department complete supervision over all administrative
transactions. If this be accomplished, nominal relations or divisions are
unimportant.[17]

The good government movement was rooted primarily in practical
considerations, i.e., the need to arrange public institutions and processes so
that they would function efficiently and economically. There is, however, a
second aspect to the reform of governmental institutions in the city. This
dimension of reform grows out of the cycle of change in the core values of a
society's governmental institutions. In what has become a classic statement of
this thesis, Herbert Kaufman has identified three core values (or objectives)
that dominate the design and performances of public institutions. These values
are representativeness, technical, nonpartisan competence, and leadership.[18]

The value of representativeness is realized by the popular election of
public officials who exercise authority over appointed officials. Alternatively, representativeness is realized by subjecting as many public
officials as possible to accountability through popular election rather than
executive appointment. The value of technical, nonpartisan competence
emphasizes training and experience as the qualifications of public office. This
value also calls for basing public decisions and actions on technical and
professional considerations rather than partisan political factors. Finally, the
value of leadership requires that the actions and decisions of public officials be
coordinated at some central point so that governmental programs are
consistent with one another, serve similar and not contradictory purposes, and
respond to the needs of the people. The value of leadership requires that the
chief executive, whether elected or appointed, possess the authority over the
administrative machinery of government necessary to direct its officers,
operations, and activities. In this way, executive leadership will be both
responsible and accountable to the citizens of the community.

Kaufman regards the development of governmental institutions as
following a pattern in which one of the core values is dominant, while others
play a secondary role. The dominance of one of the core values is reflected in
the institutional arrangements and relationships existing in a governmental
system at any given point in time. Kaufman's own presentation of this is
helpful:

At any point in history elements reflecting all three values can be
discovered in our governmental system; the three are not mutually

exclusive. Indeed, all have left their distinctive marks on governmental organization, with the result that governmental organization today represents a combination of devices introduced earlier and innovations constituting responses to more recent needs and desires. But at various stages of our development, one or another would receive more emphasis than the other two, partly because new conditions required new methods, partly because excessive emphasis on only one of the values tends to set in motion demands for redressing the balance. Thus without intimating that any of the values was ever completely ignored, it is possible to demonstrate that each had its heyday and left its impress on our government and politics.[19]

According to Kaufman, institutional arrangements can be designed to emphasize one or another of these core values. For example, during the early colonial period state governments were characterized by executive dominance, while government institutions created after the Revolution were designed to realize the value of representativeness and, at the same time, restrict and control executive authority. Representativeness as a core value reached its peak during the period between Andrew Jackson's Presidency and the Civil War. Governmental arrangements at all levels, but particularly at state and local ones, were characterized by the extension of suffrage, direct election of administrative officers such as controllers, attorneys general, superintendents of education, department heads, and judges, and the "long ballot." Voters found themselves obliged to vote for scores of state and local officials on what came to be referred to as a bed-sheet ballot, because of its great length, to say nothing of complexity.

In the late nineteenth century reformers called for separating politics from administration at the state and local levels. Civic reformers fighting the corruption of city government by political machines and administrative theorists reacting to the consequences of an uncontrolled pursuit of the value of representativeness in the post-Revolutionary period found themselves extolling the value of nonpartisan competence in government. They also sought to free city government from unwarranted interference by state government. Two main institutional arrangements were designed to realize nonpartisan competence: the commission and city-manager plans of city government.

Both commission and council-manager forms of government offered the (presumably) redeeming value of substituting a system of authority based on the principle of separation of power for one based on the principle of fusion of power. That is, where the mayor-council form of government based on separation of power contributed to the kinds of organic weaknesses reflected in the writing of Henry Jones Ford, commission and council-manager forms were designed to eliminate these organic and structural defects by having executive authority derived from and dependent upon legislative authority. The similarity to the model of parliamentary government used in England was not coincidental, nor should it be allowed to pass without mention. Under the commission and council-manager governments, citizens elect a relatively small legislative body, usually in nonpartisan, at-large elections. The legislature then delegates executive authority to an administrator of its choosing. The administrator is responsible to the legislature for the operation of government on a day-to-day basis. The institutional design of both forms assigns authority for policymaking to the legislature and responsibility for executing policy to the appointed administrator. The two forms of government are sufficiently different in specific detail, however, to warrant separate examination. However, before examining the commission and council-manager governments it is necessary to make one additional observation.

An important aspect to the support of governmental reform, particularly as it focused on the commission and council-manager forms, was the assumption that the values of nonpartisan competence would be overriding in the criteria employed to select public administrators in city government. That is, it was believed that governmental officials in the executive department would be selected because of their training, expertise, and experience in administration, rather than their political skills, abilities, or influence. Municipal reformers who supported changing the structure of city government did so in part because they believed that professional administrators were the major (if not only) hope for ridding city government of the incompetence and inefficiency of the "hacks" brought in by the political machines.

Home Rule

By the end of the nineteenth century only a few states had granted home rule powers to their municipalities. In the majority of instances states imposed severe restrictions on the powers municipalities could exercise. Most cities were established by means of special act charters that enabled the state to place numerous restrictions on municipal powers and responsibilities.

The municipal reform movement sought to change this. Along with efforts to design institutional arrangements that would enhance the efficiency and responsiveness of city governments, municipal reformers believed that these values would best be served if city government was not constrained by numerous restrictions imposed by higher (state) authority. Home rule became a plank in the reform movement. Frank Goodnow, a leader in municipal reform during the late nineteenth and early twentieth centuries, remarked that "the fact that a city is an organization for the satisfaction of local needs makes it necessary that its action be determined by local considerations. To this end it must have large local powers."[20]

Advocates of home rule for cities based their support on a number of considerations. First, they believed that it would serve the interests of democracy by making the people themselves directly responsible for government. Second, it would encourage persons of ability and experience to become involved in city government, since corporate powers would be sufficient in meeting the needs of the city population. Finally, home rule would enable cities to take positive action to deal with problems of growth and development. City government would no longer be forced to accept a passive, caretaker role in dealing with social and economic conditions within its jurisdictional boundaries.

Commission Government

The commission form of government was the first to reflect the integration of legislative and executive authority.[21] It was initially adopted in Galveston, Texas, in the aftermath of a devastating flood. A group of businessmen and civic leaders petitioned the state to assume governmental authority and respond to the crisis at hand. After that authority was granted, the group formed itself into a "commission" and later recommended far-reaching alterations in Galveston's structure of government, seeking to make the commission arrangement permanent. In 1901, the new plan, called commission government, was made permanent and the government of Galveston passed into the hands of five officials, three appointed by the governor and two elected by the voters. After 1903 all five were elected. Four of the five were in charge of individual city departments; the fifth served as ceremonial and symbolic mayor. Collectively, the commission exercised legislative authority, making policy decisions and administrative appointments. Individually, each commissioner served as administrative head of a city department and was responsible for executing the policies and decisions of the legislature insofar as they involved his/her area of administrative responsibility. Under the commission plan, the legislature or commission was composed of a relatively small number of representatives chosen at large in nonpartisan elections.

In 1907, just a few years after adoption by Galveston, the commission plan was adopted by the city of Des Moines, Iowa. Thereafter, and for the next decade or so, the commission form of government enjoyed considerable popularity. By 1910, it had spread to some 108 cities; in 1917, nearly 500 cities were using the commission plan.

City-Manager Government

Council-manager government, or city-manager government, as it is also called, was the second structural reform advocated by municipal reformers.[22] It, too, sought to eliminate the problems of separated powers and inefficient, incompetent operation of city government. The plan of city-manager government, as we have noted, was first designed by Richard S. Childs, a leader in the National Municipal League. Childs and the league were primarily responsible for the widespread adoption of the city-manager form of government.

The underlying principles of city-manager government are similar to those of commission government. Legislative and executive authority are integrated in a popularly elected legislature, usually known as a city council. The city council exercises legislative authority and makes policy and basic decisions for the city. It is usually small, numbering five to nine members who are chosen at large in nonpartisan elections. Members of the council are the only popularly elected governmental officials. Administrative authority is delegated to a manager appointed by the council. The city manager is responsible to the council for the day-to-day operation and performance of city government. The manager carries out the policies enacted by the council. There is no separation of power, inasmuch as the executive authority of the manager is derived from and delegated by the legislative authority of the council. The administration of the city is integrated under the control of the professional manager, chosen by the council presumably because of administrative training, competence, and expertise in administration. The manager's administrative responsibility is manifested in his/her authority to appoint and remove subordinate administrative officers, including heads of functional departments. The manager serves at the pleasure of the council and enjoys no fixed term of office. However, the manager is insulated from the politics of the council because he/she is not subject to popular election or recall by the voters.

Though specific council-manager governments differ from each other in various details, these are the essential principles and structural characteristics of this form of government. It enjoyed considerable and widespread popularity, measured by its adoption by cities across the nation, and still is used quite extensively. The cities of Staunton, Virginia, and Sumter, South Carolina, compete for the honor of being the first to adopt the council-manager form of government. In 1908, the Staunton city council appointed a "general manager" to oversee the administrative affairs of the city, but it retained the long ballot and the powers and duties of the manager were quite limited. When Childs conceived of the idea of combining the appointment of a professional manager with adoption of the short ballot, the city-manager plan, as it was known to municipal reformers, came into being. The first city to adopt the plan in this form was Sumter in 1912. Two years later, in 1914, the city of Dayton, Ohio, became the first large city to adopt the council-manager form of government. By 1915, there were 49 council-manager cities. Five years later, there were 158. The number of cities using the council-manager form of government has grown consistently and virtually without interruption since its inception.

Independent Boards and Commissions

No discussion of structural reform would be complete without referring to the advocacy of independent boards and commissions by municipal reformers. Such bodies, created to operate outside the formal structure of city government, were a major part of the agenda of municipal reform. The use of boards and commissions to administer selected functions of government was yet another part of the attack on the political machine and the desire to separate administration and politics. Selected functions like libraries, parks and recreation facilities, public health, art galleries and museums, public transportation, and the like were completely and structurally separated from city government. Administration of these functions was turned over to a citizen board or commission selected on a nonpartisan, or at least bipartisan, basis. Board members were insulated from city politics by holding fixed, overlapping appointments. On more than one occasion the budget for operating the function of the board or commission was fixed in the city charter, thereby guaranteeing the board a minimum level of revenue each fiscal year. Ostensibly, this would prevent the city council from "playing politics" with particular functions by using its budgetary authority to influence the decision of the board or commission. Day-to-day operations and activities were the responsibility of a professional administrator appointed by and responsible to the board or commission. There was little, if any, contact or accountability between the professional administrator and either the city council or, for that matter, the city electorate. Civil service, planning, and zoning are among the administrative responsibilities most frequently performed by independent boards or commissions. The main reason for this is the belief that these functions are among those it is most important to "take out of politics" and perform on an impartial, nonpartisan basis, using the interests of the community as a whole and relevant professional standards and norms as the only criteria in decision making.

Independent boards and commissions have been shown to be extremely useful to city officials. For one thing, they provide a vehicle through which lay citizens can participate in government on a voluntary, limited basis. For another, they provide the opportunity for a group of citizens to focus on a particular function or problem in a way that elected city councils could not. The specific focus of an independent board or commission permitted a degree of depth in deliberations not normally found in the legislature.

However, the use of independent boards and commissions to administer essential functions was not without its problems. When functions like personnel and planning were administered by independent bodies serious problems of coordination arose. The structural and legal insulation and separation of these units from city government meant that there were no formal institutional incentives to consultation and coordination between independent boards and the elected officials of city government. The potential for duplication of effort or even contradictory actions and policies was a real and serious problem. The existence of numerous separate bodies making decisions and policies for the public, with only one of those (i.e., the city council) accountable for its actions to the public, created a serious operational and practical dilemma. Oftentimes the decisions of an independent board would have far-reaching implications for city government, especially in the expenditure of revenues, yet elected city officials or their representatives had no formal authority to require an independent board to consider those implications. Any coordination and cooperation between the actions of an independent board or commission and the "regular" city government were informal. Elected officials could do nothing to require that members of boards or commissions consider the implications of their policies and actions for the rest of city government.

REFORM OF GOVERNMENTAL OPERATIONS AND PRACTICES

The third dimension of the reform movement was not exclusively municipal in focus. Rather, the effort to bring accountability, economy, and efficiency to the operations and procedures of city government required that action be taken at the state and sometimes national levels of government. Consequently, municipal reformers concentrated their efforts at these levels to gain enactment of laws that would regulate and control the way local government conducted its affairs.

Two areas of governmental operation and practices were singled out as the focus of reform in these efforts, namely personnel practices and financial administration. Municipal reformers believed that much of the corruption and inefficiency in city government were the result of procedures and practices in these areas that permitted excessive latitude in the way city officials made governmental decisions. Certainly the political machines made extensive and effective use of their control of the city's hiring practices to reward the party faithful with patronage jobs. Also, the machines' control of city administrations enabled them to use purchasing procedures to reward party supporters with preferential treatment in awarding lucrative city contracts. In addition, the relative paucity of external checks on local financial practices and accounting procedures enabled city officials to withhold or falsify information necessary to demonstrate the nature and extent of improper and illegal activity in the conduct of governmental business. Consequently, civic reformers turned their attention to the enactment of laws at the state and national levels of government that would regulate and control local government operations and practices in personnel and financial administration.

Civil Service Reform

The effort to reform personnel politics and practices was focused primarily at the national level. There, under the leadership of the National Civil Service League, reformers sought enactment of legislation that would end the preferential treatment of the spoils system and replace it with a personnel system in public employment based on the merit concept. Actually, dissatisfaction with the spoils system began to emerge during the post-Civil War period, though it did not find tangible expression until 1877 with the formation of the New York Civil Service Reform Association. Later, in 1881, the National Civil Service Reform Association was established, to become known later as the National Civil Service League. The latter organization has been at the forefront of civil service reform ever since 1883, when the league-sponsored and supported Civil Service Act, also known as the Pendleton Act, was passed by Congress and signed into law by the President.

Between 1883 and 1920 personnel administration in the federal service amounted to little more than recruiting, testing, and policing. The major thrust of actions taken by the U.S. Civil Service Commission was to develop practices that would advance the practice of merit in employment at the federal level. In a sense, personnel policy was "negative" in that its main objective was to deny political parties and elected officials the control over public employment that had been used so effectively to build and maintain machine organizations throughout the country. It wasn't until 1923, when the Classification Act was passed by Congress, that federal personnel policy began to take a more positive developmental direction. The Classification Act of 1923 established the principle of grouping positions into classes on the basis of duties and responsibilities and laid the groundwork for achieving "equal pay for equal work." It can be said that the Classification Act did for the development and expansion of civil service under the merit principle what the Pendleton Act did for the formal establishment of merit as the criteria for recruiting, hiring, and advancing public employees.

Though the development of personnel policies and practices on the basis of merit in state and local government is far from uniform, many of these units of government were pursuing their own efforts at the same time that action was occurring at the federal level.[23] For example, in the same year (1883) that the Pendleton Act was passed, the state of New York adopted its own merit-based statute for employees. This was followed the next year by Massachusetts, then by Wisconsin and Illinois in 1905, Colorado in 1907, New Jersey in 1908, Ohio in 1912, California and Connecticut in 1913, and Maryland in 1920. By 1935, almost all remaining states had enacted some form of legislation prescribing merit as the principle for public employment.

Many of the larger cities were pursuing similar developments. In the state of New York, for example, the cities of New York, Albany, and Buffalo adopted civil service in 1885. In the same year, the Massachusetts cities of Boston, Cambridge, Fall River, Springfield, and Lynn adopted civil service regulations. The civil service movement moved westward in 1895, with Chicago and Milwaukee enacting local laws and, in 1900, with San Francisco adopting a civil service law. By 1903, one hundred cities in the United States had some form of civil service coverage for their employees.

Many of the larger cities and states also undertook establishment of position classification as a way to extend and expand the merit concept. Thus, position classification was adopted in Chicago in 1912, and, by 1920, position classification spread to the states of New York, New Jersey, Colorado, Massachusetts, and Ohio. In addition, the cities of Milwaukee (and Milwaukee County), Portland, Oregon, Pittsburgh, New York, Baltimore, Cleveland, Los Angeles, St. Louis, St. Paul, and Seattle all adopted position classification programs. The list of states and cities adopting position classification programs, along with the dates of their action, is particularly significant in light of the fact that the federal law wasn't enacted until 1923. In some respects the cause of civil service reform moved along further and faster among state and local government than in the federal government.

The enactment of federal, state, and local laws prescribing merit as the criterion of entry into the public service and position classification as the mechanism for practicing it does not tell the whole story of civil service reform. However, much of what was going to be done to free municipal personnel practices from influence of city officials controlled by political machines was accomplished through civil service laws. If the machine was to be effectively taken out of the public employment system, the merit principle and position classification were major tools for accomplishing this. It remains to be seen just how effective civil service reform has been in eliminating the machine as a "middleman" in the public personnel system.

Though commissions varied somewhat from one place to another, the typical approach to legal and structural independence from city government consisted of establishing a nonpartisan, or at least bipartisan, body of lay citizens to make personnel policy. This group usually consisted of an odd number of members (three to seven was normal), with representation of both political parties (if the jurisdiction in question retained partisan elections) mandated by law. For example, if the independent commission charged with enforcement of civil service policies and practices consisted of seven members, then no more than four persons from the same political party could serve at one time. Appointments to the commission were commonly made by the chief executive and legislature, with the former nominating persons to the commission and the latter giving its advice and consent. Terms of commission members were arranged so that overlapping prevented city officials from packing the commission and thwarting the spirit or law of independence from city government and politics. Actual implementation of civil service policies and practices was the responsibility of a professional administrator in charge of personnel, appointed by and responsible to the independent civil service commission. The personnel administrator or director had responsibility for hiring a staff to provide the needed assistance and expertise in administering the personnel system.

Financial Administration

The other main area of governmental operations and practices that municipal reformers sought to improve was financial administration, broadly conceived as including governmental budgeting, accounting, and reporting. Here reformers sought to enact legislation that would regulate and control every facet of the city's financial affairs, from the preparation and submission of the budget to the purchasing of supplies and equipment to the auditing of city government expenditures at the close of each fiscal year.

The approach to controlling the budgetary and accounting practices of city governments took the form of enacting state laws and amendments to state constitutions specifying the categories of funds public moneys could be allocated to or expended from.[24] Though the number and kinds of funds employed by governments vary, the great number of specified funds brought about considerable control of financial practices. To permit effective budgetary control and establish uniformity in financial reporting and accounting, state laws were enacted to provide for a classification of funds that would include (1) a general fund, to account for revenues not allocated to specific purposes by law or contractual agreement; (2) special revenue funds, limited to a single purpose, e.g., for financing parks or schools; (3) bond funds, for revenues derived from sale of bonds; (4) special assessment funds, for charges levied against properties or persons benefiting from special services or improvements rendered by city government; (5) sinking funds, for the accumulation of moneys to retire term bonds; (6) trust and agency funds, for assets received by a governmental unit in the capacity of trustee or agent; (7) working capital funds, for service activities performed by a department or bureau for other departments or bureaus of the same governmental unit; and (8) utility or other enterprise funds, for self-supporting enterprises rendering services primarily for the public. It was a common practice for state laws or constitutional provisions to require that each fund in city government had to be self-balancing.

The major financial practices of city government—accounting, budgeting, financial reporting, and auditing—came under varying degrees of supervision and control by state government. Provisions for uniform accounting and budget format were a common approach. So, too, were requirements for budget review by a state agency and an audit of city expenditures at the close of each fiscal year. State action also included appointment by the local government of a budget officer, usually called a city treasurer, to be responsible for compliance with state laws. The treasurer was commonly appointed by the city legislature rather than the executive and enjoyed the protections of civil service laws. Finally, state laws often regulated the nature and limit of taxes a city government could levy as well as the level of debt it could incur.

State laws also were enacted to supervise and control purchasing, for it was in this area of financial administration that corruption was most common. Very often purchasing and acquisition procedures were used by city officials to give preferential treatment to party supporters in awarding contracts for government work. State statutes were enacted to require closed, competitive bidding for purchases above a certain dollar value. In addition, statutes often spelled out restrictions as to conflicts of interest for city officials and employees. Often a centralized purchasing department was created in city government, headed by a director who, like the treasurer, was included in the classified civil service. It was presumed that such protection would enable the purchasing director to resist efforts to influence or even determine purchases and contract awards by machine-supported officials of city government.

Finally, state laws were enacted to require auditing of local expenditures. Such provisions were designed explicitly to ensure compliance with state laws and to enforce financial accountability. State supervision of auditing took a number of forms. In one, a state supervisory agency may be charged with the auditing of all local governments within the state. In a second, the state simply requires that all local governments must be audited annually either by a state agency or staff, a certified public accountant, or even a public accountant licensed by the state specifically for municipal auditing purposes. Third, the state may simply require that an audit report, prepared by an independent auditor appointed by city government (usually the legislature), be filed with the state supervisory agency on a regular, usually annual, basis.

Summary

The agenda of municipal reform was varied in content and scope. By and large, reformers sought to improve the accountability and performance of city governmental institutions and politics by effecting far-reaching changes in electoral systems and rules, governmental structure, and governmental operations and procedures. The efforts of reformers were manifested in federal laws in the area of civil service, state laws imposing regulations and controls on local government budgeting and financial practices, and, at the municipal level, charter revisions that included the adoption of new forms of government and changes in electoral systems and practices.

The program of reform was sufficiently far-reaching in scope, intent, and consequences that consideration should be given to its impact on the development and performance of city government and politics. In the next chapter we turn our attention to considering this facet of urban development, paying particular attention to the extent to which various reform prescriptions impacted the performance of governmental institutions in the central cities.

NOTES

1. Lincoln Steffens, *The Shame of the Cities* (1904; reprint ed., New York: Hill and Wang, 1957).

2. A short biographical sketch of Childs is available in John Porter East, *Council-Manager Government: The Political Thought of Its Founder, Richard S. Childs* (Chapel Hill: University of North Carolina Press, 1965), pp. 3-14.

3. Richard S. Childs, "Civic Victories in the United States," *National Municipal Review* 44 (September 1955): 402.

4. See Richard S. Childs, *Civic Victories: The Story of an Unfinished Revolution* (New York: Harper & Row, 1952), pp. 47-70.

5. Lincoln Steffens, *The Autobiography of Lincoln Steffens* (New York: Harcourt, Brace and World, 1931), pp. 573-74.

6. Steffens, *Cities*, pp. 3-4.

7. Richard Hofstadter, *The Age of Reform* (New York: Alfred A. Knopf, 1955; Vintage, 1960).

8. *Ibid.*, p. 9.

9. Edward C. Banfield and James Q. Wilson, *City Politics* (Cambridge, Mass.: Harvard University Press, 1963), p. 239.

10. *Ibid.*, p. 46.

11. Hofstadter, p. 9.

12. Andrew D. White, "The Government of American Cities," *Forum*, December 1890, reprinted in *Urban Government: A Reader in Administration and Politics*, ed. Edward C. Banfield (New York: The Free Press, 1969), pp. 271-73.

13. Samuel P. Hays, "The Politics of Reform in Municipal Government in the Progressive Era," *Pacific Northwest Quarterly* 55 (October 1963): 157-69.

14. *Ibid.*, pp. 158-59.

15. Names, places, and dates of reform are taken from Ernest S. Griffith, *A History of American City Government: The Conspicuous Failure, 1870-1900* (New York: Praeger, 1974), chap. 9.

16. Charles R. Adrian, "A Typology of Nonpartisan Elections," *Western Political Quarterly* 12 (June 1959): 449-58.

17. Henry Jones Ford, "Principles of Municipal Organization," *The Annals of the American Academy of Political and Social Science* 21 (March 1904): 215-16.

18. Herbert Kaufman, "Emerging Conditions in the Doctrines of Public Administration," *American Political Science Review* 50 (December 1956): 1057-73. See also his *Politics and Policies in State and Local Governments* (Englewood Cliffs, N.J.: Prentice-Hall, 1963), chap. 2.

19. Kaufman, *Politics and Policies*, pp. 34-35.

20. Quoted in Charles N. Glaab and A. Theodore Brown, *A History of Urban America,* 2d ed. (New York: Macmillan, 1976), p. 175.

21. See Bradley Robert Rice, *Progressive Cities: The Commission Government Movement in America, 1901-1920* (Austin: University of Texas, 1977).

22. See Harry A. Toulmin, Jr., *The City Manager: A New Profession* (New York: D. Appleton, 1916; reprint ed., New York: Arno Press, 1974), and Richard J. Stillman II, *The Rise of the City Manager: A Public Professional in Local Government* (Albuquerque: University of New Mexico Press, 1974).

23. International City Management Association, *Municipal Personnel Administration,* 6th ed. (Washington, D.C.: International City Management Association, 1960), chap. 1.

24. See Lennox L. Moak and Albert M. Hillhouse, *Concepts and Practices in Local Government Finance* (Chicago: Municipal Finance Officers Association, 1975), chap. 19.

CHAPTER VI.

Aftermath of Reform

Introduction

Virtually all of the existing governmental institutions within the contemporary governing system of the city were developed between 1890 and 1917. Prior to World War I many cities adopted proposals for at-large and nonpartisan elections, the direct primary, separation of local and national elections, the city commission or council-manager forms of government, home rule, civil service, and state imposed financial regulation.

While the Progressive Era marked the emergence of municipal reform, the decade of the twenties was its pinnacle. Despite the decline of social reform on the national level in the 1920s, urban reformers were successful and optimistic about the future. The business-oriented approach that characterized the decade strengthened the cause of urban reform. The structural changes proposed prior to World War I were widely adopted during the twenties. Changes, such as at-large and nonpartisan elections, and commission/city-manager governments, seemed to guarantee that public institutions would be run by professionally trained administrators, using objective, businesslike criteria of economy and efficiency in making public decisions.

A second period of interest in structural reform developed during the period of rapid suburbanization of America after World War II. Though changing conditions in the 1920s and the post-1945 era caused modifications of earlier reforms, the basic program of Progressive Era reformers continued to influence the structure of city government.

This chapter will examine the reform movement in the years following the

Progressive Era. The two major alternatives proposed to the mayor-council system of government were the city commission and the council-manager. Both of these gained widespread support during the 1920s and the latter has continued as the favored alternative since 1945. However, the weaknesses evident in the city-manager system have led to another alternative, the chief administrative officer, which combined the benefits of the strong mayor and the city-manager systems.

Despite the attempts at removing politics from urban government, politics has continued either under new guises or in more traditional ways. The appearance of strong, dynamic mayors in large cities, amateur or club politics, and the expanding city bureaucracy reflect the persistence of urban politics in new forms. Yet, neither the alternative governmental structures nor "new politics" prevented the persistence of more traditional manifestations of urban politics, the political machine and bloc voting. The latter is the basis for the political power presently held by urban leaders.

ALTERNATIVE FORMS OF GOVERNMENT

City Commission

As we have seen in Chapter V alternative forms of government appeared after 1900. The Galveston city commission structure was widely imitated. By 1917 nearly five hundred cities had adopted this plan. The popularity of commission government has generally been restricted to smaller cities. The majority of commission governed cities have populations between 5000 and 25,000. After 1945, however, a number of cities abandoned commission government in favor of the council-manager form, and most of the conversions from the commission form were in the larger cities. Representative of the abandonment are Des Moines, Iowa, in 1949, San Antonio, Texas, in 1951, and Hoboken, New Jersey, in 1952. A few large cities still use the commission, most notably Portland, Oregon, St. Paul, Minnesota, and Tulsa, Oklahoma.[1]

Criticisms of commission government generally centered around the lack of responsibility to the public, the absence of policy leadership on the legislative body, the absence of coordination in administration of executive functions, and the prevalence of accommodation among the commissioners in their dual roles as legislators and administrators. Responsibility to the public was not clearly fixed; instead, it was divided among the several commissioners. The fact that commissioners were elected at large enabled each to use the other in fixing responsibility for the kinds and content of policy enacted by the legislature. Then, too, there was the fact that no one on the commission was responsible for taking the lead in developing programs and policies for commission consideration. Each commissioner was equal in status to the others and it was difficult for any one of them to carve out a role equivalent to that of prime minister in the British model of parliamentary government. Third, dissatisfaction with the commission form of government grew out of absence of coordination on the administrative side of matters. Each commissioner was responsible for the operation of his/her own executive function, but none was responsible for the overall operation and coordination of administrative responsibility. There was little that could be done about any overlapping or duplication of functions from one department to another. Finally, it became common practice for commissioners to hold an attitude of accommodation toward each other. Oftentimes matters of importance, particularly the approval of a city budget, were decided by a coalition of a majority of commissioners based on nothing more than an agreement for reciprocal support of each coalition member's preferences and wishes. Criticism and internal accountability were virtually absent from legislative deliberations.[2]

These criticisms gave rise to two kinds of responses. First, as noted earlier, many of the cities that had adopted the commission form during the peak of popularity abandoned it. In a number of instances respect for and support of the values of nonpartisan competence led to adoption of another reform-supported structure of government, the council-manager plan. Second, cities that retained the commission form made some major structural modifications. The most important of these involved the establishment of a centralized budget office, submission of a city budget to the commission and coordination of its execution across departmental lines and appointment of a professional administrator as the deputy head of each department, thus providing a person to handle the daily operational matters and providing the leadership and administrative skills that citizen commissioners assigned to the individual departments often lack.[3]

Council-Manager

A more popular alternative form of government was the council-manager plan which spread rapidly after World War I. By 1930 over four hundred cities had adopted this plan. This reform was the last institutional change developed during the Progressive Era. It evolved from the rise of the "public city." Society demanded and needed these additional services. And only the public sector was equipped to provide them. For example, Detroit's city government took on 228 new functions between 1860 and 1920. Such an expansion of new services led to the professionalization of those responsible for their provision. Numerous professional organizations were established, such as the Municipal Finance Officers Association in 1906. These associations reflected growing specialization and the need for specific skills in carrying out or overseeing the various functions, activities, and services of government. It was inevitable that the function of the chief administrative officer in city government would also be professionalized. Though this didn't occur until late in the Progressive Era, after other alternatives for administering the public sector were considered, the scientific management movement was applied to public services.[4]

One important reason for the spread of the council-manager plan was its endorsement by the United States Chamber of Commerce. On the local level chapters, using the arguments of business efficiency and removing government from politics, pushed the adoption of this plan. Other proponents of the plan also used the business analogy. The *Dallas Morning News* argued in its support of council-manager government:

> Why not run Dallas itself on a business schedule by business methods under businessmen?... The city manager is the executive of a corporation under a board of directors. Dallas is the corporation. It is as simple as that.[5]

While the forces of structural change were not always successful, they usually waged a good fight.

The next great surge of interest in the council-manager plan came after World War II when the number of cities using this increased from 600 to nearly 1200. The impetus behind this was the rapid suburbanization that occurred with the return of the automobile and the federally insured VA and FHA loans. To overcome the chaos caused by suburban sprawl many areas looked for professional help in the form of the city manager. As Richard Stillman writes, the suburbs "frequently found the manager government answered both their modern needs: centralized administrative authority under an expert manager, combined with direct local participation in city councils."[6] While such a government did not necessarily serve metropolitan needs and was usually, despite the "cult of efficiency," more expensive, it effectively served the immediate needs of the white, middle-class suburbanite. By 1976, 1704 cities with 5000 people or more had the council-manager form of government (see table 2). Over 50 percent of the cities with a population between 50,000 and 500,000 have this form.

As the table indicates, the mayor-council form is still the most common in the cities over 500,000. Four-fifths of these cities have maintained this. The same is true in cities between 5000 and 10,000. A majority of these cities have the more traditional form. It is generally accepted that the mayor-council form is necessary in the larger cities because of the need for elected leadership

TABLE 2
Forms of Government in Cities over 5000 Population

Population	No. of Cities	Mayor-Council	Council-Manager	Commission	Other [a]
5,000–10,000	1,569	874	559	43	93
10,000–25,000	1,362	587	624	53	98
25,000–50,000	539	172	309	41	17
50,000–100,000	257	94	145	13	5
100,000–250,000	97	40	48	9	0
250,000–500,000	30	14	14	2	0
500,000+	27	22	5	0	0
	3,881	1,803	1,704	161	213

SOURCE: International City Management Association, *Municipal Yearbook, 1976* (Washington, D.C., 1976), table 3.

[a] Town meeting and representative town meeting forms.

in a heterogeneous community, while cities under 10,000 maintain this form largely because of the cost involved in hiring a full-time professional.[7]

The council-manager form has maintained its popularity while many cities with the commission form have converted to other governmental systems. When a city did abandon the commission form, it usually did so in favor of council-manager government. However, the fact that the council-manager plan has enjoyed sustained popularity, particularly in smaller- and medium-sized cities, ought not to be construed to mean that operational and practical problems have been absent.

On the contrary, the operation of the council-manager plan, particularly in regard to the separation between politics and administration, has proven to be especially difficult to maintain. The council, more often than not, concerns itself with administrative implementation of policy, rather than restricting itself to the political role of policymaking. Many times the manager found himself/herself thrust into a political role by the very council that was supposed to monopolize politics. Individual council members quickly learned that the manager, insulated as he/she is from electoral pressures, is a convenient scapegoat for less popular decisions. Moreover, on more than one occasion a manager had to "go to the community" to engender support for a program he/she had proposed for council approval. Furthermore, a political role for the manager is established as soon as the council requests a recommendation on one or another item it is considering.

Like the commission plan, the council-manager form suffers from the absence of policy leadership in the legislative arena. Though a mayor is usually provided in the council-manager form, either by popular election or designation by the council as a whole, the role is typically not one that carries with it much authority or responsibility for providing policy leadership. Rather, the mayor in the council-manager government serves largely in a ceremonial-ritualistic capacity, doing those things that state law mandates must be performed by the mayor, e.g., signing ordinances, resolutions, etc., and representing the city at special events and occasions. Under such circumstances, the mayor's role is little more than honorific; he or she may not even be considered as a sort of "first among equals." As in the commission form, there is no one to serve as a link between the council—acting collectively as a policymaking body—and the manager—acting as administrative head of city government. Rather, each council member tends to guard his or her prerogatives jealously and deals with the manager on an individual, personal basis. Needless to say, the manager's time is often taken up in maintaining favorable relationships with individual council members, since no manager could expect to survive for long without the support of a majority of the council.

Other problems exist, however, that tend to thrust the manager into the political, as opposed to administrative, role. For one thing, the manager has a virtual monopoly over technical information and administrative expertise in the city. This surely contributes to the fact that he/she is sought out by community leaders and council members alike in their need for assistance in developing programs and policies or their drive for support to get proposals approved by the council and accepted by the community. Second, the manager sits at the very center of city government, especially on the administrative side, as the one person with administrative responsibility over all departments and at the focal point for the convergence of lines of communication between and among departments.

A number of studies have shown the extent to which managers are inextricably brought into city politics, either out of necessity, by their own choosing, or simply because it is just "good politics" for council members to maneuver the manager into taking, or seeming to take, responsibility for controversial measures. No less an analyst of public administration than Leonard D. White, writing in 1927, found the "failure" of the council to stay out of administration and restrict its role to policymaking to be "one of the startling weaknesses" of the council-manager plan. Other studies of managers and their relations with their councils have tended to confirm White's judgment.[8]

Experiences with City-Manager Government: Kansas City

Structural reforms have never fulfilled the expectations of reformers. In some cases such reforms have generated more problems than they have solved. In other cases reforms have been modified to fit local circumstances, leaving the city with a hybrid form of government in which weaknesses of both mayor-council and council-manager forms exist in a simple institutional arrangement. One of the most famous cases of failure of structural reform in the 1920s was in Kansas City. The good government people saw council-manager government as a means to oust the machine of Tom Pendergast, who was the most powerful political figure in western Kansas. He controlled not only a city with over a quarter of a million people but the county as well. But the middle class was restless and Pendergast's candidate for mayor was defeated in 1924 by a Republican reformer. Reform Democrats joined with the Republicans to propose a new charter. The charter included a council-manager form with the council elected in a nonpartisanship, semi-at-large manner. Also

> ... reports on the state of the funds were to be required from every
> department to manager, council, and public. Another important theme
> in the new system concerned the problem of personnel: all department
> heads, as well as the city manager, were to be men of special training in
> their fields, and were to be appointed on a non-partisan basis.[9]

Realizing that the majority of the voters supported charter revision, Pendergast decided to control the effects of reform. After the new charter was adopted, even though elections were to be nonpartisan, Pendergast selected his candidates at a Democratic caucus. The Republicans did likewise. The result was a close election with the Pendergast forces emerging victorious. He now controlled the council and thus could name the professional city manager. In Kansas City structural reform took place but the machine proved highly adaptable to the new institutional arrangements.[10]

Experiences with City-Manager Government: Flint

The twisting path of structural reform is also seen in Flint, Michigan. Flint, a city which grew rapidly during the first three decades of the twentieth century from 13,000 to over 150,000, faced the same problems as most industrial cities. The existing governmental structure, which dated back to the nineteenth century, was incapable of meeting the demands of a rapidly expanding city. As a result, after World War I, William McKeighan emerged as a Republican boss, building a machine on the support of the foreign-born and other recent urban migrants. It was said of McKeighan, "He inspired a great deal of love from poor people who thought of him as Robin Hood, and a great deal of hate from the affluent who saw him as Robin the Hood." In 1927 charges of corruption against Mayor McKeighan led reformers to take on the cause of charter revision. Like Pendergast, McKeighan realized it was hopeless to fight this crusade and chose to join it. A new charter was adopted in 1929, calling for a commission of nine to be elected in an at-large, nonpartisan election. The commission would appoint a professional city manager. McKeighan was elected one of the first commissioners but his forces had to wait until 1931 before they controlled the commission. The reformers dominated the first commission and they named the first city manager, a professional. But as George Washington Plunkitt said, reformers are "mornin' glories" and the middle class in Flint grew tired of the day-to-day responsibilities of governing the city. In the next election the McKeighan forces gained control of the commission and fired the manager. McKeighan then orchestrated a voter-approved amendment to the charter, changing the method of representation from at-large to the ward system. It was ironic that McKeighan, a Republican, had his political life extended by structural reform, since nonpartisan elections allowed him to run without the Republican label.[11]

Structural reform left Flint with the weaknesses of both systems. In effect it destroyed effective government through the organization of a machine and guaranteed impotence for the formally established governmental system. While the McKeighan influence ultimately disappeared, nonpartisan elections effectively precluded the emergence of other political organizations. After the war, the United Auto Workers became the single most influential political force. Because of ward elections commission members spent their time exchanging political favors. City managers frequently found themselves in the middle of political infighting among commission members. When one coalition replaced another on the commission, the city manager was in trouble, regardless of the job being done. Many management decisions were influenced not by what was best for the city but by the pressures brought to bear on the manager by commission members.

While there were periodic calls for eliminating the obvious weaknesses in the Flint charter, all attempts at charter revision were defeated until 1974. At that time a new charter was approved by the voters establishing a council-mayor form of government and providing for the appointment by the mayor of a city administrator. However, the past influenced charter revision; nonpartisan ward elections continued.

The fate of the professional city manager in Flint was similar to the fate that awaited most city managers at one time or another. In governing the city it is impossible to separate politics from administration. The city manager cannot function as the president of a corporation, responsible only periodically to his/her board of directors. The nature of services the manager oversees thrusts him/her into the center of council politics.

The Chief Administrative Officer

The city-manager system was based on the premise that administering or managing a city should be done in a neutral, professional, businesslike manner. Experiences such as those described above revealed the difficulty of maintaining the separation of politics and administration. While most larger cities saw the advantages of strong leadership from a single executive who had the support of the public, most were unwilling to turn to a strong mayor form, fearing the return of boss/machine politics. However, in the fifties it became apparent to many that the two forms were not mutually exclusive. A hybrid form combining an elected mayor with a chief administrative officer gained a great deal of support and was adopted in a number of cities.

The strong mayor, with chief administrative officer (CAO), and council form of government originated in San Francisco in the 1930–1931 charter revision campaign. It was a compromise between the strong mayor and the manager plan. The compromise also reflected the urbanization process in the state. Unlike states in the East and Midwest, most California cities developed after the era of industrialization. As a result, they did not have the heterogeneous social-economic forces found in the earlier industrial cities. Many California cities, following a middle-class ethos, adopted the council-manager form of government. Inglewood and Glendale were among the first to adopt this form in 1914. By the mid-twenties, twenty-nine cities used the council-manager government. But the council-manager form did not serve the needs of the larger cities, like San Francisco, or the counties. In San Francisco the charter revision campaign of 1930 proposed a compromise which maintained the strong mayor but retained the role of professional manager in city government. This chief administrative officer would be responsible to the mayor for the administrative operation of city government. A popularly elected mayor would have the political base of support needed to get the legislative body of the board of supervisors to adopt his recommendations. By 1952, thirty-seven cities in California, one-eighth of the state's total, accounting for 45 percent of the urban population, had the CAO. The advantages of this approach were apparent to the governing boards of the California counties, especially those that were facing urban sprawl. The CAO form provides a professional manager who is responsible to the county board and ensures that the board's policies are carried out. Los Angeles County adopted this form in 1938, and most of the other large counties have followed suit.[12]

Other cities adopting the CAO include Philadelphia in 1951, New Orleans and Hoboken in 1952, and New York, Boston, and Newark in 1953. The official title of the CAO varies. He/she might be called a city administrator, deputy mayor, managing director, or simply administrator. Whatever the title, he/she generally is appointed by the mayor and serves at the mayor's pleasure. The CAO is responsible for the day-to-day operation of the city, including most personnel matters. As a professional city administrator, the CAO provides the mayor with an important link to the city bureaucracy, especially as regards the provisions of public services.[13]

NEW POLITICS

"New Breed" Mayors

By the 1950s the nation's cities realized that old problems postponed by the Depression and the war and new ones generated by economic change and suburban sprawl could not be ignored. Some cities responded to the challenges, either by the adoption of the council-manager form or the introduction of the CAO. In other cities there was a turning to aggressive, dynamic mayors, many of whom were political amateurs. These men might be called "new breed" mayors, a term used in Zane Miller's *The Urbanization of Modern America.*[14]

In the fifties and sixties it was believed this type of mayor would halt urban decay. There were, however, differences in mayoral leadership between the two decades. In the fifties the plight of the large city was not seen in crisis terms. There were problems; there were signs that the quality of life might worsen and that the proposed solutions might not work. Yet, the overall optimism that prevailed is seen in an article which appeared in 1958 in *Fortune* and later in *The Exploding Metropolis.* The author, Seymour Freedgood, concluded that "today the big city must rank as one of the most skillfully managed of American organizations."[15] These mayors, among whom he included Raymond Tucker of St. Louis, Frank Zeidler of Milwaukee, deLesseps Morrison of New Orleans, Richardson Dilworth of Philadelphia, David Lawrence of Pittsburgh, and Richard J. Daley of Chicago, were providing social leadership and administration in city governments despite the occasional opposition of the bureaucrats and the good government forces.

While these mayors came from different backgrounds and used different methods of leadership, they had many common traits. All shared a sense of mission for their people and their cities. They were politicians, although some of them had come out of reform movements. Most importantly, they emphasized good public relations. They surrounded themselves with young dynamic aides who provided them with the expertise necessary to respond to the myriad of problems. They saw progress mainly in terms of physical renewal of the city. This included urban renewal, expressway expansion, and reinvigorating the central business district. All of these actions were very popular among the middle class and the business interests. They were, according to Freedgood, "tough-minded, soft-spoken politicians."[16]

The "new breed" mayor was the big city's answer to urban reform, just as the council-manager was the answer for the medium-sized city. When Philadelphia was undergoing charter revision in the early fifties, the supporters seriously considered adopting Cincinnati's model of a council-manager. Yet the father of the Cincinnati model, Charles Taft, told the Philadelphia delegation that he would not under any circumstances recommend his city's form of government to a city of two million people. One member of the delegation recounted, "when the Lord himself said he didn't want those ten commandments spread elsewhere, that was the death knell."[17] Philadelphia went on to adopt a strong mayor form with a chief administrative officer.

Freedgood, despite the general optimism of his article, did foresee a number of trouble spots. One of the most difficult challenges facing the strong mayor was overcoming the entrenched bureaucracy protected by civil service. This level of city government was insulated from political pressures and at times more interested in protecting its own interests than serving the people. The most protected type of bureaucracy was the "public corporation." For example, while the Port Authority of New York and New Jersey under Robert Moses was perhaps "the most efficient public works agency in the world,"[18] it was totally independent of the public and largely unaccountable to it.

However, even strong mayors, in order to gain short-term benefits, endorsed the concept of independent public authorities. One problem all mayors faced was the debt limit placed on the cities by their states. A way of getting around this was to establish municipal authorities to issue bonds and administer specific public services. In this way the mayor was able to undertake additional public works and to exert some influence through the power to make the initial appointments to these bodies. In the long run these agencies became independent of the mayor's office and other political pressures, for once appointed the members of these authorities could not be removed.[19]

Despite the problems, Freedgood believed that the large cities were generally well governed and the quality of life was improving. *Fortune* magazine rated Cincinnati as the best governed of all the cities, while Milwaukee, Philadelphia, San Francisco, New York, Pittsburgh, Baltimore, and Detroit also received good marks. Only two cities, Houston and Minneapolis, failed to be included in indices used by *Fortune* to rate city governmental systems.[20]

Despite the *Fortune* article, a concern about the lack of dynamic political leadership in America emerged in the late 1950s. John F. Kennedy played on this concern and ushered in a new era in American politics. The Kennedy campaign generated among Americans a new interest in politics. Many who were drawn into politics during his campaign remained active on the local level, seeking political office. Most of these people were liberal Democrats and political amateurs. They soon joined the ranks of prominent mayors like Joseph Barr of Pittsburgh, elected in 1957, and Richard Lee of New Haven, elected in 1953. Lee set the example for most new mayors. Although New Haven had only 150,000 people, it was seen as "the greatest success story in the history of the world."[21] While this was an exaggeration, Lee did provide the leadership which brought hundreds of millions of dollars in federal, state, foundation, and private money into New Haven. The key to Lee's apparent success in New Haven, as well as the strong mayors of other large cities, was rebuilding. Detroit elected Jerome Cavanaugh, a thirty-three-year-old attorney, who had the Kennedy flair; Minneapolis chose a university professor, Arthur Naftalin. Atlanta elected a middle-aged businessman, Ivan Allen, who promised, like Kennedy, to get the city moving.

Later in the sixties, Joseph Alioto became mayor of San Francisco and two Kennedy-type blacks, Carl Stokes and Richard Hatcher, emerged as national figures by winning in Cleveland, Ohio, and Gary, Indiana. Even Republicans appeared who had the Kennedy charisma, as evidenced by the rise of John Lindsay in New York in 1965. All of these men were characterized in article after article as hardworking, articulate, problem-solving politicians who surrounded themselves with bright, young liberals who had the technical knowledge to solve the urban crisis. For a while, these "new breed" mayors generated confidence because of the influx of federal dollars.[22]

But the problems of urban redevelopment were too much. The riots of 1965-1968 showed that rhetoric, charisma, and even President Lyndon B. Johnson's Great Society programs were not adequate to halt the visible decay of the older, industrial cities. Four of the most prominent of these mayors chose not to run again in 1969: Lee, Naftalin, Allen, and Cavanaugh. In 1971, Stokes followed suit by announcing that he, too, would not seek reelection. Earlier, in 1969, John Lindsay won reelection on the Liberal party ticket largely because the conservative vote was split between Republican and Democratic candidates.

"New breed" mayors departed the central cities in the seventies. A number of reasons can be cited for their failure to reverse the decline of central cities. First, as Plunkitt has noted, reformers were mornin' glories.[23] They lacked the will to meet the drudgery of day-to-day administration, especially when this involved day-to-day crises. Rhetoric, money, charisma, and Ph.D.'s did not bring about the promised utopia. Second, by the late sixties, the Republican administration of Richard Nixon had reduced and sometimes stopped the flow of federal funds to central cities. This made matters only worse and it marked the end of the dream of the Great Society. The riots and the chaos associated with the antiwar movement led the American people to elect law-and-order candidates. Even in Minneapolis, the home of the Farm Labor party and a city with few minorities, Naftalin was succeeded by a tough law-and-order cop.

The Club Movements

The municipal reform movement attacked the political machine from a number of directions. Structural and procedural reforms of government and politics were among the most consequential changes designed to weaken machine organizations and loosen their control of governmental institutions. In addition, the reform movement also brought a new type of individual into the local political arena. He/she did not participate in local politics and party organization because of tangible and material rewards but because of the opportunities to realize ideological and issue-oriented goals.

These political activists were not professional politicians. That is, participation in party politics was not precipitated by dependence on the rewards of the political machine. Instead, these political "amateurs" saw reform of the party organization and its internal decision-making processes as an end in itself. Since amateur politicians were middle class in background, their livelihood did not depend upon the material rewards and patronage of machine politics. They could support positions on issues without being concerned with incurring the wrath of the bosses. The motivational base of the amateur politician was ideological and substantive. They sought to democratize the internal processes of the party by broadening the base of participation in organizational decision making, especially the process of nominating candidates to public office. In addition, they viewed election of the party's candidates not as an end in itself, but rather as a means to improving the conditions and solving the problems facing the city. As a result, amateurs were issue-oriented, that is, they wanted the party's candidates to appeal to voters on the basis of positions on substantive issues relevant to city life. This was, of course, anathema to the political machine inasmuch as its candidates appealed to the city electorate on the basis of more parochial and less substantive considerations like ethnic identification, patronage, etc.

The amateur movement, as it came to be called, really didn't get off the ground till after World War II and the presidential candidacy of Democrat Adlai E. Stevenson. Then, in a number of cities across the nation, "clubs" of amateur Democrats began to form within existing party organizations.[24] They appeared under different names in the various locations but shared certain common characteristics, a main one being the tendency to develop within the organization of the Democratic party in the central cities. In California, for example, they were referred to most generally as the "club movement" and more precisely as the California Democratic Council. In New York City amateurs took on the label of the "Lehman group" after one of their chief leaders, former United States Senator Herbert H. Lehman. In Illinois, on the other hand, there were two groups of amateur Democrats, one known as the Independent Voters of Illinois and another as the Democratic Federation of Illinois.

Since the term "amateur" is so closely associated with the party reform movement it should be made clear that its use is not intended to imply any irreverence for politics or party organization. As James Q. Wilson indicates,

> By amateur is not meant a dabbler, a dilettante or an inept practitioner of some special skill; many amateur Democrats have a highly sophisticated understanding of practical politics and have proved their skills in the only way that matters—by winning at the polls. . . .
>
> Nor does amateur here mean a person who is in politics for fun or as an avocation, rather than for money or as a career. . . .
>
> An amateur is one who finds politics *intrinsically* interesting because it expresses a conception of the public interest. The amateur politician sees the political world more in terms of ideas and principles than in terms of persons. Politics is the determination of public policy, and public policy ought to be set deliberately rather than as the accidental by-product of a struggle for personal and party advantage. Issues ought to be settled on their merits; compromises by which one issue is settled other than on its merits are sometimes necessary, but they are never desirable.[25]

The two most important processes and decisions in the party organization for the amateur are the determination of policies and the choice of officials, and there is a decided and explicit interconnection between these activities. Candidates for office should be chosen by the party not because of any shared ethnic or racial characteristic with voters, but rather because they support policies and programs espoused by the party's leaders and activists. Furthermore, it is assumed that the party's candidates will, if elected, work for the achievement of those policies and programs rather than dispense patronage and preferential treatment to party supporters.

The club movement has attracted different kinds of people, but to a great extent they share some important socioeconomic and political characteristics. They are young, well-educated professional people, including a large number of women. They are distinctly middle and upper class; they share a commitment to ideas and ideals often described as "liberal." The principal reward of politics to the amateur is the sense of having satisfied a perceived obligation to participate. This, in turn, is seen as a means to the interrelated goal of democratizing the party organization and working for the implementation of substantive programs and policies for the benefit of the entire central city.

While the club movement was especially strong in the early sixties, it declined later in the decade. It accomplished some positive goals in various cities, especially in New York City, where the Democratic party was reinvigorated. It brought into politics a number of young, dynamic reformers; it gave the Jewish community a voice in local and state politics proportionate to its population. Political clubs in Illinois, frustrated by defeat after defeat, turned to more substantive issues, such as civil rights. In California the conflicts between reformers and the regular Democrats paved the way for a number of conservative Republican victories.[26]

Club politics peaked in the mid-sixties. The national election of 1964 presented to the electorate what the reformers desired, namely, political parties divided largely along the lines of programs and issues. In addition, reformers made gains in making the political process of the Democratic party more democratic at the local and national level. The idealism and energy of the amateurs in the first half of the sixties seemed to prove that politics did not have to depend on material incentives.

One result of the politics of President John F. Kennedy's New Frontier and President Johnson's Great Society was to encourage urban reformers to look to the national government for the solutions to local problems. Local government and politics were seen as too cumbersome and were unresponsive to proposed change. Reformers saw civil rights and poverty as the great issues. In the late sixties the war further divided reformers and dissipated their energies for local reform.

In the early seventies the idealism of reformers almost destroyed the national Democratic party. Party reformers had so weakened the organization of the Democratic party that it was unable to retain party workers and to appeal to a broadly based electoral constituency. At the local level the city electorate proved to be more interested in material concerns than substantive issues and politics.

New Machines

Structural reformers in the twentieth century advocated more accountability and efficiency in city government. These two goals partially explain the strong support after 1945 for the council-manager system in the larger "bedroom" communities. In the older industrial cities reformers called for taking politics out of government. They urged that the cities be turned over to professionals. This meant the adoption of the council-manager system and professionalization of rank-and-file city employees through civil service. It was assumed that "there is no Republican or Democratic way to clean a street."

Theodore Lowi argues that as a result of reform the cities are better run than ever before but not necessarily better governed. The reform movement did not abolish politics, but altered it. In New York and other cities, the bureaucratic agencies of trained professionals became the "new machines." They are machines because they are not responsible to any authority. Their leaders are self-perpetuating yet make public policy. The problem with the new machines is that they are independent of one another, as well as independent of the mayor and council. These professionals are interested in expanding and perpetuating the power of their respective agencies. They tend to be less concerned with the community as a whole. The desire of agencies to expand their scope of operation, combined with the recognition that urban problems are multidimensional from a functional standpoint, leads to intense intra-agency competition. Through all of the competition the mayor is essentially powerless to effect coordination and direction to the operation and performance of the city bureaucracy.[27]

The emergence of powerful bureaucracies is especially evident in New York. Lowi argues that the 1961 city election in New York was "one of the most significant elections in American urban history." The reason is that the candidate for mayor, incumbent Robert Wagner, attempted to create a coalition that reflected the political power of the bureaucracies. His slate included the former commissioner of sanitation for president of the City Council and the city budget director for comptroller. In addition a former fire commissioner and a former police commissioner were influential figures in Wagner's campaign organization. Lowi concludes that the destruction of the machine in New York did not eliminate the need for political power; rather, it only altered the means of putting it together. Wagner balanced his slate just like the earlier Tammany machine had done; he just recognized that the locus of power in city politics had changed.[28]

The urban bureaucracies were undoubtedly exerting an increasing influence on local politics. Writing in the late sixties, Lowi described what he saw as a trend in urban government. While he did not know what the end result would be, he did feel that the new machines, the entrenched bureaucracies, were less positive forces on the local level than the old ones. In fact, he argued that the old machines, if they had not been weakened by reform, might well have had higher regard for the interests of the public than these new machines. The last of the Tammany leaders, Carmine DeSapio and Edward Costikyan, certainly were more public regarding than their predecessors.[29]

Edward N. Costikyan, one of the last Tammany leaders, argues that reformers are naive in their belief that removing political leaders from the government will put an end to corruption. Corruption comes with power and not with politics. When the locus of power moves from the politician to the civil servant, so does the possibility of corruption. An example of this was in 1961, when New York newspapers gave a daily tally of the scandals in the Wagner administration. Of the twenty or so scandals, only one involved a political leader or his appointees; the others all involved civil servants. Another example cited by Costikyan is an urban renewal program administered by Robert Moses. Moses was responsible to no one, and since he was a civil servant, no one questioned his actions. His exercise of administrative authority in the urban renewal program was characterized by arbitrariness, favoritism, and the lack of any public accountability. Though the program failed, Moses' reputation did not suffer, for he was not a politician. He went on to a new job and other honors.[30]

Much of the corruption in contemporary city government is of the "white-collar" variety, what George Washington Plunkitt called "honest graft." Influence, although nonpolitical, still determines who gets what, such as urban renewal projects, public works contracts, and franchises.[31] Many of these decisions are made by civil servants who are not easily held accountable to elected city officials. As mentioned earlier, many strong mayors supported the establishment of independent public authorities because they both increased the amount of money that could be spent on projects and because they were more easily controllable, at least initially, than agencies in the city bureaucracy. After a time, however, even these public authorities were difficult to control.

Another critique of urban bureaucracies comes from the radical left. While the ostensible focus of these attacks is largely the national Democratic party program, it is generated by the failure of local government. Richard Cloward and Frances Fox Piven are two of the most vocal critics of the urban public bureaucracies. They argue that the Kennedy and Johnson administrations introduced a broad range of urban programs. Those programs did not result, as expected, in ending poverty but in enlarging the white-dominated urban bureaucracies. These bureaucracies, especially in cities without effective political machines, expanded their own power and kept the poor dependent. Billions of federal dollars benefited not the poor but the urban bureaucrats, including teachers, social workers, police, and other public employees. The irony is that the more incompetent the bureaucracy, the larger it grew, as the failure of programs and restlessness of the urban poor were met with ever more money from the federal government. The professionalism and experience of the urban bureaucracy were cited to justify the ever larger role in dealing with urban problems.[32]

Cloward and Piven argue that urban programs have not the poor but the urban bureaucracy as their real clientele. The poor have few rights, leaders, or responses. When a leader does emerge, he/she is co-opted; when a response might work, it is preempted. For example, the Community Action Program did not organize the poor but destroyed whatever indigenous organization the poor had.[33] There are numerous examples to support the Cloward-Piven thesis that federal money for the cities has failed to reach the poor. However, responsibility for the failure of federal programs is usually directed at the poor. No one blames the banks, Federal Housing Administration, or contractors for the failure of federally subsidized housing; no one blames the doctors for the enormous costs of Medicaid programs; no one blames the school systems for the lack of improvement in reading skills among central city students. While these programs are not directly a part of city government, they involve agencies of city government that are attempting to make the city more livable.

THE PERSISTENCE OF MACHINE POLITICS

The preceding pages have considered the impact of various new forces on the governance and development of cities. The club movement was an attempt to reform American politics both on the national and the local level. It sought to weaken the control of politics and government by professional politicians. In most cities the impact of the club movement and amateur politicians was weak and short-lived. Though the club movement was successful in leaving its mark only on New York, "new machines" are found in almost every central city. In some cities, like Chicago, the city bureaucracy is still very much part of the old machine. But in most cities the bureaucracy employs the cry of reform to influence government and politics while operating essentially beyond the reach of public accountability. Detroit's 1977 mayoral election pitted incumbent Mayor Coleman Young against another black, Ernest Browne. Young was attacked as a machine politician, while Browne portrayed himself as the candidate of good government. He was supported actively by the predominantly white city bureaucracy, including the police, fire, and sanitation departments. Young won handily because he had the almost unanimous support of blacks, the upper-class business establishment in Detroit, and the liberal community, especially the leadership of the United Auto Workers. Yet, the city bureaucracy in Detroit is able to resist and often prevent change; its main interest lies in maintaining the status quo. Protection of civil service, combined with the development of powerful municipal unions, have made the new machines, the city bureaucracies, far more difficult to reform or to remove than the traditional political machines.

Despite the reforms of political processes and governmental institutions and practices, political machines have been able to survive in many cities. In some instances they are more aggressive and healthier than before reforms were initiated. A number of reasons explain this persistence. First, reformers have failed to govern the city or improve its conditions. Second, the incentive system on which political machines relied has remained viable, despite civil service and other reforms. Third, old-style politics and politicians seem to be more successful than new-style politicians. Finally ethnic politics and voting patterns that support political machines are still very much a part of city politics.

Failure to Govern the City

The experience of the last three decades indicates that the urban reform movement has failed to realize its goals. More specifically, the reforms of the Progressive movement failed to make politics more democratic and the cities more livable. Urban reform has not only failed to give the lower classes a more effective voice in government but has, by some accounts, reduced their influence. The introduction of nonpartisan elections, for example, has increased the time and money needed to seek elective office. These resources are generally more available to the middle and upper-middle classes. Furthermore, the introduction of at-large elections has reduced the participation and influence of the lower classes, especially ethnic and racial groups, who tend to live in residential enclaves. Officials elected at large usually come from middle-class neighborhoods and are less likely to take responsibility for action taken in a particular neighborhood. In 1974, for example, the majority of the members of the city council in Cincinnati came from two middle-class neighborhoods. In 1973 the nine-member school board in Flint, Michigan, did not have a single member from the working-class neighborhoods in the northern half of the city.

Reformers also attacked the inefficiency and lack of expertise resulting from the absence of specialized, professional administrators. Today, with the technically trained personnel, inefficiency still exists and expertise is still nonexistent in most city governments. The middle-class ideal of honesty, efficiency, and impartiality has led to an emphasis on procedure rather than substance. In many cities there has emerged a bureaucracy that is insulated from public pressures in its decision making. The result has been agency-based decentralization of political power, duplication of services, red tape, and a concern for self-preservation. The interests of the lower classes, especially blacks and other minorities, are easily ignored or manipulated in such an arrangement.

The style and approach of reformers has not brought effective government. Reformers are amateurs; politics is an avocation. Reformers want to change policy by changing structure. When this does not occur, they grow tired an pursue other crusades. Politicians, on the other hand, are professional: they persist in defeat as well as victory. Professionals take losses stoically but with renewed determination regroup their forces, work out compromises, and try again at a later time. Among reformers defeat usually leads to intraorganization battles or dropping out, further narrowing their political base. In many cities this situation leads to a "cycle of reform," in which the control alternates between the machine and the reformers.

Incentive System Continues

Reform sought to destroy the political machine by changing the incentive system on which it depended. Civil service supposedly reduced the number of both low-level and middle-level patronage jobs. Interest in these jobs, it was believed, diminished as second- and third-generation immigrants moved into the middle class. But the incentive system of the machine still operates on many levels. Despite civil service, mayors in Chicago and New York have thousands of jobs at their disposal, jobs that are filled with temporary employees who soon become permanent. In Chicago each ward committee person has approximately seven hundred jobs over which he/she has some control. Since the early sixties federal dollars have generated tens of thousands of new jobs, many of which become political appointments. Jobs are available on the lower level for those who need and want work. At the middle levels, political appointments still represent a way of social mobility into the middle class. The incentive system does not begin and end with public jobs. Many politicians find positions for their friends and supporters through contacts in the private sector.

Middle-level politicians are not always employed by the city. However, because they are lawyers, insurance agents, or realtors, they find their political connections valuable in providing all the business they can handle. Thus, machine leaders have the incentives of income plus power, prestige, and sociability. Amateur politicians and reformers generally fail because they are unable to establish an ongoing, effective political organization. And this is because they lack a tangible reward system.

Old-Style Politics

It is argued that machine politics disappeared because "old-style" politics is no longer effective. Voters were not influenced by personal contact. A study carried on in the mid-fifties supported this by showing that less than 20 percent of the voters in Northern cities were contacted before an election.[34] But in 1968 an innovation was introduced, the door-to-door campaigning of the McCarthy volunteers. The same phenomenon occurred in the Democratic primaries in 1972. While there were many differences between the machine precinct workers and the idiologically committed McCarthyites or McGovernites, their methods were similar and to a certain extent successful.

"Old-style" politics survives not only in terms of methods, but also personalities. The "old-style" politician was relegated to history after the emergence of "new-style" politics. The years of prosperity following the Korean War and the Kennedy mystique produced scores of dynamic mayors. These "new breed" mayors emphasized public relations, utilized energetic, bright young assistants, developed programs for urban renewal, expressway building, and central city redevelopment, and had great ambition. Most of them had left public office by the end of the sixties because of the failure of their policies and the bankruptcy of the Great Society.

One mayor who survived the sixties was Richard J. Daley, who was in many ways the stereotype of the "old-style" political boss. An interesting comparison can be made between Richard J. Daley and John Lindsay. Lindsay in the mid-sixties seemed to be the Republican Kennedy—young, dynamic, and charismatic. He was a WASP who could rap with ghetto blacks and empathize with Jewish liberals. But he found the politics of the city in the mayor's office less conducive to his style than his "silk-stocking" congressional district. He could not govern New York City because he had no machine. He tried to create one but failed because he could not relate to the predominantly white ethnic city bureaucracy. In 1969 Lindsay barely won reelection, but not as a candidate of the Republican party. In 1973 he chose not to seek another term as mayor.[35]

Richard J. Daley has been praised as "the most successful mayor of America" and attacked for making a farce of the electoral system. In his book *Boss*, Mike Royko had little positive to say about him. Chuck Stone charged

"Boss Daley has built a Chicago Dynasty on syndicated crime and subsurface corruption." Few liberals could say anything good about Daley after the 1968 debacle.[36]

But what allowed Daley to survive the sixties and then go on to win reelection in 1971 and in 1975 by overwhelming margins? First, Daley survived because he was a typical Irish politician—he wanted nothing more than to hold on to power. He occasionally practiced what he preached, that "good government is good politics," not as an end in itself but as a means to maintaining his power. Daley had no ambitions beyond being mayor of Chicago.[37]

Second, he survived because of his ability to organize the many different interest groups in Chicago—downtown businessmen, unions, suburbanites, ethnics, blacks, and certain less respectable elements. Conflict among these groups occasionally erupted and when it did Daley was usually able to bring off an acceptable solution. While Daley relied on his machine, he also maintained the neutrality if not support of the middle class. Like the "new breed" mayors he used an extensive construction program to maintain the support of the middle class, business interests, unions, and the Chicago media. His administration built an expressway system and convention center to instill new life in the Chicago Loop. In response, private corporations have invested hundreds of millions of dollars in Chicago's business district.

Third, Daley's survival in city government and politics depended on the Cook County Democratic organization. Daley's power in Chicago rested not on his position as mayor, but on his position as chairman of the Cook County Democratic party organization. Daley moved up through the machine, loyally serving as ward committeeman, state legislator, and state revenue director. In 1953 he replaced Jacob Arvey as chairman of the Cook County Democratic Committee and two years later was elected mayor. The Chicago machine depends on controlling not so much the fifty aldermanic offices but the fifty ward committee persons, who control hundreds of jobs and the aldermen and -women. Because of the number of wards in Chicago, many wards tend to be dominated by a single racial or ethnic group. Thus is forged a link between ethnic politics and the political machine. Daley never had to deal with more than a handful of aldermen or ward committeemen who were not part of his machine.

Daley's good relationship with Washington was a fourth reason for his success. His influence with Chicago's congressional delegation and his link to the White House were necessary to keep federal intervention to a minimum and federal money at a maximum. An example of this strategy occurred after the passage of the Economic Opportunity Act in 1964. Daley, through his control of the Chicago congressional delegation, used the poverty program to strengthen his machine. Chicago obtained and spent more Community Action Program dollars per poor family than any other major city. Daley accomplished this by keeping community representation to a minimum. In cities where liberals succeeded in providing representation for the poor in poverty programs, internal conflicts and bureaucratization kept new services and programs to a minimum. Liberal reformers attacked Daley because he channeled the new welfare programs through his machine rather than organizations of the poor, yet he was far more successful than the reformers in distributing poverty funds. Thus Daley the politician did more for the poor in Chicago than well-meaning liberals in New York, Philadelphia, and other cities. In these cities the poor neither responded to the reformers' dream of participatory democracy nor received much in material benefits.[38]

While Chicago politics, both with Daley and without him, is a model of the "classic" machine, it is not the only effective machine in existence. New York provides examples of two very powerful machines, one suburban and Republican, the other urban and Democratic. Both machines are based on fund raising, patronage, and legislative influence. These activities produce benefits which allow the machines to perpetuate themselves. New York State Assemblyman Joseph M. Margiotta heads the Nassau County Republican organization which has been called the "most effective political machine east of Chicago." Margiotta's organization brings in about a million dollars a year for deserving Republican candidates. This money comes from traditional party dinners, big donors, and an annual contribution from the seventeen thousand county and town employees, amounting to 1 percent of their salaries.[39]

Meade H. Esposito heads the most effective machine in New York City. His Brooklyn Democratic organization is run in a more traditional manner than Margiotta's. Esposito must deal with a racially and ethnically mixed organization. He has been successful in balancing the various interest groups through his control over patronage, which comes through the courts, the city administration, and state government. Because Esposito controls almost all of Brooklyn's state representatives, Governor Nelson Rockefeller had to provide him with a considerable amount of state patronage. After Abraham Beame became mayor of New York in 1974, Esposito's organization received additional patronage.[40]

These machines are examples of the more successful ones. Other machines are operating, although some not as effectively. In any case, it is clear that political machines have not disappeared as municipal reformers had intended. The cycle of reform politics and machine politics is very much a part of city politics today, just as it was seventy years ago.

Ethnic Politics

The persistence of ethnic politics provides a fourth reason for the persistence of political machines in contemporary America. This does not mean that ethnic groups are necessary for the functioning of political machines. Margiotta's machine in Nassau County lacks an ethnic base.[41] But ethnic politics tends to support machine politics.

Ethnic politics continues to exist in America. Immigrants became involved in politics soon after their arrival in the industrial cities. They found that in exchange for votes, a person could receive tangible rewards as well as group recognition. Individuals were encouraged to come together and identify as ethnics not only because of common cultural ties, but also because they were identified as such by the dominant society. For example, the politician was one of those who identified the immigrants from Sicily and Tuscany as Italian-Americans.[42] The establishment of relatively homogeneous neighborhoods also was conducive to ethnic politics. These neighborhoods, if they were small, might coincide with the boundaries of a precinct; if large, with a ward. It was only natural for the political machine to develop ties to immigrant neighborhoods through the indigenous activists.

An understanding of contemporary ethnic politics requires a knowledge of the nature of ethnicity and its impact on America. In the past it was held that the immigrants and their children were being assimilated into American society. As a result, liberals did not foresee the rise of ethnicity in the 1960s because they believed that it had disappeared. Ethnicity to them was a carry-over from the era of immigration. It was not an American experience. Liberals failed to realize that ethnicity was a combination of European and American experiences. Glazer and Moynihan argue that ethnicity is not a relic of the past, but a social form, continually being re-created by new experiences. They believe that while the Italian-American might share precious little with Italians of Italy, in America he/she is part of a distinctive group that maintains itself, is identifiable, and gives something to the person who shares in that identity, just as it also infuses burdens that those in the group have to bear.[43]

In 1967, political scientist Michael Parenti argued that ethnics were an important political force because they had not assimilated and were only partially acculturated. He saw that residual cultural values and attitudes remained within ethnic groups. As a result ethnic social and political institutions were alive and well. Parenti also questioned whether ethnic mobility really occurred. He rejected the idea that the ethnics had moved up to the middle class; rather, he argued, overall changes in the national economy had raised nearly everyone. The ethnics' position relative to the dominant group in society remained essentially unchanged. Even those ethnics who did move up the socioeconomic ladder still maintained separate social structures. He believed that the "unassimilated ethnic should be seen as very much alive and with us today."[44]

The ethnicity prevalent today is essentially conservative. In politics it is conservative because it attempts to hold on to the past and fears the implications of the liberal ideology of the 1960s and early 1970s. Ethnicity both in the past and the present manifests itself through ethnic politics. Ethnics believe that by acting together as a political interest group they will achieve both tangible and intangible benefits. For most white ethnics, group politics is more effective operating through a political machine than outside it.

Even in those cities where the political machine is not functioning, ethnic politics still plays a role, allowing specific ethnic groups to gain political influence. This political influence for the ethnics has been strongest in the older central cities of the Midwest and Northeast. It was in these cities that reformers were less successful in establishing major changes in the existing political and government structure. Ethnic politics tends to be most effective in cities with ward rather than at-large elections, partisan rather than nonpartisan nominating procedures and ballots, and with mayor-council rather than the council-manager form of government.

Only one group, the Jews, functions more effectively in reform politics than in machine politics, especially in New York City. The reasons for this include the large concentration of Jewish immigrants in New York City and its surrounding communities, the high level of literacy among the Jewish immigrants, rapid educational and economic mobility, the cultural characteristics of self-help, involvement in social reform, and support for civil liberties. During the early twentieth century Jews in New York voted independently, dividing their vote among Republican, Democratic, and Socialist candidates. The Jewish vote tended to support liberals regardless of party.

The influence of ethnic politics lessens as immigrants and their children move out of the central city. The inability of the older cities to expand their boundaries has led to the creation of scores of suburbs. In these small political units ethnic politics tends to be weak. The number of ethnics is generally not large enough to bring about the dominance of a single group. Yet, in the cities where the ethnics still make up a large percentage of the population, ethnic politics is viable and effective. Sometimes it works through the existing political machine; other times it works outside of the machine; rarely does ethnic politics coincide with reform politics.

BLACK POLITICS: A NEW PHENOMENON
IN URBAN POLITICS

It is not clear that blacks will follow a pattern of political activity similar to that of the ethnics. As the black urban population increases, the political power of the group increases. For blacks, however, the city is a different place than what it was for the immigrant. Blacks face a more explicit type of discrimination. As a result, black politicians face problems that immigrant and ethnic politicians did not have to confront. Racism and the fact that they were the last major group to arrive in the city have made it more difficult for blacks to achieve effective political influence. Like the immigrants earlier, blacks found that they had a greater opportunity for political power with ward as opposed to at-large elections. At least with wards, they could gain representation on the city council, while at-large elections would preclude such access until they reached a near majority of the population. Detroit and Cincinnati are examples of reformed cities. With at-large elections blacks failed to have substantial representation on the city council in Detroit until the early 1970s. In Cincinnati in the mid-1970s, blacks did not have one member on the council.

Because of racism, middle-class blacks have not had, until recently, the opportunity to move to the suburbs. Thus blacks remain largely in the central city. It is in these cities that black political power is manifested. Because of the political gains that have been made in the cities, blacks generally oppose metropolitan-wide government reform. They also are the most vocal supporters of greater decentralization of political and administrative authority, especially in the service bureaucracies and school districts. Blacks are suspicious of the small but visible in-migration of middle-class whites to central cities. Some have become very alarmed by this, seeing it as an erosion of their gains in political power in the city. Along with the return of some whites to the central city, there is also a beginning of outmigration of middle-class blacks to inner-ring suburbs. This movement, which reflects a lessening of the more blatant forms of racism, also erodes black political strength by reducing their numbers and removing potential black leaders. This factor has made it possible for whites to regain control of the mayor's office, as in Cleveland after Carl Stokes's two terms in office.

The future of black political power is linked to what happens to the older central cities in the Midwest and Northeast. The future of both depends on which political strategy black politicians select. Black politicians must select a political strategy that will allow them to deal effectively with the groups that reside in the suburbs but retain economic interests in the city, the white-dominated city bureaucracy, the white ethnics in the city, and the large, black lower class. Possible strategies include (1) separatist, (2) reformist, (3) ethnic, and (4) pragmatic.

The separatist strategy was given the most publicity not by a black mayor but by Congressman Adam Clayton Powell. Powell entered Congress in 1945, a time when there was no effective political machine in New York because of the reforms of Fiorello La Guardia. So Powell built his own machine in Harlem, basing it on the Abyssinian Baptist Church which he had taken over from his father as minister in 1937. He became the personal embodiment, the projective personality of his congregation. The rewards which he offered his constituents were intangible—he challenged "Mr. Charlie" and won. Powell could indulge his personal desires without fearing any backlash from the voters back home. The weakness of this strategy is that it provided only transitory, intangible rewards for the black masses and ultimately brought down the politician himself. However, some Black Power advocates supported this model at the National Black Convention in Gary, Indiana, in 1972. The proponents of this strategy call for a separate black party which they hope will hold the balance of power in America. A more likely result will be failure, indecision, and further frustration for the black community.[45]

The reformist strategy is represented by "new breed" black mayors, men like Carl Stokes, Richard Hatcher, and Kenneth A. Gibson in his first administration. These men gained the support of Black Power advocates and white liberals to win in Cleveland, Gary, and Newark, New Jersey. Each won a close election, carrying better than 90 percent of the black vote but less than 20 percent of the white vote. The weaknesses of this strategy are identical to those found among white reform mayors. The mayors promised great change but could deliver very little because of the extent of the decay found in the cities, dependence on federal money, and an inability to work with the political machines. These men saw themselves as torchbearers for the fulfillment of the dreams of the New Frontier and the Great Society. They hoped to develop a viable community by throwing out "old politics." They had the additional problem of facing criticism from black militants when they worked with white interests and from black moderates when they did not. Carl Stokes followed the path of most white "new breed" mayors by not seeking reelection in 1971. Richard Hatcher endured, winning a second four-year term in 1971 with 60 percent of the vote and a third term by a comfortable margin in 1975. When the local Democratic machine put up black candidates in 1971 and 1975, Hatcher defeated both, but the white ethnic precincts solidly supported the machine candidates.[46]

Throughout his years as mayor, Hatcher has found himself isolated from the ethnic-dominated Lake County Democratic organization. In his first administration, he was characterized as a strong mayor who had centralized politics in Gary, mobilized community resources, and brought about substantial innovation. His success was due to the millions of dollars of federal money and the support he had from liberals in Washington and New York. But in Gary he failed to compromise with his opponents in the Democratic machine. Many of his innovative programs ended with the reduction in federal funds after 1969. His power in Gary was also reduced when the Lake County Democratic machine joined with downstate legislators to pass legislation in the Indiana General Assembly to weaken the power of the mayor of Gary.[47]

The ethnic strategy in its first stage provides social services for black newcomers and token recognition for black leaders through the political machine. This recognition includes appointments to boards and middle-level management positions, as well as slating of candidates to represent black wards or districts. Congressman William L. Dawson of Chicago was an example of the black politician benefiting from the ethnic strategy. Dawson started out as a street-corner speaker with a magnetic personality. He was a Republican alderman in Chicago until 1939, when he switched to the Democratic party. After serving as a powerful ward committeeman, he was selected by the Kelly machine to be the congressman from the black South Side in 1942. Despite his election to Congress he remained ward committeeman and also brought three other South Side wards under his control. In Congress he was an integrationist politician, shunning race issues and having only two blacks on the fifty-man staff of his House Committee on Operations. In Chicago he was the machine politician, handing out tangible rewards to his loyal followers, reportedly having ties with the policy racket and the jitney drivers, and making deals with Richard J. Daley. The major weakness of this strategy is that the leader is co-opted with tangible rewards for himself and for some of his constituents. Social reform is checked; social mobility occurs only for a few; the serious problems in the black community are ignored. Since Dawson's death in 1970, the black submachine in Chicago has continued to be part of the Daley machine.[48]

If black politicians hope to be successful in governing cities, they must somehow develop a pragmatic strategy which combines the best of the ethnic and reformist model. This is seen in Newark where Kenneth A. Gibson has been more successful than Hatcher or Stokes in bridging the gap between blacks and ethnics. In 1974 Gibson won reelection by decisively defeating State Senator Anthony Imperiale. In black wards Gibson won more than 90 percent of the vote; in white wards he won 30 percent. In this election he had the support of some influential whites, including John P. Caulfield, director of the fire department, and Stephen Adubato, founder of the federally funded cultural center in the Italian section. This support offset Gibson's break with Imamu Baraka (LeRoi Jones), the black nationalist poet, whose ticket did poorly against Gibson's more moderate one.[49] Coleman Young in Detroit is another example of a black leader who has come to terms with established power groups. As noted earlier, Young was reelected easily in Detroit in 1977. While he had failed to develop an effective working relationship with Detroit's ethnic community and the white bureaucracy, he did assemble a solid coalition of lower- and middle-class blacks, important banking and industrial interests, and the United Auto Workers. Like Daley, Young is successful in working with the economic elite. Unlike Daley, he has not been able to work with lower- and middle-class ethnics. Only the future will tell if Young will be effective in making Detroit livable.

Harvard University scholar Martin Kilson believes that if black politics is to be successful, then the black middle class must control it. The more militant blacks would serve as ward and precinct leaders, bridging the gap between the middle and lower class. To maintain this power, patronage must be available, especially in terms of federal funds flowing out of Washington.[50] With the federal policy of the seventies of employing block grants, local governments acquire a new source of patronage and influence. It also is a way for blacks to move into the white-dominated bureaucracy. The hiring of blacks need not require the firing of whites.

Summary

In this chapter we have examined the continuation of urban structural reform. These reforms had been proposed in the late nineteenth century, enacted in the early twentieth century, and expanded after the 1920s. We also have seen the continued conflict between the forces for structural reform and those opposing it. In the period after the 1920s neither the reformers nor the machine politicians were able to improve the quality of life in the older, industrial cities of the Midwest and Northeast. In many instances action or lack of action by both groups accelerated central city decline. In some cases, such as Cincinnati, the structural reformers were successful in establishing good government and a livable environment, at least for most groups in the city. In Chicago, the political machine of Richard J. Daley did the same. But these are exceptions. To understand the importance of both the reformers and the machine, as well as the reasons why other responses were proposed for urban decay, responses such as metropolitanization and the community power movement, one must look at the socioeconomic forces that change the makeup of urban society in the twentieth century. In the following chapter we will examine this eclipse of the central city.

NOTES

1. Bradley Robert Rice, *Progressive Cities: The Commission Government Movement in America, 1901-1920* (Austin: University of Texas Press, 1977), p. 53; Demetrios Caraley, *City Governments and Urban Problems* (Englewood Cliffs, N.J.: Prentice-Hall, 1977), p. 89.

2. Rice, pp. 90-94.

3. Charles R. Adrian and Charles Press, *Governing Urban America*, 5th ed. (New York: McGraw-Hill, 1977), pp. 167-68.

4. Richard J. Stillman II, *The Rise of the City Manager: A Public Professional in Local Government* (Albuquerque: University of New Mexico Press, 1974), pp. 7 and 20.

5. Harold A. Stone, Don K. Price, and Kathryn H. Stone, *City Manager Government in the United States: A Review After Twenty-five Years* (Chicago: Public Administration Service, 1940), p. 27; quoted in Stillman, p. 21.

6. Stillman, p. 24.

7. John H. Baker, *Urban Politics in America* (New York: Charles Scribner's Sons, 1971), p. 186.

8. Leonard D. White, *The City Manager* (Chicago: University of Chicago Press, 1927); see also Gladys M. Kammerer et al., *City Managers in Politics* (Gainesville: University of Florida, 1962), and Ronald O. Loveridge, *City Managers in Legislative Politics* (Indianapolis: Bobbs-Merrill, 1971).

9. A. Theodore Brown, *The Politics of Reform, Kansas City's Municipal Government, 1925-1950* (Kansas City, Mo.: Community Studies, 1958), pp. 31-32, quoted in Lyle W. Dorsett, *The Pendergast Machine* (New York: Oxford University Press, 1968), p. 78.

10. Dorsett, pp. 75-89. For a discussion of Kansas City after Pendergast, see Stanley T. Gabis, "Leadership in a Large Manager City: The Case of Kansas City," *The Annals* 353 (May 1964): 52-63.

11. Karolatta Beauchamp, "The Origin of Flint's Commission-Manager Form of Government" (typed copy in possession of The Department of History, The University of Michigan-Flint), quote from p. 8.

12. John C. Bollens, *Appointed Executive Local Government: The California Experience* (Los Angeles: Haynes Foundation, 1952), pp. 6-17. See also Loveridge, *City Managers*.

13. Stillman, pp. 24-26.

14. Zane L. Miller, *The Urbanization of Modern America* (New York: Harcourt Brace Jovanovich, 1973), pp. 182-84.

15. Seymour Freedgood, "New Strength in City Hall," in *The Exploding Metropolis*, ed. Editors of *Fortune* (Garden City, N.Y.: Doubleday, 1958), p. 62.

16. *Ibid.,* p. 63.

17. *Ibid.,* p. 77.

18. *Ibid.,* p. 82.

19. *Ibid.,* pp. 86-91.

20. *Ibid.*, pp. 69-73.

21. Fred Powledge, "The Flight from City Hall," *Harper's*, November 1969, pp. 69-86.

22. *Ibid.*, 69-86.

23. The term "mornin' glories" is taken from William L. Riordon, *Plunkitt of Tammany Hall* (New York: McClure and Phillips, 1905), p. 30.

24. The phrase "amateur Democrat" is part of the title of one of the most comprehensive studies of the movement. See James Q. Wilson, *The Amateur Democrat: Club Politics in Three Cities* (Chicago: University of Chicago Press, 1966).

25. *Ibid.*, pp. 2-3.

26. *Ibid.*, pp. vii-viii.

27. Theodore J. Lowi, Foreword to 2d ed., *Machine Politics: Chicago Model*, by Harold F. Gosnell (Chicago: University of Chicago Press, 1968), pp. viii-xii. See also Lowi, *The End of Liberalism* (New York: W. W. Norton, 1969), pp. 200-206.

28. Lowi, Foreword, pp. viii-xv.

29. *Ibid.*, p. xvi.

30. Edward N. Costikyan, *Behind Closed Doors* (New York: Harcourt, Brace and World, 1966).

31. *Ibid.*

32. Richard A. Cloward and Frances Fox Piven, *The Politics of Turmoil: Essays on Poverty, Race and the Urban Crisis* (New York: Pantheon, 1975), pp. 314-40.

33. *Ibid.*, p. 5.

34. Fred I. Greenstein, *The American Party System and The American People* (Englewood Cliffs, N.J.: Prentice-Hall, 1963), p. 46.

35. For an interesting comparison of Daley's Chicago and Lindsay's New York see Lowi, Foreword, pp. vii-xii.

36. David Halberstam, "Daley of Chicago," *Harper's*, August 1968. p. 25; Chuck Stone, *Black Political Power* (Indianapolis: Bobbs-Merrill, 1968), p. 118. Also critical of Daley, James Q. Wilson and Edward C. Banfield, *City Politics* (New York: Vintage, 1963),pp. 124-25; Mike Royko, *Boss* (New York: E.P. Dutton, 1970).

37. Halberstam, pp. 25-36. See also newspaper articles in *Chicago Tribune* on primary election in Illinois, March 1974; William F. Gleason, *Daley of Chicago* (New York: Simon and Schuster, 1970); Royko, *Boss*; Len O'Connor, *Clout: Mayor Daley and His City* (Chicago: Regnery, 1975).

38. J. David Greenstone and Paul E. Peterson "Reformers, Machines, and the War on Poverty," in *City Politics and Public Policy*, ed. James Q. Wilson (New York: John Wiley, 1968), pp. 267-92.

39. Frank Lynn, "Suburban to City, Bosses Differ a Bit in Style," *The New York Times*, July 7, 1974, E5.

40. *Ibid.*

41. Another example of machine politics without an ethnic base is Vigo

County, Indiana. See David S. Broder, "Old Style Politics," *The Washington Post*, June 15, 1975, p. 1.

42. Walter A. Borowiec, "Perceptions of Ethnic Voters by Ethnic Politicians," *Ethnicity* 1 (October 1974), pp. 267-78.

43. Nathan Glazer and Daniel P. Moynihan, *Beyond the Melting Pot*, 2d ed. (Boston: M.I.T. Press, 1970), p. xxxiii.

44. Michael Parenti, "Ethnic Politics and the Persistence of Ethnicity, *American Political Science Review* 61 (September 1967): 717-26; quote from p. 726. Supporting Parenti on the persistence of ethnicity but critical of his broad generalizations are Raymond E. Wolfinger, *The Politics of Progress* (Englewood Cliffs, N.J.: Prentice-Hall, 1974), pp. 34-35, and Daniel N. Gordon, "Immigrant and Municipal Voting Turnout," *American Sociological Review* 35 (1970): 665-81. For a critical view, see Martin Plax, "Uncovering Ambiguities in Some Uses of the Concept of Ethnic Voting," *Midwest Journal of Political Science* 15 (August 1971): 571-82.

45. Dwaine Marvick, "The Political Socialization of the American Negro," reprinted in *Ethnic Group Politics*, eds. Harry A. Bailey, Jr., and Ellis Katz (Columbus, Ohio: Charles E. Merrill, 1969), p. 126; Chuck Stone, pp. 178-201.

46. Mark R. Levy and Michael S. Kramer, *The Ethnic Factor* (New York: Simon and Schuster, 1972), pp. 69-72; Chuck Stone, pp. 203-22; Alex Poinsett, "Black Take-Over of U.S. Cities?" *Ebony* 26 (November 1970), 77-86; Jeffrey Hadden et al., "The Making of the Negro Mayors, 1967," *Trans-action* 5 (January 1968): 21-30. See also Alex Poinsett, *Black Power: Gary Style* (Chicago: Johnson, 1970); Charles H. Levine, *Racial Conflict and the American Mayor* (Lexington, Mass.: D.C. Heath, 1974), pp. 51-106; and a general work by Hanes Walton, Jr., *Black Politics: A Theoretical and Structural Analysis* (Philadelphia: Lippincott, 1972); William E. Nelson, Jr., and Philip J. Meranto, *Electing Black Mayors: Political Action in the Black Community* (Columbus, Ohio: Ohio State University Press, 1977), pp. 67-335.

47. Levine, *Racial Conflict*, p. 81; Godfrey Hodgson and George Crile, "Gary: Epitaph for a Model City," *The Washington Post*, March 4, 1973, p. B1.

48. For a discussion of William Dawson, see Chuck Stone, pp. 170-78; for a comparison of Dawson and Powell, see James Q. Wilson, "Two Negro Politicians: An Interpretation," reprinted in *Ethnic Group Politics*, pp. 207-27 and Marvick, "The Political Socialization of the American Negro," p. 126. For a later discussion of black politics in Chicago, see Norman Bonney, "Race and Politics in Chicago in the Daley Era," *Race* 15 (January 1974): 329-50.

49. Chuck Stone, "Re-election of a Black Mayor: A New Milestone," *Detroit Free Press*, May 23, 1974.

50. Martin Kilson, "Black Politics: A New Power," *Dissent*, August 1971, pp. 333-45.

CHAPTER VII.

Eclipse of the Central City

Introduction

In the preceding chapter we examined the impact of municipal reform on the development of governmental and political institutions in the twentieth century. We also showed how the differing styles and concerns of amateur and professional politicians influenced the performance of urban public institutions in providing services and dealing with the problems created by urban development. Today most governmental institutions represent an accommodation between the ideals and goals of the urban structural reformers and the needs and realities of the cities mediated through the process of charter revision. The decade of the 1920s can be said to be the high point of urban reform; reform efforts thereafter were modified in response to the opposition of strongly entrenched political interests, the Great Depression, and the eclipse of the central city.

This chapter examines the factors affecting urban development in the decades since World War I. We find that the shift in focus of reform from the central city to other governmental units reflects our view that those committed to improving the quality of life in the central city no longer see urban problems solely in terms of intraurban institutional arrangements and processes. Reformers now look beyond the existing governance structure when seeking to meet the challenges facing urban America. In fact, the two major contemporary movements for structural reform, metropolitan government and decentralization-community control, transcend the traditional and legal institutions of city government. It might even be argued that urban reformers have given up on the city per se, seeing the problems it faces as beyond the capacity of local government to solve. Reformers now feel that no meaningful change can come from restructuring city government. There is no longer a generally accepted long-term solution for the urban crisis. In the short term the struggling cities of the Midwest and Northeast rely on funds from both the federal and state governments, with the latter coming grudgingly and in small amounts. At the same time these cities, even with additional sources of revenue, have been forced to curtail services. This has resulted in a return to the "private city" of the mid-nineteenth century with the solid middle class paying for services and the poor doing without.

THE 1920s: THE PINNACLE OF THE CITY IN AMERICA

Urban America's Dominance Established

The 1920s marked the pinnacle of the industrial city in America. It was the decade when the forces of rural America were routed and the supremacy of the industrialized, urbanized society was established. Rural America had a brief moment of glory with the passage of the Eighteenth Amendment. But this victory was followed by weak enforcement in cities. Other attempts by rural interests to control a rapidly changing society also met with frustration. The crusade of the Fundamentalists to halt the advances of Darwinism suffered a mortal wound with the fiasco at Dayton, Tennessee, and the death of William Jennings Bryan shortly thereafter. In national politics rural dominance ended with the nomination of Al Smith at the 1928 Democratic convention. The radio, the automobile, and movies further eroded the agrarian values of the nineteenth century. Rural America underwent a final transformation during the decade as thousands of families were pushed from the countryside by the twin forces of continued mechanization in agriculture and the decade-long agricultural depression. These migrants were drawn to the city by the possibilities of jobs, not only in the traditional sectors of industrial employment, like iron and steel, but in the new ones, like the automobile, chemical, rubber, and appliance industries.

But the victory of industrialization over agrarianism was only one reason why the 1920s was the decade of the city. More important to the city were the changes occurring within it. Structural reform was one such change. Reformers in the developing cities in the West and Southwest were most successful because they faced few entrenched interest groups or established ethnic or class biases to impair the pursuit of structural reform. However, the success of reformers in the older cities of the Midwest and Northeast depended on a number of variables. If a city was small, ethnically homogeneous, and had a relatively high socioeconomic status, it would most likely adopt structural reform. If these factors were not present, reform was more difficult to achieve, though it was not necessarily precluded. In some cities exceptional leadership, tight organization, or catastrophic events overcame the forces opposing reform.[1]

Successes in charter revision and structural reform were not the only reason for the confidence shown by middle-class reformers during the decade. Other reforms improved the quality of life in the city. Prosperity and a greater sense of social responsibility by American business met the challenge of growth. In city after city, corporations became involved in solving problems created by economic expansion. This was manifested in welfare capitalism, which was an industrial philosophy whereby employers attempted to fulfill the reasonable wants of the workers as defined by themselves. Welfare capitalism peaked in the twenties. Corporations sought to improve the quality of life of its workers through subsidized housing, support for recreational and educational opportunities, and plans for profit sharing and fringe benefits for skilled workers. Local chambers of commerce took the lead in reaching out to the worker as a means of guaranteeing a stabilized work force for those companies or persons interested in economic investment in the area. The decade was a period when there was a link between business and politics. Corporations, like U.S. Steel and General Motors, devoted substantial sums of money to improving the quality of life of cities as a means to ensure that their investments were protected. It was assumed that businessmen and management would be active politically, usually in the Republican party. The interest of upper-level management in city politics was due also to their belief that the principles of business efficiency could be applied to governing the city.[2]

The twenties brought more than just economic expansion in the form of greater industrial investment. Economic expansion was also seen in the brick and mortar projects appearing in the central business districts and newly emerging residential neighborhoods. The decade was one of construction. One writer, referring to Gary, Indiana, in the twenties, called it "The Augustan Age."[3] Office buildings, hotels, and apartments appeared almost overnight. The housing problems that had characterized the cities prior to 1920 were greatly reduced. Of course, the newcomers who were poor usually inherited the slums, but not always. For example, in Harlem, blacks moved into middle-class housing because of a surplus created by speculation. New working-class neighborhoods appeared. In Flint and Pontiac, Michigan, a subsidiary of General Motors, Modern Housing Corporation, built hundreds of houses at moderate prices for its workers, especially skilled tradesmen. Workers also provided housing for themselves. Despite relatively low hourly pay, the long hours and six-day week gave many semiskilled and skilled workers the opportunity to save and ultimately invest in housing. Immigrants especially took pride in home ownership and sought to make this possible by building an income-producing duplex or small basement apartment. Realtors also pioneered in working-class residential developments. In Chicago, Detroit, and Philadelphia, speculators built working-class developments in the cities.[4]

Signs of the Eclipse

During the 1920s the movement of the middle and upper class into commuter developments outside many cities was accelerated. In Detroit, they moved into the Grosse Pointe villages. As a result only 50 percent of the Establishment families lived in the city by 1930, compared to 90 percent in 1910. In Chicago, communities such as Oak Park, Evanston, and Wilmette developed along the commuter railroads. Similar exclusive communities were established west of Philadelphia along the Pennsylvania Railroad's Main Line. While this exodus of the solid middle class provided additional housing for the working class, it was also an omen of future problems. For example, Michael McCarthy in an article, "On Bosses, Reformers, and Urban Growth," argues that the reason for the lack of effective reform politics in cities like Detroit, Chicago, and Philadelphia is due to the growth of solid middle-class communities outside the city rather than within the city. On the other hand, he believes that cities such as New York, Los Angeles, Minneapolis, and Seattle have had reform politics because middle-class communities developed within the city limits during the twenties.[5]

The twenties marked the end of the expanding industrial city. For a number of reasons, the older cities in the Midwest and Northeast were unable to expand their boundaries to keep up with this exodus of the middle class. The 1920s marked the end of an era of easy annexation for the industrial cities. This era of the expanding industrial city began approximately seventy years earlier when changes in intraurban transportation made it possible for those who could afford it to move out from the central city. These middle-class commuters in moving out also wished to maintain their political influence in the community where they had their economic interests. As a result they joined with land speculators to champion the cause of annexation. Their influence surpassed their numbers, but this generally did not matter since many states did not require the issue of annexation to be placed before the voters for approval. Thus the most important factor allowing for virtually unlimited annexation was the supportive position from the state. Another factor favoring annexation was the "booster" spirit found in the cities. The city boosters, usually those with major economic investments in the central city, would go to almost any length to surpass rival urban centers. One mark of a dynamic city was growth and this meant the expansion of boundaries. The business concept in the late nineteenth century that a large organization was more efficient than numerous smaller ones was another telling argument in favor of annexation. Consolidation, it was believed, would offer substantial savings for both the central cities and the outlying areas.[6]

However, by the 1920s most cities in the Midwest and Northeast had ceased expanding. For example, the twenty largest cities, showing a declining population in 1970, have added only 83 square miles since 1930, compared with 1602 square miles added before 1930.[7]

There are many reasons for this virtual cessation of annexation. Most industrial state legislatures, under the control of rural and suburban interests, have made annexation much more difficult, if not impossible. This is due to the changing character of the communities surrounding the central cities. The communities that grew up, especially after 1920, were middle-class suburbs which found that they could have the best of both worlds. For example, in some states, central cities are expected to provide the new communities with services at central city rates. There has also been an increase in the use of special service districts. These districts, which administer services such as schools, public health, port facilities, parks, water and sewage, make it possible for the suburbs to avoid responsibility for functions and activities that primarily benefit the lower classes. A second reason evident in the 1920s was that suburbanization made it possible for the middle class to escape responsibility for the welfare of the poor in the central city. The middle class blamed first the immigrants and then blacks for the poverty found in society, the political corruption of the machine, and the social pathologies evident in the cities. A third reason is that the technology that produced the automobile allowed for the unplanned and uncoordinated development of the outlying areas. Earlier the location of streetcar lines had exerted a form of control on expansion. Developing areas were usually contiguous to the city and were relatively high density areas. But this was no longer true after the appearance of the automobile and the efficient commuter railroads.[8]

Since the 1920s middle-class residents in the suburbs found that they could effectively exclude undesirable influences through incorporation. As Theodore Lowi writes, "They did the impossible; they divided the indivisible."[9] They separated the legal and the economic boundaries of the city. Cities previously had been responsible for accommodating the vast numbers of newcomers because they had the total resources of the "real" or economic city at their disposal. But after the 1920s this became less true as the suburbs refused to share their resources with the central cities. The suburbs became parasites on the cities, expecting them to continue to provide jobs, as well as the amenities of urban life like museums, opera houses, and libraries, and all the time protecting them from the impact of the city's poor. From the 1920s until the 1960s the cities continued to provide jobs for all classes, subsidize the cultural interests of the middle class, and protect the middle-class suburbs from the poor. Only since the sixties have the central cities been unable to meet such demands.

Many cities in the Sunbelt do not face the same problems because they developed after the industrial age. As a result these cities are today surrounded by vast open spaces, rather than by other industrial cities or incorporated suburbs. There is little opposition either locally or at the state level to annexation of vast areas of undeveloped land. But in Northern states many industrial cities developed in close proximity to one another and could not annex even if they wished to. At the same time the solid middle-class suburbs did not develop in contiguous areas but far removed from the city. This type of residential development was a means by which the middle class could leave behind the Southern and Eastern European immigrants found in the central city. The middle-class fear of immigrants was quickly reinforced by the large-scale migration of Southern blacks to the Northern cities. In the South and West the immigrant was never seen as a major problem. This was due to the limited number of immigrants in these cities and the fact that the growth of cities in these two regions occurred largely after the restriction of immigration. While the South had a black population and the Southwest and West a Mexican-American one, these groups were never seen as primarily urban. Every community, whether rural or urban, had small minority neighborhoods or barrios. In addition, the dominance of the Anglo-American over these two groups was such that there was little to fear because the minorities lacked political or economic power. It was different in the North, where immigrants and their children were urban and held at least the potential for economic and political influence.

Cities in 1930

Despite the cessation of annexation, or maybe because of it, the older industrial cities achieved a sense of stability during the twenties. Many, while continuing to increase in population, showed a growing stability; they lost the boom-town atmosphere that came with having a large part of the population made up of newcomers, the majority of whom were young, unattached males. Instead, the number of families increased along with home ownership, school age children, and the influence of such institutions as the public school system and settlement houses. This trend of increased stability probably would have carried through into the 1930s if the Depression had not intervened.

TABLE 3

	Towns 2,500+		Small Cities 10,000+		Medium Cities 50,000+	
	No.	*Pop. (000s)*	*No.*	*Pop. (000s)*	*No.*	*Pop. (000s)*
1920	1,970	9,354	608	12,110	119	11,784
1930	2,183	10,615	791	15,523	154	14,032

Large Cities 250,000+		Great Cities 1,000,000+	
No.	*Pop. (000s)*	*No.*	*Pop. (000s)*
22	10,765	3	10,146
32	13,720	5	15,065

SOURCE: *Historical Statistics of the U.S., 1976*, part 1, p. 11.

The economy also matured during the twenties. The boom times of the pre- and postwar years would not again appear. The growth that was expected would be a slow but steady increase. As the industrial cities moved into the thirties, they had in fact met the challenges of the twenties. Most had adopted or attempted structural reform, the central city building boom had occurred, the challenge of acculturating the immigrants and their children had been met, and corporate paternalism was successful. There was a feeling of satisfaction among urban spokesmen as the decade of the 1930s approached. The decade of the 1930s was expected to be one of prosperity but not of accelerated growth. Instead it brought a new challenge to the city—the challenge of survival.

On the eve of the Great Depression, the statistics of the 1930 census indicated that in the previous decade substantial growth had occurred in cities of all categories (see table 3).

The urban population had increased from approximately 54 million to 69 million. Detroit and Los Angeles had joined New York, Chicago, and Philadelphia as cities with more than a million population. These great cities held over 20 percent of the urban population in the United States. Twelve new cities entered the category of large urban centers having between 250,000 and 1 million people, bringing the total to 32. The cities experiencing the greatest increase in terms of population relative to class of city were the smaller ones, those with populations between 10,000 and 50,000. These 791 urban communities held slightly more people than the five great cities.

Industrial communities, such as Flint, Michigan, and Gary, Indiana, had matured. There would be growth in the future, but not the helter-skelter or boom-town type of growth that had occurred earlier. The physical city had been formed during the twenties. Industrial cities had caught up with the demands for services, facilities, and governmental institutions. Vast public works had been undertaken in order to meet the needs of the urban working class. To cover the cost of these public facilities and the increase in services, cities went into debt and raised property taxes. Detroit is an example of growth, as it went from being the ninth to the fourth largest city in the United States between 1910 and 1930. The automobile was the reason for this change. It transformed Detroit's diversified industrial base to one very dependent on the automobile. Of all great cities, it was the most industrial, the one that most resembled the smaller industrial cities of the Midwest and Northeast. As it grew in population it also expanded its boundaries. This allowed for the creation in the 1920s of numerous working-class neighborhoods within the city. But the 1920s also marked the flight of the Establishment from the city.

THE 1930s: THE COLLAPSE OF THE INDUSTRIAL CITY

The Depression

The collapse of the national economy destroyed the optimism of the twenties. In Matthew Josephson's 1929 essay, "Detroit: The City of Tomorrow?" one General Motors Corporation executive was quoted: "... Never in the history of the world have such great numbers of men been so prosperous and physically contented." A year later Detroit was much different. Helen Hall detailed the suffering among unemployed autoworkers in her article, "When Detroit's Out of Gear."[10] Detroit epitomized the "boom and bust" cycle of American industry. Detroit and many other cities found that they stood isolated, unable to obtain the necessary assistance either from the rural-dominated state legislatures or the Republican-controlled federal government. President Herbert Hoover's principle of "local responsibility" kept both the legislative and the executive branches from taking effective action. Hoover believed that the transfer of local obligation to the national government would undermine the "spirit of responsibility of states, of municipalities, of industry and the community at large, which is the one safeguard against the degeneration of that independence and initiative which are the very foundations of democracy."[11] Even as the third winter of the Depression approached, the President held steadfast in his belief that "this task is not beyond the ability of these thousands of community organizations to solve....I am confident that the generosity of each community...will meet the needs of the nation as a whole."[12]

This policy was rejected by most urban spokesmen. Witness after witness appearing before the La Follette subcommittee studying federal aid for unemployed relief in 1932 and 1933 pleaded for an end to Hoover's policy of "local responsibility." Critic Edmund Wilson sarcastically attacked Hoover's policy:

> It is a reassuring thought, in the cold weather, that the emaciated men in the bread lines, the men and women beggars in the streets, and the children dependent on them, are having their fibre hardened.[13]

The plight of cities was described in article after article. *Fortune* reported on "New York in the Third Winter," the *New Republic* on "The Collapse of Local Government," *Forum* on "Why Cities Go Broke," and *Atlantic* on "The Hungry City."[14]

Despite the crisis, Hoover felt that the federal government could not undermine the doctrines of rugged individualism and local responsibility. Cities attempted to organize in order to exert pressure on Congress and the President. Led by Mayor Frank Murphy of Detroit, twenty-nine mayors met in Detroit in June 1932 to demand federal aid. Welcoming the mayors, Murphy stated, "We have done everything humanly possible to do, and it has not been enough. The hour is at hand for the Federal Government to cooperate." In the keynote address, Mayor James Walker of New York, in one of his last appearances before being driven from office, summarized the condition of most cities:

> We of the cities have diagnosed and thus far met the problem; but we have come to the end of our resources. It is now up to the Federal Government to assume its share. We can't cure conditions by ourselves. Let us make it known just whose responsibility this now becomes.[15]

A Murphy-led delegation to Washington calling for $5 billion in federal works money came away with only $300 million dollars in loans from the Reconstruction Finance Corporation. This money was to be shared by all local governmental units and had to be repaid. With such token support, Detroit and other cities could not survive. Forty percent of Detroit's taxes were delinquent and the debt service on bonds issued during the 1920s consumed nearly 70 percent of the city's income. By late 1932, six hundred urban centers had defaulted on various kinds of payments, including Detroit, Chicago, and Philadelphia.[16] Cities could not simultaneously meet the increased demands for relief assistance, continue the heavy interest payments on bonded indebtedness, and maintain necessary public services and facilities.

Intervention of the Federal Government

The Depression and the changing political patterns in the cities brought about a new relationship with the federal government. This relationship generated some immediate relief to the short-term problems facing the cities. However it has also complicated the urban crisis of today. Beginning in the 1930s the cities became very important in the election of Democratic Presidents and liberal Democratic senators from the industrial states. As a result, the federal government under Democratic control became more responsive to the needs of the cities and less under Republican leadership. This has created a cycle in which years of substantial federal moneys accompanied by federal regulation are followed by years of "salutary neglect." Both phases of the cycle create problems for the cities. The linking of the cities to the Democratic party led to equating national social problems with urban problems and these, in turn, with the political fortunes of one of the two national parties. Thus, the problems facing the cities are seen in terms of national politics.

The changing political pattern in the cities of the Midwest and Northeast was evident in the 1928 presidential election. Al Smith's candidacy stimulated the growing political awareness among immigrants and their offspring. Though the Republican party had an urban base as early as the 1890s, it developed a complacent attitude toward its urban constituency. This was compounded by the exodus of the white middle class from the city to the outlying suburbs. It was this class, far more than the immigrants, that made up the Republican party's urban constituency. For the urban working class disillusionment with the Republicans was guaranteed by the economic slowdown that began in 1929 and continued into 1930. On the local level Democrats gained victory after victory. Republican support in the Northern cities was limited largely to upper-middle-class neighborhoods and the black ghettos. The large cities of the nation gave Roosevelt a substantial plurality in 1932. While Roosevelt was not an urban man, he was responsible for creating the numerous ties between the federal government and the cities, especially the large cities. It was in these cities that the problems associated with the Depression were most visible. The Works Progress (Projects) Administration worked directly with local authorities rather than through the states. By the late 1930s, 50 percent of WPA funds went to the fifty largest cities holding one-quarter of the American people. Mark Gelfand, author of *A Nation of Cities*, writes of the thirties,

> As never before, municipal officials influenced the writing of federal laws and regulations and participated in the national decision-making process. With the passage of the Housing Act of 1937, federal municipal ties were placed on a permanent, though not very secure or broad, foundation; there would be no turning back.

Louis Brownlow, director of the Public Administration Clearing House in the early 1930s, commented, "Municipalities in this country are no longer mere political subdivisions of the several states. We are now entering upon a recognized new relation of the urban citizenry with the citizenry of the nation itself."[17]

The cities in the Depression faced the challenge of survival. They could only survive if they received enough federal assistance to meet the needs of their citizenry and if government could stimulate the economy so that the unemployed could again become wage earners. However, assistance that reached the cities tended to be direct aid to individuals in need. For the most part the New Deal programs were not seen as being urban. In some cases public works projects fostered cooperation between the cities and other local governments. For example, it is estimated that nearly thirty special districts were created in this way, ranging from sanitary and park districts to housing authorities.[18]

While the Democrats did not deal with the urban problems directly, they did come to depend more and more on an urban constituency. By 1934, large numbers of northern blacks had voted Democratic for the first time. In 1936, most Northern cities were under the control of local Democratic party organizations which in turn generated large pluralities for Roosevelt and Democratic congressional candidates. The national Democratic party, recognizing the basis on which its position as the majority party was built, was responsive to its urban majority. Because of the size of the Democratic majority in the cities, Republicans tended to ignore or openly to oppose programs proposed for assisting the cities. Republican indifference was also fostered after World War II as more of the city's middle class moved to the suburbs. As the suburbs became increasingly Republican, the "crabgrass curtain" became more evident, making it impossible for the city to expand its legal boundaries so as to coincide with its natural economic area. Then, too, assistance from rural-dominated state governments was harder to come by.

The cities met the challenge of the 1930s in the sense that they survived. However, the older industrial cities would never return to their previous condition of growth and stability. The survival of the cities was due more to the economic upturn precipitated by the war than to either self-initiated efforts or state or federal assistance. The experience of the 1930s left a lasting imprint; never again would the city operate in a vacuum. In the future the federal government would play an ever-increasing role in the survival of the cities. And the growing dependency of the Democratic party on the cities would influence the role that the federal government would play.

THE CITY AFTER 1945

The Metropolitanization of America

In the years immediately following World War II, America was transformed from an urban to a metropolitan nation. This transformation from an urban nation, with a substantial portion of the population residing within the central cities, to a metropolitan one, with a substantial portion of the population residing in suburban communities, came about much more rapidly than the earlier transition from rural to urban.

By 1960, 112.9 million people, or 62.8 percent of the population, lived in the nation's 212 metropolitan areas. Ten years later, 139.4 million, 68.6 percent, lived in 243 metropolitan areas. Much of the growth in metropolitan areas since 1950 has come at the expense of the older, industrial cities of the Midwest and Northeast. Between 1950 and 1960, in nine of the ten largest Standard Metropolitan Statistical Areas (SMSAs), the central cities experienced absolute declines in population with losses ranging from a low of 1.4 percent in New York City to a high of 13 percent in Boston. The comparable figures for the ten years ending in 1970 show that the rate of decline in population in the older central cities has slowed. The data reveal that during the period of the 1960s eight of ten central cities experienced absolute losses in population, ranging from 1 percent in Washington, D.C., to a high of 17 percent in St. Louis. During the same period, the outlying areas continued to show a substantial increase, ranging from 4.4 percent in the Pittsburgh SMSA to 60.3 percent in Washington, D.C. SMSA (see table 4).

Despite the shifts in population, the fifteen years after 1945 were ones of optimism. The problems of the city were still seen as largely under the control of local residents. The belief again prevailed that with the right leaders working in the right governance structure cities could get moving again. The plight of cities was blamed on the lethargy of local voters and the lack of concern of the federal government. By the late fifties many cities responded to these admonitions by electing new and dynamic candidates to major public offices. To many this signaled the revival of urban America. All that remained was the emergence of a national figure to get the country turned around. In 1960, the promises of the New Frontier generated considerable enthusiasm in urban America. Scores of new urban programs were proposed. The New Frontier was followed in 1964 by the Great Society, and many proposed programs were enacted into law by the federal government. But instead of the hoped-for utopia, urban America collapsed. The two decades of optimism that followed World War II gave way to ten years of decline and decay in the central cities. It was manifested first in the urban riots, beginning with Watts

TABLE 4
Percentage Change in Population
in Ten Largest SMSAs, 1950–1960 and 1960–1970

SMSA	Total SMSA		Inside Central City		Outside Central City	
	1950–1960	1960–1970	1950–1960	1960–1970	1950–1960	1960–1970
New York	11.9	8.2	– 1.4	1.5	75.0	26.0
Los Angeles–Long Beach	45.5	16.4	27.1	12.5	66.6	20.0
Chicago	20.1	12.2	– 2.0	– 5.2	71.5	35.0
Philadelphia	18.3	10.9	– 3.3	– 2.7	46.3	22.6
Detroit	24.7	1.6	– 9.7	– 9.5	79.3	28.5
San Francisco–Oakland	24.0	17.4	– 4.5	– 2.8	57.9	31.9
Washington, D.C.	37.7	37.8	– 4.8	– 1.0	86.0	60.3
Boston	7.5	6.1	–13.0	– 8.1	17.7	11.3
Pittsburgh	8.7	– 0.2	–10.7	–13.9	17.2	4.4
St. Louis	19.9	12.3	–12.5	–17.0	50.8	28.5

SOURCE: *U.S. Bureau of the Census, 1970 Census of Population, Number of Inhabitants, United States Summary*, PC (1)-A1 (Washington, D.C., 1971), table 34.

in Los Angeles, and later in the financial collapse and near bankruptcy of New York City.

The question why the last thirty years have been so traumatic and disappointing for the central cities has not gone unasked. Nor are we lacking for answers. However, the older, industrial cities still find themselves unaware of how to reduce the pace of their decline, if not end it. Institutional reforms have been proposed and, in some cases, implemented, but the social and political influences impacting the governing of cities in the mid-twentieth century need to be understood.

The Changing Economy and Urban America

The city cannot escape the role it plays in our economy. A city reflects its economic function. Without a healthy economic base, the city will not be able to grow and prosper. As seen earlier, one of the major problems confronting many cities is that the political entities are no longer coterminous with the economic entities. The urban crisis of today is found specifically in the old, industrial cities. It is natural for these cities to be in crisis, for the nation's economy has been transformed and the cities are unable to adjust very quickly to the changes. As America moves from an industrial to a postindustrial age,

American cities will be changed. For some, it will mean prosperity; for others, decline and decay.

The dramatic increase of service-related jobs, when viewed in the context of an industrial work force, will have serious consequences for American cities. As obsolete factories are phased out, the industrial cities will remain the homes of thousands. As new factories are constructed in other cities, machines will replace semiskilled workers. Those workers finding employment will be skilled and white collar. The growth areas in our economy are in the service-related fields. The workers to fill jobs in these areas must possess skills that are far different from the ones needed fifty years ago. And it is impossible for the industrial city to supply the labor for modern industrial America. For example, as the energy crisis forces the auto industry to design and produce smaller cars, constructed out of lightweight carbon fiber, the declining steel industry will be hit even harder. Because of the reduced demand, many steel mills will close. In addition, others will work at less than full capacity. This will reduce profits, making it difficult for the steel industry to modernize existing facilities or to build new mills. Inefficiency in production will cause the price of steel to rise and this, in turn, will encourage steel consumers to turn to cheaper, foreign steel. In all of this the steel cities have little chance of maintaining the resources needed to respond to the urban crisis. The pattern repeats itself in other industries as well.

The economy of the United States is based on growth and growth generates obsolescence, not only in products, but also in factories, machinery, and in the men who work in production jobs. While successful corporations adjust to ever-changing economic conditions through increased automation and abandoning obsolete factories, blue-collar workers and the industrial cities cannot adjust. These urban centers inherit the outworn factories as relics of technological improvement. When General Motors closes one factory, it might well be mortally wounding an urban center. Yet, it also generates another when it decides to build elsewhere. As one urban center booms, it usually does so at the expense of another. The human and social costs are borne neither by the corporation nor by the new boom town, but by the older, industrial city.

Corporate America has responded to changes in transportation by decentralizing its factory system. The expressway system has created the age of the truck. Since the mid-fifties American industry has come to depend on the truck rather than on the railroad. Trucking is a particularly efficient means of transportation especially within a five-hundred-mile radius. This dependence, as well as the factor of obsolescence and an interest in combating the strength of organized labor, has caused corporations to decentralize their industrial facilities. Because the general growth areas are in the South and

West, industry is drawn to these regions in order to supply the expanding market. As Sam Bass Warner points out in *The Urban Wilderness*, we now have three megalopolises in the United States, the Northeastern seaboard and the Pittsburgh/Buffalo to Chicago/Milwaukee and the San Diego to San Francisco complex. There is probably another in the making from Florida to Texas. These megalopolises become almost self-contained, supplying many of the products consumed and the services needed to support their populations. The truck and the expressway also allowed corporations to move plants and office facilities out of the central cities to locations along the interchanges, where land is relatively inexpensive and transportation networks are more than adequate. [19]

These economic changes have transformed American society in general and urban America in particular. The 1970 census showed the results. In a ten-year period, the number of jobs in the fifteen largest metropolitan centers increased. But the location of these jobs changed. Jobs available in the central cities dropped from 12 million to a little over 11 million, while jobs in the suburbs increased from more than 7 million to 10 million plus. In only two cities, Dallas and Houston, was there a significant increase in jobs. This occurred because these two cities expanded their boundaries. New York City showed a decline of 10 percent in jobs, while Detroit lost 23 percent of its jobs. The era of the suburbanite as commuter is coming to an end. The changing economy has brought about a decentralization of industrial production both within the metropolitan area and within America. As a result, outer-ring suburbs of the Midwest and Northeast and the emerging metropolitan areas of the South, West, and Southwest show increases in jobs and in population. When we combine this with the changing nature of jobs, from manufacturing to service, we find that serious problems have been created for society in general and for the older cities in particular.[20]

Race and Urban America

Two population trends have influenced urban society in the twentieth century. Beginning in 1915, race became a national rather than a sectional issue. The Great Migration caused a dramatic relocation of blacks. In 1910, less than 10 percent of blacks lived in the North and only one-fourth lived in cities. By 1970, 50 percent lived in the North and nearly three-quarters in urban centers. Because blacks were unskilled, they were drawn to the same industrial centers which had previously relied on the unskilled labor of Southern and Eastern European immigrants. Cities like Chicago, Cleveland, Detroit, Pittsburgh, and Gary provided jobs and homes for black newcomers. With the fair employment order issued by President Roosevelt in 1941, and the demands for unskilled labor generated by the war, other cities came to have substantial black populations. Despite the existence of de facto segregation, blacks were drawn to the older industrial cities because of the possibility of employment. Furthermore, public assistance benefits were far superior to those in the rural South.

A second trend was the establishment of black ghettos, which led to equating race with poverty. Blacks and other minorities, especially Puerto Ricans and Mexican-Americans, are stigmatized not only by their poverty but by race as well. Like other urban newcomers who entered the city with little, blacks were forced into substandard housing in the central cities. However, unlike the immigrants, blacks found it nearly impossible to leave the central cities. Two reasons for this were the changing economy and racism. Blacks came in at the bottom and found it impossible to move up the socioeconomic ladder because the economy had changed. No longer is economic expansion in America based on the blue-collar work force. With blue-collar workers becoming fewer in numbers, blacks have little opportunity for employment if they are unskilled. High unemployment rates for young black males will probably continue into the foreseeable future. The blue-collar jobs that are available continue to be largely in the hands of the immigrants and their children because these workers were in the industrial centers first. Lower-class blacks will continue to be the largest group in the substandard neighborhoods of the industrial cities. They can make no contribution to the economic expansion taking place in America and they will reap no benefits from this expansion.

The second reason for the concentration of blacks in the central cities is racism. The dominant society made it very difficult for black neighborhoods to expand, and if expansion was necessary, influential forces were able to control the pace and direction of expansion. It is only a recent phenomenon that middle-class blacks have greater choice in housing. As overt racist practices against middle-class blacks are eliminated, the older industrial cities will suffer even more. It might be argued that because of racism the black middle class was kept in the city, thus artificially keeping up property values. The black middle class, finding fewer barriers, will move to middle-class suburban communities like their white counterparts. In other words, the weakening of racism will in fact accelerate the decline of the older, industrial cities by further homogenizing its class base.

We have in America tended to equate race, poverty, and the urban crisis. This was especially true in the programs of the Great Society. While the majority of the poor are white and rural, Great Society programs were largely directed to lower-class blacks in the cities. The lumping of broad social problems together made it impossible to solve any of them. And as we have already seen, the city cannot solve them because it faces social problems with inadequate governmental authority over economic resources.

Politics and Urban America

Cities have been affected by the political changes that have occurred during the past thirty years. The industrial cities suffered from inadequate representation during their years of growth. State legislatures failed to reapportion themselves, thus allowing rural interests to dominate well into the twentieth century. It was not until 1962 that the Supreme Court reversed its earlier decision that apportionment was entirely in the hands of the legislative branch of state government. In the 6 to 2 decision in *Baker* v. *Carr*, the Court ruled that unequal representation denied equal protection of the laws. This led the federal courts to intervene, forcing state legislatures to redistrict. Unfortunately, reapportionment came too late to help many cities in the Midwest and Northeast. By the 1960s, suburban areas had grown to a point that representatives from these communities held the balance of power in many state legislatures. State legislatures have shown little sympathy or concern for the needs of the industrial cities. It is only with great reluctance that state governments respond to urban needs and problems. The New York State government, in both the executive and the legislative branches, reacted slowly to the deepening financial crisis of New York City. In Michigan the governor dispatched state police to patrol the expressways in Detroit only when it became obvious that the Detroit police could not protect the suburban commuters and other visitors in their trips to the central business district. Suburban communities feel no responsibility for the social ills facing the central cities. Only when these ills directly threaten the outlying areas will state governments consider taking action.

If the suburban communities have an inordinate share of the political power in the state, the central cities seem to have a disproportionate influence at the national level. The Electoral College system allows cities to hold the balance of power in presidential elections. If a Democratic presidential candidate runs strong in the industrial cities of a large state, he has an excellent chance of winning that state's electoral votes. If the Democratic candidate is unable to maintain strong support from both urban blacks and ethnics, the candidate will not carry the industrial states.

Richard A. Cloward and Frances Fox Piven argue that in the late 1950s the national Democratic party realized that black ghettos had enormous political potential. As a result, Presidents Kennedy and Johnson pushed civil rights legislation and introduced a broad range of social programs for cities. It was expected that these programs would produce an even greater allegiance of blacks to the Democratic party and this would be reflected in an ever-increasing percentage of blacks voting. Unfortunately, these programs did not strengthen the party but instead generated a white backlash and divided it.[21] Despite the election of Jimmy Carter in 1976, the Democratic party was still divided. Carter was elected without articulating a comprehensive program of federal aid to the cities. Black Americans, finding the national Democratic party incapable of responding to their problems, find the Republican less receptive. The cities thus find themselves suffering the consequences of massive government interference from the Democrats and "benign neglect" when the Republicans are in power. The city and the related issues of poverty and race have become political footballs for the two major parties. This has resulted in a worsening of the urban crisis for the cities of the Midwest and Northeast.

The Increasing Role of the Federal Government

Urban America has suffered from the involvement of the federal government. Federal actions, whether directly or indirectly affecting the cities, have left numerous scars on the urban landscape. The government in Washington has accelerated the movement of people out of the Northeast and Midwest to the South and West. In the 1930s and 1940s the federal government consciously located military bases in the South and West and gave defense contracts to corporations in those areas in order to subsidize the economies of these regions. Despite the obvious shift in wealth to the South and West and the shift in poverty to the Northeast and Midwest, tax dollars are still flowing to the Sunbelt. In fiscal 1976 it was estimated by the *National Journal* that the Northeast and Midwest had a deficit of $32.7 billion, while the South and West received $23 billion more from the federal government than they paid in taxes. Indirect government subsidies include expensive public works programs, making possible massive irrigation projects and the creation of large urban centers in areas which have only a limited natural water supply. Social Security benefits allow those who retire to seek out the sun. This migration of millions of retirees to the South and Southwest also draws others who provide services needed by the expanding population.[22]

The single most significant piece of urban legislation passed by the federal government is the Federal Highway Act of 1956. This act affected the city in many different ways. While the expressway system and the automobile are not solely responsible for suburbanization, they made possible the new, low-density, multicentered metropolis. As mentioned earlier, the truck and the expressway system enabled manufacturing belts to be reorganized into four megalopolises. Though not intended to, the Highway Act of 1956 brought dramatic change to urban America. It accelerated the process of suburbanization and the establishment of new manufacturing, distribution, and management centers far removed from the older central cities. Jobs followed the expressways. In addition to enlarging both suburbia and exurbia, the expressways have to be brought into the central city in order to make these areas viable. The cost of constructing these multilane freeways in cities is more than just the dollars pocketed by the "road gang." In human costs, many lower-class and lower-middle-class neighborhoods are destroyed because they are in the path of proposed roads. As people are dislocated, they push into other neighborhoods, creating serious social problems if race and/or poverty differences are involved. A domino effect occurs as neighborhood after neighborhood feels the shock waves of bulldozers plowing through the city. The city also suffers an immediate loss of revenue when millions of dollars of property taxes are taken off the tax rolls. Cities hope to recover these revenue losses by encouraging businesses to remain in the central business district. For example, Chicago's Mayor Daley fought long and hard for a crosstown expressway which he hoped would keep hundreds of suppliers, distributors, and factories in the city. Neighborhoods fought the proposal and the Democratic governor refused to allow the state to put up the 10 percent required for federal funding. Daley then had the federal law changed to permit Chicago to put up the 10 percent. However, after Daley's death the Republican governor agreed to allow the state to fund its share and the project was continued.

As of 1977 the price tag for the federal highway system was three times what was estimated in 1956. Still 4000 of the 42,000 miles of roads are to be built. This system, while benefiting America in a number of ways, has had numerous unforeseen results. It is an indirect subsidy to the trucking industry and middle-class Americans alike. The trucking industry, while paying various taxes into the highway trust fund, receives far more in benefits. All gasoline is taxed to pay for the construction, but only 15 percent of passenger miles occur on these expressways. It is middle-class rather than the lower-class Americans who use the roads, even though the lower class pays the same gasoline taxes. It is the middle class that benefits from freeways in terms of work, residential location, and recreation.[23]

The Highway Act, in combination with the housing policy of the federal government, accelerated the decline of central cities in the 1960s and inner-ring suburbs in the 1970s. The construction of expressways through the central cities destroyed thousands of homes belonging to the lower classes. This usually coincided with the pressures of urban renewal on the low-income housing market. In St. Louis, nearly 10,000 housing units were destroyed to make room for expressways. Many of these units were low-income, because it is usually low-income neighborhoods that are targeted by the government as routes for the highway system.[24]

Charles Leven and his coauthors argue in *Neighborhood Change* that neighborhood decay is due not to the age of housing or race but to the change in neighborhood income level. As the income level of a neighborhood drops, so, too, do housing values. This change affects not only the immediate neighborhood but those adjacent to it. A low-income neighborhood, if it is stable, will not have an impact on the surrounding area, but if a middle-income neighborhood becomes a low-income one, the contiguous neighborhoods will be impacted. A contributing factor to changing neighborhoods is a mismatch of supply and demand of housing, something the federal government is very much responsible for. The policies of the FHA and the expressway system have generated surplus of middle-class housing in the cities, while urban renewal and expressways created a shortage of lower-class housing. As a result, urban neighborhoods changed in income level at almost a revolutionary pace.[25]

The policies of the federal government subsidize this exodus. And it is natural for the middle class to take advantage of the situation. Since local government provides a disproportionate share of benefits to the low-income groups, the middle class is encouraged to move into homogeneous income suburbs where they feel protected and removed from responsibility for the lower classes. Federal tax laws, allowing the deduction of interest and taxes, directly benefit the higher-income groups and encourage this outward movement. With the expressways destroying distance, the middle class can seek safety even beyond suburbia.

But the primary impetus to the middle-class exodus comes from the Federal Housing Administration. Leven argues that the purpose of the FHA is not to create decent housing but to stimulate the construction industry. There is no housing shortage but a housing surplus. In most central cities between 5 and 10 percent of the decent housing is vacant. If the FHA's role were limited only to that of insuring loans, thus reducing the risk to the lender, the impact on the cities would be manageable. But the FHA, through the Federal National Mortgage Association, uses the borrowing power of the federal government to stimulate the construction industry. Capital that might have gone into other sectors of the economy is redirected to housing starts for the middle class. Originally, the FHA practiced redlining, thus making it very difficult to buy housing in the city. After redlining was prohibited, the FHA also made it easier for the middle-class home owner to sell to a low-income family. Such FHA policies have assisted sellers rather than purchasers. While it is true that the flight of the middle class provides improved housing for the lower classes, this is only a short-term benefit. After moving into a structurally sound housing unit, many lower-class families are unable to maintain it. And as the neighborhood changes in income level, the housing that was purchased by the low-income family loses its value and is not worth the mortgage. Unable to maintain it and unable to sell it, the family abandons it. For example, between 1968 and 1973 low-income groups were able to buy new housing and older housing through section 235 of the 1968 Housing Act. As a result, in Detroit the federal Department of Housing and Urban Development took over 25,000 houses, or 13 percent of all homes in Detroit, after the owners had defaulted on FHA and VA mortgages. In St. Louis County, 2700 houses were repossessed between 1965 and 1973, roughly 8.5 percent of FHA activity in the city and the county.[26]

Housing and urban renewal programs of the government have been established not to benefit lower-income groups but rather other sectors of the economy. The primary benefits have come to the construction industry, both builders and workers. The indirect benefits have come to the middle class that seeks the safety of the suburb. The lower class might receive a short-lived improvement in housing, but that is all. It is the cities, especially the industrial cities, that bear the consequences of these federal programs.

If the above examples of federal intervention are not enough to burden the city, other federal activities also accelerate the decay of the central cities. Pollution standards for mills and factories encourage corporations to abandon their already inefficient operations in the older cities. Pittsburgh, Buffalo, Youngstown, Detroit, Chicago, Cleveland—the list is almost endless—are examples of cities with vacated operations.

Decisions by the courts concerning busing and policies established by HEW and other federal agencies covering affirmative action all add to the constraints imposed on the central city's survival. Busing has become an end in itself with little regard for the question of education. Again, the middle class has an out, through subsidies provided directly and indirectly by other governmental agencies. As the proportion of black students in central city school systems increases, integration becomes less attainable and meaningful. Yet, busing is pushed, further eroding the few stable, middle-class neighborhoods that remain in the city. Affirmative action programs, while necessary to break down the racial barriers of the past, have also added considerably to the costs of local government with little relief provided by the federal government.

Summary

This chapter provided an overview of the social, economic, and political changes affecting urban America since World War I. These changes have brought the older, industrial cities to the brink of collapse and, perhaps, death. The cities that have survived and appear healthy are ones that have been able to grow, to expand their legal boundaries to make them coterminous to their economic orbit. For example, the twenty largest cities showing population growth annexed 1207 square miles before 1930 and 3160 after that.[27] Those cities that have been unable to expand find themselves with an increasing lower-class population and decreasing sources of revenue. Such cities to survive find themselves becoming ever more dependent upon the federal government. Yet, as we have traced the history of federal involvement, we find that the programs established by the federal government lack a continued commitment to the cities and many times hasten the decline. Many federal programs that have been established to solve other national problems, such as housing and transportation, have also accelerated the decline of the older cities. The cities that are in crisis have little hope of obtaining assistance from their states and no expectation of support from their affluent neighbors. As we examine the urban crisis we also see that two of the proposed solutions are outside the traditional governmental structure of the city. The next two chapters will examine these two solutions, metropolitan government and community control.

NOTES

1. Richard M. Bernard and Bradley R. Rice, "Political Environment and the Adoption of Progressive Reform," *Journal of Urban History* 1 (February 1975): 149-74.

2. Irving Bernstein, *The Lean Years: A History of the American Worker, 1920-1933* (Baltimore: Penguin, 1966), pp. 157-89; David Brody, *Steelworkers in America: The Nonunion Era* (New York: Harper Torchbooks, 1969), pp. 263-78; Elbert H. Gary, "Workers' Partnership in Industry," *World's Work* 48 (June 1924): 197-203; "GM Employees Benefit," *Automotive Industries* 42 (February 1, 1930): 175.

3. I. James Quillen, "The Industrial City: Gary, Indiana" (Ph.D. diss., Yale University, 1942).

4. Gilbert Osofsky, *Harlem: The Making of a Ghetto* (New York: Harper & Row, 1966); Joan M. Meister, "Civic Park: General Motors' Solution for the Housing Shortage," in *A Wind Gone Down: Smoke into Steel* (Lansing, Mich.: Michigan History Division, Department of State, 1978), pp. 5-14.

5. Michael P. McCarthy, "On Bosses, Reformers, and Urban Growth," *Journal of Urban History* 4 (November 1977): 29-35; Melvin G. Holli, ed., *Detroit* (New York: New Viewpoints, 1976), pp. 122-24, 141-43; see also Roderick D. McKenzie, *The Metropolitan Community* (1933; reprinted:, New York: Russell, 1967), pp. 183-84.

6. Kenneth T. Jackson, "Metropolitan Government versus Suburban Autonomy," in *Cities in American History*, eds. Kenneth T. Jackson and Stanley K. Schultz (New York: Alfred A. Knopf, 1972), pp. 448-52.

7. *Ibid.,* p. 453.

8. *Ibid.,* pp. 452-56. See also Sam Bass Warner, Jr., *Streetcar Suburbs: The Process of Growth in Boston, 1870-1900* (Cambridge, Mass.: Harvard University Press, 1962).

9. Theodore J. Lowi, *The End of Liberalism* (New York: W. W. Norton, 1969), p. 195.

10. Matthew Josephson, "Detroit: City of Tomorrow?" *Outlook* 151 (February 13, 1929): 243-46, 275, 278, with quote from p. 246; Helen Hall, "When Detroit's Out of Gear," *Survey* 64 (April 1, 1930): 9-14, 51-54.

11. From President Hoover's speech of December 13, 1930, quoted in Irving Bernstein, *The Lean Years* (Boston: Houghton Mifflin, 1966), p. 287.

12. From President Hoover's speech of October 18, 1931, on the opening of the national drive to assist private relief agencies, quoted in Albert Romasco, *The Poverty of Abundance* (New York: Oxford University Press, 1965), p. 158.

13. Quoted in Harris G. Warren, *Herbert Hoover and the Great Depression* (New York: W. W. Norton, 1967), pp. 193-94.

14. "New York in the Third Winter," *Fortune* 5 (January 1932): 18-29; "The Collapse of Local Government," *New Republic* 69 (January 20, 1932): 254-55; Lothrop Stoddard, "Why Cities Go Broke," *Forum* 87 (June 1932): 375-79; Joseph Hefferman, "The Hungry City," *Atlantic* 149 (May 1932), 538-46.

15. Quotes taken from Mark T. Gelfand, *A Nation of Cities: The Federal Government and Urban America, 1933-1965* (New York: Oxford University Press 1975), p. 36.

16. *Ibid.,* p. 38; Blake McKelvey, *The Emergence of Metropolitan America, 1915-1966* (New Brunswick, N.J.: Rutgers University Press, 1968), p. 81.

17. Gelfand, pp. 45, 65; quotes from p. 65.

18. McKelvey, p. 104.

19. Sam Bass Warner, Jr., *The Urban Wilderness* (New York: Harper & Row, 1972), pp. 55-149.

20. Department of Commerce, *Nineteenth Census of the United States, 1970.*

21. Richard A. Cloward and Frances Fox Piven, *The Politics of Turmoil: Essays on Poverty, Race and the Urban Crisis* (New York: Pantheon, 1974), pp. 267-70.

22. Joel Havermann, Neal R. Peirce, and Rochelle L. Stanfield, "Federal Spending: The North's Loss Is the Sun Belt's Gain," *National Journal: Weekly on Politics and Government* 8 (June 26, 1976): 878-91; see table on p. 881.

23. William V. Shannon, "The Untrustworthy Highway Fund," *The New York Times Magazine* (October 15, 1972), pp. 31ff. Robert Lewis, "Heavy Trucks Being Blamed for Abnormal Wear on Roads," *The Flint Journal*, January 3, 1978, p. C8; Richard O. Davies, *The Age of Asphalt* (Philadelphia: Lippincott, 1975), pp. 28-35; Warner, *Urban Wilderness*, pp. 37-52.

24. Charles L. Leven et al., *Neighborhood Change* (New York: Praeger, 1976), p. 163.

25. *Ibid.,* pp. 34–50, 98, 142–45.

26. *Ibid.,* pp. 149–60, 179–81.

27. Jackson, p. 453.

CHAPTER VIII.

Metropolitan Reform
and Urban Development

Introduction

In the previous chapter we described the social changes in the cities and nation at large that contributed to the metropolitanization of America. A variety of factors account for this development, including technological changes involving the automobile and mass transportation, extensive federally supported highway construction, federally supported housing construction and mortgage programs, and the flight of the largely white middle class from the cities to the suburbs. The population remaining in cities was predominantly poor and nonwhite.

The growth of suburban areas created both a challenge and an opportunity in urban development. As a challenge, the cities had to find a way to continue meeting the needs of their residents for public services and facilities. In many cases these needs were more substantial and pressing than before. Cities had to contend with competition among and between independent and autonomous units of local government. The economic and social conditions in the cities remained inextricably intertwined with those of the suburbs, but there was no formal or legal mechanism for effecting coordination or equity in patterns of development. Our purpose in this chapter is to examine the consequences of this aspect of urban development for governmental institutions and their ability to meet the needs of the metropolitan area for expanded public services and facilities.

GOVERNMENTAL ORGANIZATION
IN METROPOLITAN AREAS

Proliferation of Governmental Units

The single most significant characteristic of governmental institutions in metropolitan areas is their sheer number and variety. There has been an explosion in the number and variety of governmental units exercising authority over the metropolitan population. The proliferation of governments in metropolitan areas has created serious problems for urban development. By 1972, 263 Standard Metropolitan Statistical Areas (SMSAs) contained a total of 22,185 units of local government, despite the fact that these metropolitan areas encompassed only about one-ninth of the nation's land. This number consists entirely of independent units of government, i.e., those formally established by state governments and possessing independent corporate powers and territorial boundaries. In other words, each unit of government has its own set of officials, service delivery system, and powers to raise and expend revenues. Furthermore, since each is a separate and legally independent unit it may act unilaterally and without concern for the impact of its action on adjacent communities and governmental units. The number of independent governmental units varies considerably from one SMSA to another. The Chicago SMSA, for example, contains over 1000 units, while the Houston SMSA has 304. A few metropolitan areas have as few as 20 units of government and some have even less. The average, however, is 86 local governments per SMSA for the entire United States.[1]

The number of governments doesn't tell the whole story. In addition to the magnitude of governmental units we must also consider the scope or range of functions and services provided, since the problems of urban development are at least in part a matter of meeting needs for public services and facilities. In examining the scope of public services and functions, one finds a bewildering maze of complexity from the large number of local jurisdictions. Different categories of local governments can be identified. First, there are "general purpose" governments, including counties, cities, townships, incorporated and unincorporated villages, and, in some instances, boroughs. These units are called general purpose because they provide a wide variety of services and functions, including police protection, fire protection, sanitation, parks, etc. In 1967, counties, municipalities, and towns/townships made up just over 40 percent (actually 41.7 percent) of the units of local government in metropolitan areas. By 1972, these units of local government still made up about 40 percent (41.2 percent) of the number of governmental jurisdictions in all SMSAs.[2]

A second category of local government in metropolitan areas is the school district. Traditionally, public education has been governed by a separate and autonomous system in the United States. In 1967, school districts made up 24.2 percent of the local governments in SMSAs; by 1972, after some consolidations, they made up 21.4 percent of the local governments of metropolitan areas and had declined 12.2 percent. However, school districts are a special category of government in metropolitan areas because they are autonomous units that restrict the use of their corporate powers to public education. In only a few instances, most notably New York City, are school districts financed by monies from municipal government. The general pattern has been to establish and maintain a separate system of government for public education.

A third type of local government is the special district, so named because of its functional specialization in a single service or activity. Special districts became increasingly popular in the period of the municipal reform movement and especially in the post-World War II era. They offered a way of overcoming the resistance and unresponsiveness of autonomous governments in growing metropolitan areas to demands for new programs and services. Special districts are independent units that exercise their own taxing and borrowing powers. They are usually created to administer a single function or provide a single service. In a few cases, special districts may be empowered to perform a limited number of interrelated functions. In most instances, however, they are unifunctional.[3] Special district governments provide a variety of specialized functions, including sewage disposal, water treatment and supply, libraries, parks and recreational facilities, air pollution control, airports, and health care facilities. We have seen the evolution of special districts from colonial times to the present. They were created not only because special service problems existed but also because of the intransigence of existing governmental bureaucracies.

Municipal reformers espoused the use of special districts in the early part of the twentieth century as a way of taking politics out of the administration of public services and facilities, especially those viewed as specialized and technical in nature. The prevailing attitude was often expressed in terms of wanting to remove the administration of functions from the politics of city hall, thus enabling citywide or areawide considerations to be paramount. After 1950, the "new breed" mayors used the special district as a means of getting around entrenched bureaucracies and state-imposed limitations on local taxing and borrowing powers.

In addition to the considerations of good government reformers, special districts were often adopted in metropolitan areas in an effort to overcome jurisdictional boundary problems facing general purpose governments.

Boundaries of special districts often transcend those of general purpose local governments, as the names of those cited above indicate. Furthermore, special districts have been established that cut across the boundaries of counties and even states. Examples of such entities are the Port of New York Authority, serving New York and New Jersey, and the Bi-State Development Agency in the St. Louis area.

The proliferation of governmental units in metropolitan areas can be traced to many factors. Certainly one of the most important considerations was the desire to escape the central city and its growing economic and social problems. Many of those who moved to the suburbs, particularly since the late 1950s, wanted to escape what they regarded as inadequate and deteriorating services, particularly in public education, as well as increasing rates of property taxation. New communities were chartered as separate and independent townships, towns, and villages. Second, the tradition of local autonomy and self-government has always been an integral part of the American political culture. Beginning in colonial times, citizens have placed a high value on the practice of autonomy in local government and control of local institutions by residents of the areas served by them. States, for the most part, have bent over backward to protect and defend the right of independent communities to govern themselves, despite the fact that the practice of local self-government has had unintended and sometimes undesirable consequences for residents of other governmental jurisdictions in metropolitan areas.

Consequences of Proliferation

The number and variety of legally independent and functionally autonomous units of government in the metropolitan area have had serious consequences for urban growth and development. More often than not, these consequences have been unintended and negative. They have made it difficult to develop and pursue a comprehensive program for dealing with the social and economic problems generated by urban development. As a result, most recent proposals for governmental reorganization have tried to deal directly with the consequences of the proliferation of governmental units in the metropolitan area. Some of the same arguments used by the good government municipal reformers in the early part of the twentieth century were dusted off, polished up, and used to support metropolitan government reform. By the mid-1960s, however, supporters of metropolitan government organization were confronted by a counterprogram, the community revolution.

Since both metropolitan and central city government reformers pointed to the same deficiencies created by the proliferation of governments in metropolitan areas, it is useful to examine the nature of these deficiencies before considering the contrasting reform programs put forward by the two groups. Robert Lineberry has identified four consequences of the proliferation of governmental units in metropolitan areas: externalities, fiscal and service inequities, absence of political responsibility, and duplication and lack of coordination.[4]

"Externalities" is a concept used by economists to describe the consequence of changes in one part of an interdependent system on the other parts. In the metropolitan area, externalities exist when one unit of government, acting in its capacity as an autonomous municipal corporation, initiates a program or activity that produces changes, often unintended, in other parts of the total region. Spillover effects is another term to describe what happens in such circumstances, since the effects of the program or activity often spill over into surrounding communities in the area. The metropolitan area is indeed an interdependent system, as changes in almost any public service or program readily demonstrate. Take land-use, zoning, and taxing policies, for example. If a small and independent community adjacent to the central city seeks to attract certain types of businesses to its jurisdiction, it may rezone an area of land deemed suitable for such purposes and establish a program of incentives and preferential property taxation, perhaps by granting lower rates of property taxes for a specified number of years after relocation. Indeed, this occurrence has taken place on more than one occasion. The enterprises attracted by such incentives almost always include businesses and commercial establishments that had been operating in the business district of the central city. As a result, the vacating of commercial properties in the central business district leaves the central city with less of a variety of businesses and, of equal importance, a diminished tax base. The erosion of the central city's tax base through the relocation of business and commercial enterprises to outlying communities within the metropolitan area is one of the most serious problems confronting city residents and government officials. Oftentimes, however, there is little central city officials can do, since the zoning and tax incentives that lure businesses to suburban areas are adopted by officials of other governmental units exercising legitimate corporate powers granted by the state. The benefits accruing to one community thus constitute commensurate costs to another.

Spillover effects can be seen in other functional service areas, including law enforcement and crime prevention, public education, transportation, and parks and recreational facilities. Not long ago, when Coleman Young was elected to his first term as mayor of Detroit, Michigan, he announced in his inaugural address that he was committed to reducing the rate of crime in the central city of Detroit. This, he said, would manifest itself in a law enforcement program that would drive the criminal element "north of Eight

Mile Road." Eight Mile Road just happens to be the northern boundary of the central city. It is doubtful that Mayor Young seriously considered the effects of his rhetoric on the residents of three suburban communities whose southern border is Eight Mile Road.

Fiscal and service inequities are another consequence of the proliferation of governmental jurisdictions in metropolitan areas. This term is used to express the concentration of service needs in the central city and greater availability of resources for meeting them in outlying communities adjacent to the central city. The *Report of The National Advisory Commission on Civil Disorders* revealed the existence of two Americas, one Black and one White, separate and unequal. The imbalance between central city and suburban service levels, needs, and resources is an excellent example of this conclusion. The area of public education offers an excellent example of the segregation between needs and resources in public services. In metropolitan Detroit, for example, twenty-five suburban school districts spent up to $500 more per child per year to educate their children than the city of Detroit. In the central city of Detroit, on the other hand, almost one-third of the school buildings were constructed before the turn of the present century. In the New Jersey metropolitan area, one suburban community had an assessed valuation of $5.5 million per pupil, while an adjacent community had a valuation of $33,000 per pupil.[5]

The proliferation of governmental units in metropolitan areas makes it difficult for local residents to hold public officials accountable for their actions. In the Flint area, for example, there is one county government, nine city governments, seventeen township governments, eight village governments, and thirty-two independent school districts. Ideally, each resident should know enough about his or her public officials to hold them accountable in primary and general elections. But the typical resident must vote on all of the following public offices:

Elected Public Officials in the Flint Metropolitan Area

County executives, including:
  a clerk
  a treasurer
  a register of deeds
  a prosecuting attorney
  a sheriff
  a drain commissioner

Municipal executives, including:
  in the cities, a mayor

in each of the townships, a supervisor, clerk, and treasurer
in each of the villages, a president, clerk, and treasurer

County legislature consisting of one representative
from each of fourteen districts

Municipal legislatures from among the following:
in the cities, up to nine council members (some elected from wards,
some at large)
in the townships, a board of trustees
in the villages, a council

School boards, numbering thirty-two in the area, whose members
number from nine to thirteen, all elected at large within their
respective districts. Furthermore, the territorial boundaries of
school districts do not all coincide with boundaries of existing
general purpose governmental units. In fact, one of the small cities
in the area is served by five different school districts.

This list doesn't include officials of state government, including a governor,
two legislators, six district court judges, five circuit court judges, three
probate court judges, twelve judges on the state court of appeals, and seven
judges of the state supreme court, or federal officials. In addition, each of the
major universities of public higher education is governed by its own board of
education or trustees, each popularly elected. The maze of public institutions
and officials makes it very difficult for citizens to gain sufficient relevant
information to make the idea of accountability meaningful or effective. Most
voters lack accurate, relevant, and timely information with which to make
electoral judgments concerning public officials acting in their capacities in
public institutions. Equally serious is the fact that in some instances public
officials use the confusion to evade responsibility for their actions. As a
consequence, even the most informed and concerned citizen may be unable to
identify those responsible for local and metropolitan problems.

The fourth consequence of proliferation is the duplication of services and
lack of coordination among decision making and service delivery units. Each
unit of government in the metropolitan area, acting independently as a
corporate entity, establishes its priorities and pursues the course of action it
deems appropriate for itself. Rarely, however, is there serious consideration
given to whether the resources and problems of a neighboring community are
relevant to proposed solution. In the delivery of services, duplication of
functions is more the rule than the exception. In public safety, for example,
numerous small villages, towns, and townships maintain their own police
force, despite the fact that each police agency has only one, two, or three
full-time officers and limited equipment. Alternatively, when communities
fail to coordinate educational programs and services, there may be gaps in the

programs and activities of one school district that make another more attractive to residents in the metropolitan area. Duplication of functions in public services and facilities creates overlapping responsibilities and resources that artificially and unnecessarily increase the costs of running government. Cooperation and coordination between units of government in metropolitan areas tends to be informal and voluntary, pursued more to protect the autonomy of each community and prevent "encroachment" on local prerogatives and corporate powers than to assure economy, efficiency, and accountability of public officials and the institutions they administer.

METROPOLITAN REFORM AND REORGANIZATION

Concerns of Metropolitan Reform

The growing number and independence of governmental units in metropolitan areas gave rise to a metropolitan reform movement. Like its predecessor, municipal reform, metropolitan reform was less a coherent, systematic movement than it was a set of proposals designed to remedy the major structural and functional weaknesses of governmental institutions in metropolitan areas. Unlike municipal reformers, however, metropolitan reformers were less immediately concerned with the honesty and integrity of public officials; they were more interested in establishing governance arrangements that would enable public institutions to operate in an efficient, economical, and responsible manner. The major difference between the two movements lies in the fact that metropolitan reformers were singularly committed to alleviating the consequences of governmental fragmentation in metropolitan areas. Though a variety of institutional arrangements were prescribed for alleviating these consequences, the prescriptions shared in common the belief that the only way to eliminate the inefficiencies and diseconomies of governmental fragmentation was to replace the many small and autonomous units of government with a single, integrated structure of government for the entire metropolitan area. Institutional arrangements proposed by metropolitan reformers borrowed heavily from the concept of "economy of scale."

The concept of economy of scale was used by metropolitan reformers to help determine the optimum size of the metropolitan area governmental unit. In the metropolitan area, the optimum size for such a unit would be one in which the boundaries for supplying public goods and services coincide with those within which demands for such goods and services are articulated to public officials.[6] The provision of public goods and services by a single, integrated government serving the entire metropolitan area reduces the per-unit cost of producing them. Furthermore, the single, integrated governmental structure purported to eliminate the boundary problem created when costs and benefits of public goods and services do not coincide with the jurisdiction of the governmental unit producing and delivering them. In other words, spillover effects can be substantially reduced when everyone who benefits from the availability of a public service contributes to the costs of producing it.

There are many instances of *dis*economies of scale in the provision of public services and facilities. For example, in a metropolitan area many units of government provide parks and recreational facilities to their residents. However, nonresidents are usually able to "consume" or use these facilities, though normally they do not help to pay for them. On rare occasions a city may establish entrance or other forms of user fees for nonresidents, but these are usually inadequate to meet the operating and capital costs of continuing to provide parks and recreational facilities to resident users. The solution to such a situation proposes metropolitanizing the park system so that all residents in the metropolitan area not only benefit from the presence of facilities but also contribute to the cost of providing them.

Despite the singular concern of metropolitan reformers with the issue of scale in metropolitan area governmental organization, the intellectual roots of the movement go back to principles of good government reformers in the Progressive Era. In fact, a substantial intellectual and philosophical debt is owed by metropolitan reformers to the good government movement of the early twentieth century.

Principles advanced by Woodrow Wilson in the last decades of the nineteenth century can be recognized as the building blocks of institutional arrangements proposed by metropolitan reformers in the mid-twentieth century. For example, it was Woodrow Wilson, in his classic study of the American system of government, who observed that "the more power is divided the more irresponsible it becomes."[7] Wilson believed that the American system of checks and balances lay at the heart of the failure to create smooth, harmonious relationships in government. He comments that checks and balances had "proved mischievous just to the extent to which they had succeeded in establishing themselves as realities."[8]

Further evidence of the debt metropolitan reformers owe to good government municipal reformers is reflected in comparing the initial recommendations of the latter with the institutional prescriptions of the former. In 1925, for example, William Anderson summarized the major recommendations of municipal reform as follows:

(1) Each major urban area should be organized by only one unit of local government.

(2) The voters in each major urban area should elect only the most important policy-making officials, and these should be few in number....
(3) The traditional separation of powers should be eliminated from the internal structure of the single consolidated unit of local government.
(4) The function of administration, on the other hand, should be separated from that of politics....
(5) Administration should be organized into an integrated command structure....[9]

Writing some forty years later, the Committee for Economic Development issued a report diagnosing the problems facing local governments in metropolitan areas. Published under the title *Modernizing Local Government*, the report found that very few units of local government were large enough to employ their fiscal resources or legal powers to deal effectively with current or future problems. The existence of overlapping layers of government was identified as a major source of weakness inasmuch as it engenders a parochial or localistic view of problems and solutions; it also impairs popular control over government by creating widespread confusion over who is responsible for various services and activities. Finally, it identified structural and functional fragmentation of authority as the main cause of institutional unresponsiveness to problems of urban development and governmental performance.[10]

The CED report proceeded to the establishment of a single integrated structure of government for the entire metropolitan area. The exact recommendations to accomplish this are worthy of examination:

1. The number of local governments in the United States, now about 80,000, should be reduced by at least 80 percent.
2. The number of overlapping layers of local government found in most states should be severely curtailed.
3. Popular elections should be confined to members of the policy-making body, and to the chief executive in those governments where the "strong mayor" form is preferred to the "council-manager" plan.
4. Each local unit should have a single chief executive, either elected by the people or appointed by the local legislative body, with all administrative agencies and personnel fully responsible to him; election of department heads should be halted.[11]

The report gained widespread support among metropolitan reformers. It served as the basis of numerous proposals to improve the performance of local government in delivering public services and increasing the accountability of local officials by consolidating the numerous small units in the metropolitan area into a single, integrated structure of government exercising authority over the entire area. Consolidation or merger to reduce the multiplicity of jurisdictions serving a metropolitan area became the centerpiece of metropolitan reform proposals throughout the nation.

The most accurate statement that can be made about the metropolitan reform movement is that, like municipal reform, it consisted of numerous prescriptions for alleviating the alleged structural deficiencies of governmental institutions. Advocates of a single, integrated structure of government for the entire metropolitan area had not one but many ways of accomplishing their objective.

It is possible to identify two instrumentalities by which a single, integrated governmental system is created in a metropolitan area. These are annexation, i.e., the absorption of adjacent unincorporated municipalities, and consolidation, i.e., the union or merger of two or more incorporated municipalities with larger county government already operating in the area.

Metropolitan Reform Proposals: Annexation

We have already discussed the earlier history of municipal expansion through annexation and consolidation.[12] Generally speaking, municipalities expanded by annexing areas that were less urbanized if not uninhabited. Also, state constitutional and statutory provisions permitted incorporated municipalities to absorb adjacent territories with minimal interference of higher authorities.

While annexation was not a viable alternative for the larger cities of the Midwest and Northeast, many smaller cities undertook annexations as a means of accommodating the strains of development and growth. In 1945, for example, 152 cities with 5000 or more population extended their boundaries through annexation. Two decades later, in 1971, almost 1100 municipalities with populations of 5000 or more effectively completed expansion through annexation. It is important to note, however, that in the great majority of instances, annexations took place in the newer cities and suburbs of the metropolitan areas. It is also important to note that for the most part the amount of land involved in the successful annexations was relatively small. In only a few instances have large tracts of land been successfully annexed by an existing municipality.

This is not to say that all cities with large populations have refrained from attempting annexation. On the contrary, data from the U.S. Bureau of the Census and other sources indicate that between 1950 and 1972 40 cities possessing a 1970 population of 100,000 or more have added between 40 and 100 square miles to their original boundaries.[13] As many as 19 of these annexed more than 100 square miles of territory, most of it unincorporated. These include Oklahoma City, which added 584.9 square miles to its jurisdiction, Houston, which annexed 279.5 square miles, Phoenix, 239.9 square miles, and Kansas City, Missouri, 235.7 square miles. Other heavily populated cities in Oklahoma and Texas added over 100 square miles to their boundaries through the instrument of annexation.

What accounts for these exceptionally large land acquisitions? As we have seen, cities like Oklahoma City, Tulsa, Phoenix, Houston, Dallas, and Kansas City have expanded because of highly favorable annexation laws not found in most states.[14] In almost every case, existing annexation legislation does not allow the residents of the target area to vote for or against the proposed expansion. And in a few instances, annexation is regarded as the lesser of evils when compared to the alternative of even more comprehensive governmental reorganization in the metropolitan area.

Metropolitan Reform Proposals: Consolidation

Whereas annexation was essentially an incremental strategy for expanding the jurisdiction and boundaries of the central cities, consolidation offered the opportunity to establish a single, integrated, and comprehensive governmental system for the entire metropolitan area in one sweep of the reform broom. Metropolitan reorganization through consolidation involves the elimination of the multiple, independent governmental jurisdictions within a county and their replacement by a single, areawide government exercising authority over the entire area and responsible for all public functions and services provided within its territorial jurisdiction. To be truly comprehensive, consolidation would reorganize all the smaller villages, townships, and cities, as well as the larger central cities, into a single unit of government for the entire metropolitan area. In both structure and scope of authority, city-county consolidation meets the basic principles and objectives of governmental reorganization and reform proposed by William Anderson in 1925 and the Committee for Economic Development in the mid-1960s.

Like annexation, the history of city-county consolidation can be divided into two historical periods. The first experiences with consolidation predate the twentieth century. They involved New Orleans (1813), Boston (1821), Philadelphia (1854), and New York (1898). In each case, consolidation was effected by an action of the state legislature, and voter approval of the proposed reorganization was not sought. Equally important, each of the consolidations was less than fully comprehensive, since more than one government continued to operate in the same territorial jurisdiction.

Between 1900 and the end of World War II, governmental and civic reformers expressed considerable interest in city-consolidation but demonstrated little ability to bring it about. Many of the same forces that were able effectively to oppose annexation by the central cities began to coalesce to resist city-county consolidation. Newly emergent suburban communities developed a strong sense of community identity and local autonomy and fought to maintain their separation from the central cities. A coalition of suburban and rural representatives in state legislatures made it virtually impossible to gain passage of enabling legislation that was required before a proposal for consolidation could be brought to the voters for their approval, or could take effect. Furthermore, many states adopted provisions for municipal home rule, the effect of which was to prohibit consolidations of incorporated municipalities without the approval of the residents of the affected areas through a local referendum on the proposal.

Given these conditions and attitudes, it is not surprising that very few proposals for city-county consolidation even reached the stage of voter approval. Most efforts failed to secure passage of the state constitutional amendment or enabling legislation needed to bring a consolidation proposal before the voters for their approval. In fact, between 1900 and 1950, only four proposals for city-county consolidation reached the stage of voter approval. Three were defeated. The three defeated proposals involved St. Louis and St. Louis County, Missouri; Macon and Bibb County, Georgia; and Jacksonville and Duval County, Florida. One city-county consolidation proposal gained voter approval: that involved Baton Rouge and East Baton Rouge Parish (county), Louisiana, in 1947. According to one analysis, the successful experience with this proposal was due in large measure to a set of highly favorable conditions and features of the plan that made it something less than a comprehensive reorganization of city and county governments.[15]

As in the pre-1900 reorganizations, the Baton Rouge-East Baton Rouge Parish consolidation provided for the retention of both the city and parish governments. It also continued the independent existence of two small municipalities and established three different taxing and service zones, identified as urban, industrial, and rural. Under the plan, responsibility for services varies throughout the area, with city government providing some services within its own boundaries and parish government providing other services for the entire area. Residents in the rural zone do not receive urban zone services from the parish government unless special taxing districts and arrangements are set up to pay for them. Thus there remains at least two levels of government, city and parish, and three areas or zones determining the scale and types of services provided by the respective governmental jurisdictions.

The real push for city-county consolidation began in 1950 and continues to the present. By one account, of twenty-five attempts at areawide governmental reorganization between 1950 and 1973, all but three resulted in defeat of the proposals.[16] In quite a few cases, proposals were resubmitted to city and county voters a second time and, in a replay of the initial vote, were defeated. For example, voters rejected city-county consolidation proposals in Albuquerque-Bernalillo County, New Mexico, in 1959 and again in 1973; in Macon-Bibb County, Georgia, in 1960 and 1972; in Durham-Durham County, North Carolina, in 1961 and 1971; in Memphis-Shelby County, Tennessee, in 1962 and 1971; in Chattanooga-Hamilton County, Tennessee, in 1964 and 1970; in Tampa-Hillsborough County, Florida, in 1967 and 1971; and in Tallahassee-Leon County, Florida, in 1971 and 1973.

Given this record, the successful attempts at city-county consolidation would seem to warrant some attention, since they constitute the exception rather than the rule. During the same time span (1950-1973) that so many proposals for reorganization by consolidation were defeated, three efforts at metropolitan reorganization gained state legislative and/or voter approval. The three involved Nashville and Davidson County, Tennessee, in 1962; Jacksonville and Duval County in Florida in 1967; and Indianapolis and Marion County in Indiana in 1970. However, it must be pointed out that in each instance the reorganization of government in the metropolitan area was less than comprehensive. Significant features of each plan prevented the implementation of a single, functionally comprehensive government for the entire area. In each case, some number of smaller municipalities were permitted to remain outside the jurisdiction of the newly reorganized countywide government, and service zones were set up to provide multiple scales and levels of responsibility for public services, functions, and facilities.

In the Nashville-Davidson County consolidation, for example, reorganization involved the creation of two service districts, one for urban services and the other general services.[17] The urban services district consists only of the city of Nashville, while the general services district consists of the entire county, including the central city. Functions are carried out by the areawide government on two different scales corresponding to the two service districts. Residents of the urban services district pay for and receive fire and intensified police protection, sewage disposal, water supply, streetlighting and cleaning, and wine and whiskey supervision; residents of the general services district are provided with schools, public health, police, courts, public welfare, public housing, urban renewal, streets and roads, traffic control, transportation, library, refuse disposal, and building and housing codes. Though provision was made for the expansion of the urban services district so as to be coterminous with the general services district, only the boundaries of the city of Nashville coincide with those of the urban services district. Six suburban municipalities with a total population of 16,000 at the time of consolidation remain outside the urban services district but are included in the general services district and subject to the jurisdiction of the unified county government for areawide functions and controls.

Reorganization between the city of Jacksonville and Duval County, Florida, also presents a case of less than complete structural and functional integration of city-county government. For one thing, when presented to the voters for approval, the plan gave each municipality in Duval County the right to remain outside the jurisdiction of the proposed areawide government. Four small municipalities with a total population of about 20,000 decided against participating in the consolidated government. Though they receive services from the reorganized and consolidated government, they are not structurally part of the unified governmental system for the officially named City of Jacksonville.

More important, however, is the fact that the consolidated area is divided into two service districts in which different scales determine the provision of public functions and services. The general service district covers the entire consolidated territory, and the unified areawide government provides such services as airports, electric power, fire and police protection, health, recreation and parks, schools, streets and highways, and welfare. These functions are financed with tax revenues raised throughout the jurisdiction. However, in the urban services district, the boundaries of which are coterminous with the old city of Jacksonville, the unified government provides additional services for water, sewage, streetlighting and cleaning, and garbage and refuse collection, all paid for by additional revenues collected only from among the residents of the urban services district. Thus, as in the case of consolidated Nashville-Davidson County, there exists at least two service areas with different scales of operation and functional responsibility for the areawide government.

Leaving aside the fact that consolidation of Indianapolis and Marion County, Indiana, was effected by an act of the state legislature and involved no local popular referendum in the affected communities, city-county consolidation under Unigov, as it is called, is additional evidence of departure from the model of comprehensive integration of governmental structure and function as advocated by metropolitan reformers.

From the perspective of governmental structure, the areawide government that went into effect in 1970 excludes eleven school districts, four suburban municipalities, and nine townships. These remain separate and autonomous units of government, not under the authority and jurisdiction of the consolidated county goverment. Functionally, there exist two service areas, one for urban-type services and the other for general functions. The former include health and hospitals, planning and zoning, roads and streets, parks, and urban renewal; the latter, police, fire, sanitation, libraries, and public housing. Urban-type functions are provided on a county- or areawide basis and paid for with revenues raised on an areawide basis. The general functions are furnished through a series of special service and taxing districts that vary in territorial size. Needless to say, the varying territorial size of the service and taxing districts for the general functions is a potentially confusing and complicating factor for the average resident, in addition to being a significant departure from functional integration under a unified, areawide government.

The experiences of city-county consolidation in the post-World War II period, including the Baton Rouge-East Baton Rouge Parish plan, reveal the difficulty encountered in trying to implement a fully comprehensive and integrated governmental system for the entire metropolitan area. Even in Indiana, where the state legislature implemented a reorganized system of consolidated county government without a local popular referendum on the plan, exceptions and departures from the "model" of metropolitan reform were made. The reality confronting metropolitan reformers and their supporters in state legislatures is that the demand for local identity and autonomy remains strong enough to prevent comprehensive reorganization. Local communities, particularly in the suburban areas outside the central cities, have been generally able to retain a dregree of structural and/or functional autonomy from the consolidated areawide government.

Metropolitan Reform Proposals: Metropolitan Federation

Failure to effect areawide governmental reorganization led metropolitan reformers to propose yet a third approach to governmental reorganization in the metropolitan area. This approach has attempted to respect the desire of small suburban municipalities to retain both their identity as a community and autonomy as a unit of government. The approach is modeled on the federal relationship between the national and state governments and, in fact, goes by the name of metropolitan federation.

Also known as the "two-tier" approach, metropolitan federation proposes the creation of not one but two levels of government. One system of government exists at the metropolitan level and exercises authority and responsibility over functions and services provided on an areawide or regional basis. A second system consists of the numerous small units of government at the local level. These units exercise authority and responsibility over local, specific, and specialized concerns. They are designed to meet the demand of suburban communities for local identity and autonomy within the larger metropolitan area. The "model" of two-tier metropolitan federation, if one exists, is the report of the Committee for Economic Development, *Reshaping*

Government in Urban Areas.[18] It lays out both the rationale for a federated approach to governmental reorganization in metropolitan areas as well as a plan for assigning functional responsibility to the various levels of metropolitan and local government.

It is generally conceded that the only major metropolitan reorganization along lines proposed by the federated or two-tier approach in the United States involves Miami and Dade County, Florida.[19] When its charter went into effect in July 1957, metropolitan Dade County became the first metropolitan area in the United States to adopt a two-tier system of government. Thus far, there have been no other two-tier or federated governmental systems adopted in metropolitan areas in the United States, though metropolitan Toronto in Canada has been governed by such a system since 1954.

Governmental reorganization in metropolitan Dade County provides for both areawide and local systems of government. The areawide county or metropolitan government possesses broad and extensive powers over the independent municipalities, which presently number twenty-seven, though at the time of reorganization they numbered twenty-six. Nineteen of the original twenty-six municipalities of metropolitan Dade County had fewer than 10,000 each at the time of reorganization.

The metropolitan government of Dade County not only provides most services on an areawide basis, it exercises broad regulatory control over planning and development matters as well. It is authorized, for example, to prepare and enforce comprehensive plans for the development of the county, something other metropolitan governments created through city-county consolidations cannot undertake. In addition, the metropolitan government is granted authority to adopt and enforce zoning and business regulations throughout its territorial jurisdiction.

The regulatory powers of the metropolitan government are enhanced by two additional provisions. First, municipalities at the local level can be created and annexations completed only upon the authorization of the metropolitan governing body, though provision is also made for a popular referendum to approve such proposals. However, the areawide government exercises substantial control over the creation and combination of municipalities within its territorial boundaries. Second, the metropolitan government has the authority to set minimum service levels for all governmental units within its jurisdiction. Metropolitan government is empowered to take over an activity if a municipality fails to comply with established service standards. In this way municipalities retain functional responsibility, but metropolitan government retains authority over the conditions under which that responsibility is exercised.

The existence of only one case of metropolitan government in the United States presents an insufficient base from which to evaluate the two-tier or federated approach to governmental reorganization in metropolitan areas. Though analyses of the Miami metropolitan federation abound, the mere fact that no other metropolitan areas have experimented with federated government indicates that, for a variety of reasons, the plan lacks widespread appeal and support. In fact, in view of the large number of governmental systems in metropolitan areas and the small number that have adopted any proposal for structural reform, we would have to conclude that the forces working against governmental reorganization in metropolitan areas are stronger than those supporting it.

ALTERNATIVES TO STRUCTURAL REORGANIZATION

Interlocal Functional Cooperation

The fact that governmental reorganization through structural integration has fared relatively poorly did not dampen the enthusiasm of metropolitan reformers, nor did it alter their belief that the proliferation of numerous small, autonomous units of government leads to the kinds of undesirable consequences discussed at the outset of this chapter. Metropolitan reformers remained committed to the view that governmental institutions in metropolitan areas should and could be more responsible and accountable, as well as economical and efficient in their performance. However, since structural reorganization was so difficult to achieve, reformers developed and pursued an alternative strategy for accomplishing their goals and objectives, one that does not depend upon altering the institutional arrangements of the governmental systems in metropolitan areas.

The new strategy seized upon by metropolitan reformers attempts to achieve economy and efficiency in providing public services and facilities by fostering cooperation between units of government at the metropolitan level. A variety of informal mechanisms and arrangements have been developed to achieve functional cooperation and, in some instances, integration, without altering the basic structural independence and autonomy of the municipalities in the suburbs and central cities of the metropolis.

A number of factors account for the increased interest in interlocal governmental cooperation centering on public services and facilities rather than comprehensive reorganization.[20] For one thing, effecting interlocal cooperative agreements between units of government in metropolitan areas is less administratively complicated and politically controversial than proposals to reorganize government through annexation, consolidation, or federation.

Interlocal agreements can be negotiated by administrative officials of the cooperating governments, ratified by their respective city councils or town boards, and put into effect immediately upon passage of the necessary ordinances or resolutions. It is not necessary to secure the passage of an amendment to the state constitution, nor do such agreements require enabling legislation from the state. In almost all instances, they do not even require the approval of local voters in a popular referendum on the proposed agreement. In other words, the adoption procedures for interlocal cooperation on functions, services, and facilities are easier to carry through to implementation.

Second, the growth in number and complexity of urban areas has made the interdependence of communities in metropolitan areas compellingly clear and indisputable. The mutual needs and difficulties of suburban and central city communities have been realized by all concerned. Interlocal agreements and cooperation make it possible to pursue joint solutions to common problems, especially in the area of reducing costs of services and facilities, without threatening the autonomy and independence of the small municipalities. Since the residents of the smaller municipalities adjacent to the central cities have been particularly concerned about their potential "takeover" or absorption by the larger units of government, interlocal cooperation offers the opportunity to share resources in meeting mutual needs without threatening community identity and autonomy.

A related consideration is the fact that local voters will often support interlocal cooperation as a way of avoiding even the appearance of structural reorganization. In a very real sense, interlocal agreements are acceptable for political reasons rather than because large numbers of people believe they will either reduce the cost of providing services and facilities and/or enable units of government to provide higher levels of service and facilities without increasing the costs of doing so.

Fourth, many county governments have been reorganized and expanded, especially in terms of the scope and variety of functions performed on an areawide basis. County government in the United States has been upgraded organizationally, with many counties adopting the county manager or county executive forms of government. These organizational changes, along with other administrative reforms, have enhanced the functional capacity of county government and its credibility in the eyes of metropolitan area residents. Residents of the small municipalities as well as the central cities now tend to be more confident of the ability of county government to meet their growing and mutual needs. In some cases they are even looking to county government to play a more active and integral role in meeting the problems attendant on urban development and growth in the metropolitan area.

Finally, actions taken by national and state governments and agencies have had the effect of endorsing the spread of interlocal cooperative agreements. Some states have gone so far as to enact legislation making intergovernmental cooperation legally possible. Two states in particular, Alaska and Hawaii, have included permissive provisions on interlocal agreements and cooperation in their constitutions. Most other states, however, have acted statutorily to make cooperation between local governments possible. Then, too, national agencies such as the Advisory Commission on Intergovernmental Relations, a body created by and reporting to Congress, and the Council of State Governments, the official voice of all fifty states, have advocated the use of interlocal cooperation and agreements. The National League of Cities, representing the thousands of municipalities throughout the United States, and the National Association of Counties, have also endorsed cooperation between local governments in metropolitan areas.

As a broad and inclusive term, interlocal agreements and cooperation take many forms and shapes. They include informal and unwritten understandings among local administrators and technicians in the same substantive field as well as formal contracts signed by a sizable number of local governments to do something jointly, such as operate a sewage treatment plant or build a major facility. Oftentimes the informal, unwritten agreements and understandings can be as important in effecting cooperation and meeting mutual needs as the formal arrangements expressed in a contractual agreement signed by the parties involved.

It is almost impossible, however, to consider the informal agreements, for the simple reason that there is no permanent and public record of their existence, the obligations they impose on the parties, etc. Therefore, any review and analysis of interlocal agreements must focus on formal arrangements of one kind or another. Generally speaking, two kinds of interlocal agreements have been formalized and put into operation. One type relates to specific functions or services; the other establishes a mechanism for reaching consensus among local officials on problems and policies with an areawide scope and impact.

Interlocal Service-Oriented Agreements

It is virtually impossible to catalog the entire range of services, facilities, and functions embraced by interlocal cooperative agreements. Virtually every conceivable service, function, or facility owned, operated, or provided by a public agency is subject to cooperation by any combination of metropolitan area local governments. Some of the important activities include airports, public buildings, correctional and detention facilities, hospitals, air pollution control, crime laboratories and investigative services, water supply, libraries, sewage disposal and treatment, parks and recreational facilities, road construction and maintenance, tax assessment and collection, election administration, flood control, etc. The list could go on endlessly, and it would include direct and indirect services, administrative procedures and practices, and physical facilities of all kinds.

Joseph Zimmerman has conducted an extensive survey of interlocal service agreements and identified a number of their significant characteristics.[21] First, most agreements involve two governments and concern a single activity. For example, the county government may contract with the smaller municipalities to operate a fee-based communications center for law enforcement. Second, though interlocal agreements have been reached for the construction and operation of physical facilities such as hospitals, civic centers, and the like, they are used more frequently for services, e.g., public health nurses, libraries, protective activities. Third, despite their contractual nature, interlocal agreements are not necessarily permanent. Often the contract specifies a termination date or provides that either party can terminate the arrangement with adequate notice in advance. A fourth feature of interlocal agreements is that many are of a standby or emergency nature. That is, they operate only under specified conditions such as a flood, epidemic, fire, civil disorder, or the like. Finally, interlocal agreements are often based on specific state legislative authorizations, each allowing cooperation in a particular field or activity.

The contract system has proved to be very popular because of its simplicity of initiation, operation, and flexibility. Services are provided within the framework of existing governments, and contracts can be negotiated and approved without popular referenda or additional state action. One city may decide to contract for the services of one police car on a twenty-four-hour basis, while another city of the same or similar size may contract for the services of three cars. Each city negotiates its own arrangement with county government.

Metropolitan areas of all sizes in all areas of the United States use interlocal agreements for specific functions, services, and facilities. Perhaps the best known of these is the Lakewood Plan that operates in the Los Angeles SMSA.[22] Initially developed in 1954, between the city of Lakewood and Los Angeles County government, the Lakewood Plan is a system of contractual arrangements whereby a municipality receives a package of municipal services—as many as it wishes to negotiate and pay for—from the county government under contracts and through city-administered districts. The plan makes it possible for cities to contract from the county government for as many services as they wish. Some cities contract for all services the county has to offer; others contract only for those they don't want to (or can't) provide themselves. One redeeming feature of the arrangement is that it enables cities, especially smaller ones, to control their own administrative overhead, capital, and personnel costs. It is possible for a city to contract for all public services and activities from the county and thus maintain a minimal administrative structure of its own. However, such a city would still have legal status as a municipality; it would have full taxing and borrowing powers, elect its own city officials to adopt ordinances and set policies, and do all the things done by a city with its own administrative structure providing services and activities to its residents.

The contract system is by no means limited to the Los Angeles area; the metropolitan areas of Philadelphia, Cleveland, and Detroit, three of the largest in the United States, also have far-ranging systems of interlocal contractual agreements.[23] Furthermore, it should be noted that municipalities also contract with one another for the performance of services. Central cities provide services on a fee basis to neighboring suburbs, and it is not unusual for one suburb to provide services to another on a contract or fee basis. If carried to its fullest, functional integration of services will almost certainly reduce if not eliminate some of the undesirable consequences of governmental proliferation and fragmentation that are such an anathema to metropolitan reformers.

Mechanisms for Interlocal Coordination

A second kind of interlocal cooperation attempts to establish an institutional mechanism to bring together officials of local governments in metropolitan areas to discuss common problems, issues, and policies and coordinate their efforts to deal with them. This effort is oriented only to creating a formal, institutionalized setting within which local officials can exchange views on matters of interlocal consequence and, hopefully, coordinate efforts to solve mutual problems. To serve this purpose, many metropolitan areas are joining in the metropolitan or regional Council of Government (COG) movement, a form of institutionalized cooperation dating from the 1950s but enjoying its most widespread popularity since the mid-1960s. COGs come in different shapes, sizes, and with different names. As of 1972, over six hundred COGs have been established across the nation, including nearly all the metropolitan areas. There is little doubt that the growth of these associations is due in part to their designation as clearinghouses for federal grant applications by the federal government.[24]

COGs are distinguished from other voluntary associations in the metropolitan area by their basis of membership; representation on a COG is based on governmental units. A COG is an association *of* governments and is not a government in itself. Every effort is made to involve representatives of every governmental unit in the metropolitan area, regardless of size as measured by land area, population, or anything else. In fact, COGs may be composed of equal numbers of representatives from each unit of government in the metropolitan area, so that all have an equal voice in whatever discussions are held. The meetings of COGs are little more than a forum for officials to get together on a regular basis and exchange views. In some areas, the COG is often the only opportunity for such interchange and communication, making it more important than a mere elaboration of its functions would imply. The underlying goal of these associations, to promote cooperative action among member governments, is facilitated by the presence of a research staff which gathers data and prepares reports on matters of areawide concern. On some occasions, the staff may be asked to make recommendations to the COG membership. However, COGs usually lack the authority to implement their recommendations; they usually are limited to adopting resolutions and recommendations that are taken back to the respective constituent governments for consideration, adoption, and implementation.

COGs, or whatever name they go by, have proved to be useful institutionalized mechanisms for facilitating a thorough and open exchange of views about common problems, issues, and strategies associated with urban development in the metropolitan area. In the final analysis, it remains the responsibility of each unit of government in the metropolitan area to implement policies or programs deemed appropriate to its particular problems of growth and development. This means that the possibility of lack of coordination among units of government remains present, since each local government retains the legal and political autonomy to pursue its own program of action to deal with the problems of urban development. The COG approach only creates the forum within which common problems and solutions can be discussed; it cannot affect any action on its own. In this respect, COGs or other voluntary associations resemble a confederation of constituent organizations. They are no more powerful than the willingness of its members to share views and cooperate with each other. There are no sanctions or penalties for failure to comply with association recommendations and there is nothing to prevent a member government from terminating its participation in these institutionalized arrangements.

METROPOLITAN REFORM: THE UNFINISHED AGENDA

Two additional obstacles now confronting metropolitan reform are the opposition of the residents of the emerging black majority in the cities and census data showing the exodus of factories and jobs from city into suburbia and exurbia. Blacks, Puerto Ricans, Chicanos, and other nonwhite groups have come to regard annexation, consolidation, and metrofederation as a means of denying them access to governmental and political power in the cities that their numbers seem to make inevitable.

It is possible to portray the opposition of nonwhite minorities to metropolitan governmental reorganization as based on a desire for community identity and autonomy similar to that expressed by suburban populations. However, in the case of the central city population, the expression of community identity and autonomy manifests itself in demands for decentralization of city government and local neighborhood control of public services, programs, and policies. These demands and the institutional responses to them are among the most significant developments affecting governmental arrangements in central cities since the mid-1960s. We turn to decentralization and community control in the next chapter.

NOTES

1. U.S. Department of Commerce, Bureau of the Census, *Census of Government* (Washington, D.C.: U.S. Government Printing Office, 1972), 1:10.

2. *Ibid.*, p. 20.

3. The most comprehensive analysis of special districts has been done by John C. Bollens. See his *Special District Governments in the United States* (Berkeley: University of California Press, 1957) and *The Problem of Special Districts in American Government* (Washington, D.C.: Advisory Commission on Intergovernmental Relations, 1964).

4. Robert L. Lineberry, "Reforming Metropolitan Governance: Requiem or Reality?" *Georgetown Law Journal* 58 (March-May 1970): 675-718.

5. These figures are found in National Commission on Civil Disorders, *Report of The National Advisory Commission on Civil Disorders* (Washington, D.C.: U.S. Government Printing Office, 1962), and Robert C. Wood, *1440 Governments* (Garden City, N.Y.: Doubleday, 1961).

6. See Robert Bish, *The Public Economy of Metropolitan Areas* (Chicago: Markham Publishing, 1971), chap. 3, for a discussion of the concept and its implications for metropolitan governmental organization. Further exploration of this concept can be found in Werner Z. Hirsch, "The Supply of Urban Public Services," reprinted in *Issues in Urban Economics*, eds. Harvey S. Perloff

and Lowdon Wingo, Jr. (Baltimore: Johns Hopkins Press, 1968).

7. Woodrow Wilson, *Congressional Government* (1885; New York: Meridian Books, 1957), p. 77.

8. *Ibid.*, p. 187.

9. William Anderson, *American City Government* (New York: Henry Holt, 1925), pp. 641-42.

10. Committee for Economic Development, *Modernizing Local Government* (New York, 1966), pp. 11-12.

11. *Ibid.*, p. 17.

12. The early annexation activities of a number of large cities are described in Richard Bigger and James Kitchen, *How the Cities Grew* (Los Angeles: University of California Bureau of Governmental Research, 1952), and Kenneth T. Jackson, "Metropolitan Government Versus Political Autonomy," in *Cities in American History*, eds. Kenneth T. Jackson and Stanley K. Schultz (New York: Alfred A. Knopf, 1972), pp. 442-62.

13. See U.S. Bureau of the Census, *Land Area and Population of Incorporated Places of 2,500 or More: April 1, 1950* (Geographic Reports, Series GEO No. 5, January 1953) and *1972 Boundary and Annexation Survey* (Washington, D.C., 1973).

14. Analysis of these laws as they affect annexation success can be found in Raymond H. Wheeler, "Annexation Law and Annexation Success," *Land Economics* 41 (November 1965): 354-60.

15. See Thomas H. Reed, "Progress in Metropolitan Integration," *Public Administration Review* 9 (Winter 1949): 1-10. Also William C. Havard, Jr., and Floyd L. Corty, *Rural-Urban Consolidation: The Merger of Governments in Baton Rouge Area* (Baton Rouge: Louisiana State University Press, 1964).

16. John Bollens and Henry J. Schmandt, *The Metropolis: Its People, Politics, and Economic Life*, 3d ed. (New York: Harper & Row, 1975), p. 252.

17. See David A. Booth, *Metropolitics: The Nashville Consolidation* (East Lansing, Mich.: Institute for Community Development and Services, 1963), and Brett W. Hawkins, *Nashville Metro: The Politics of City-County Consolidation* (Nashville: Vanderbilt University Press, 1966).

18. Committee for Economic Development (New York, 1970).

19. See, for example, Joseph Metzger, "Metro and Its Judicial History," *University of Miami Law Review* 15 (Spring 1961): 283-93; Edward Soften, *The Miami Metropolitan Experiment* (Garden City, N.Y.: Anchor Books, 1966), and "Quest for Leadership," *National Civic Review* 57 (July 1968): 346-51.

20. The movement for greater interlocal governmental cooperation is treated in W. Brooke Graves, *Interlocal Cooperation: The History and Background of Intergovernmental Agreements* (Washington, D.C.: National Association of Counties Research Foundation, 1962), and *American Intergovernmental Relations: Their Origins, Historical Developments, and Current Status* (New York: Charles Scribner's Sons, 1964).

21. Joseph F. Zimmerman, *Intergovernmental Service Agreements for Smaller Municipalities* (Washington, D.C.: International City Management Association, Urban Data Service, 1973).

22. On the Lakewood Plan, see Robert Warren, *Governments in Metropolitan Regions: A Reappraisal of Fractionated Political Organization* (Davis: University of California Institute of Government Affairs, 1966).

23. On these, see Matthew Holden, Jr., *Intergovernmental Agreements in the Cleveland Metropolitan Area* (Cleveland: Cleveland Metropolitan Services Commission, 1958); George S. Blair, *Interjurisdictional Agreements in Southeastern Pennsylvania* (Philadelphia: University of Pennsylvania Institute of State and Local Government, 1960); and Vincent L. Marando, "Inter-Local Cooperation in a Metropolitan Area," *Urban Affairs Quarterly* 4 (December 1968): 185-200.

24. The best summary of the activities of associations like COGs is the one by the Advisory Commission on Intergovernmental Relations, *Alternative Approaches to Governmental Reorganization in Metropolitan Areas* (Washington, D.C.: U.S. Government Printing Office, 1962), and *Metropolitan Councils of Governments* (Washington, D.C.: U.S. Government Printing Office, 1966). See also Nelson Wikstrom, *Councils of Government: A Study of Political Incrementalism* (Chicago: Nelson, Hall, 1977).

CHAPTER IX.

The Community Revolution
in the Central Cities

Introduction

The sixties was an important decade in urban development for it marked the beginning of widespread and, in some cases, intense dissatisfaction with and alienation from governmental institutions in the central cities. Responses of city, state, and federal governments to this dissatisfaction have had a decided impact on the ability of the city's public officials and institutions to respond to social and economic problems of development. Social commentators like Daniel Bell and Virginia Held have described the events of the sixties as the "community revolution."[1] Janice Perlman suggests that the community revolution has given rise to a "plethora of grassroots associations involving local people mobilized on their own behalf around concrete issues of importance in their communities."[2]

The demand for local control of public institutions and services did not originate with the community revolution of the sixties. Rather, the proliferation of autonomous governments in metropolitan areas was a direct result of the desire of suburban residents for legal, political, and social independence from the central cities. One of the main reasons for the incorporation of suburban municipalities was the desire to control the size of governmental organization and make public institutions more responsive to local citizens. This is also one of the reasons for the failure of efforts at municipal annexation, city-county consolidation, and even metropolitan federation in the post-World War II period. Moreover, the success of agreements of interlocal functional corporation and coordination was due in large part to their informal nature and service emphasis, as well as the fact that they could be established without prior approval of a local electorate.

The community revolution in the central cities is a counterpart to suburban opposition to metropolitan reform. A major difference between suburban and central city attitudes and responses to metropolitan reform proposals lies in the fact that the suburban population is predominantly white and middle class while the central city population has become increasingly nonwhite and working class. However, experience in some cities indicates that there is substantial support for community organization in white, middle-class neighborhoods. Residents in these neighborhoods view neighborhood-based organization and control as a way of retaining the essential character, distinctiveness, and stability of their own area.[3]

The community revolution did not develop overnight. Interest in and support for local control of governmental institutions and services was a result of many years of unmet expectations in both society at large and the central cities themselves. It gained momentum as a result of federal legislation dating back to the mid-1950s that promoted grass-roots involvement in policymaking by local institutions.

SHAPING THE COMMUNITY REVOLUTION

Social Changes

By the mid-sixties, fully a decade had passed since the landmark decision of the United States Supreme Court in *Brown* v. *Board of Education*. Many expected the *Brown* decision to effect an immediate cure to patterns and practices of segregation in public facilities. Only ten years later it was already apparent that such an expectation was unwarranted. While the *Brown* decision most certainly lent the federal government's support to integration of public accommodations and struck broadside at de jure segregation in the South, it had little impact on de facto segregation in the cities of the Northeast and Midwest. Consequently, for minorities in the central cities of these areas, the mid-sixties produced a realization that efforts to integrate neighborhoods, schools, and other public facilities were less than fully effective. The attention of leaders of minority groups soon turned inward, i.e., toward improving conditions and facilities in their own neighborhoods. Increasingly, demands for integration were replaced by demands for Black Power.

Two features of the municipal reform movement have contributed to shaping the community revolution. First, some political machines had been in prolonged decline by the decade of the sixties. This meant that there was no longer a structural mechanism available for expressing and transmitting the demands of minority groups to governmental institutions and officials. City government came to be perceived as increasingly unresponsive to the demands and needs of minority groups.

Second, the municipal reform movement greatly changed the nature of the city's primary representative institution—the city council. By replacing the election of city council members from wards with an at-large system, minorities found their access to and control of the local legislature greatly diminished. Under the ward system, minority groups were almost always guaranteed election of one of their members to the city council, since ward boundaries were usually drawn to conform to the boundaries of residential enclaves throughout the city. Thus, a predominantly black or Puerto Rican ward could reasonably expect to elect a member of their group to the city council. At a minimum, this produced a sense of satisfaction at having acquired access to and membership in at least one branch of city government. At-large elections meant that the votes of minority groups in different neighborhoods had to compete with each other for election of members to the council. At the same time, white middle-class voters, who generally turn out to vote in larger numbers, cast votes for their own candidates. In consequence, minority groups saw their ability to elect members of their own group to the city council seriously impaired. This compounded their perception of city government as unresponsive and unrepresentative.

The bureaucracy of city government was getting larger, more difficult to understand, and less responsive to citizen demands. Increased use of independent boards and commissions to administer functions like personnel, planning, and zoning made it all but impossible for even elected officials in city government to influence policy in these functional areas. City residents had no opportunity to hold members of boards and commissions accountable for their actions, and these bodies were generally unresponsive to the particular concerns of class-based interests. Furthermore, the city bureaucracy itself was becoming more professionalized and unionized. In combination these two developments increased the insularity of public servants from the demands of citizen-consumers in different neighborhoods throughout the city.

Still another factor contributing to the community revolution lies in the nature of urban public services. Whereas many public goods are indivisible, i.e., they are provided for the entire population, some urban public services are locally specific and highly divisible. Police patrols, garbage collection, snow removal, street maintenance, and parks, for example, are among some of the urban public services and facilities provided on a neighborhood-by-neighborhood basis. As a result, it is relatively easy for city residents to judge for themselves whether government is providing adequate levels and kinds of services. A substantial body of data has been collected and analyzed suggesting that urban public services are distributed unequally in different sections of the central city. Most important is the conclusion that neighborhoods inhabited by low-income and minority groups receive lower levels of services and express widespread dissatisfaction with the services they receive.[4] Such feelings of dissatisfaction with urban public services reinforce the view that city government is unresponsive to individual needs and demands, and support the conviction that responsiveness will improve with increased citizen participation in decision making.

Finally, local autonomy and control of public institutions have always been dominant themes in America. Beginning in colonial times, governmental institutions have been designed to respect and institutionalize popular control of public institutions and officials. The demand for Black Power and community control in the central cities can be viewed as a contemporary manifestation of a traditional, widely shared and supported principle of American government.

Federal Government Support

Against the backdrop of these social developments, the effect of actions by the federal government promoting citizen participation in local institutions and programs must also be considered. Three federal programs are important to the shaping of the community revolution.

First, the Housing Act of 1954 promoted citizen participation in the urban renewal program by requiring municipalities, as a condition of eligibility for federal funds, to develop a "Workable Program" for urban renewal. The Workable Program was to consist of seven elements, one of which was the provision for citizen participation in the planning and development of the urban renewal program. The Department of Housing and Urban Development describes the requirement of citizen participation as "the keystone of a community's Workable Program" because participation enables citizens to inform themselves of community needs, assist in the development of improvement goals, and learn the means by which the goals can be achieved.

Ten years later the passage of the Economic Opportunity Act of 1964 launched a major effort to encourage widespread citizen participation in federally supported programs. The antipoverty program was conceived as an effort to raise some thirty-five million people above the poverty level by involving them in the design, development, and implementation of programs to alleviate the conditions associated with being poor. The Economic Opportunity Act of 1964 consisted of seven Titles loosely tying together a wide range of old and new programs to combat poverty. The commitment to citizen participation was expressed in Title II-A, Section 202(a) (3), authorizing the creation of Community Action Programs (CAPs), which were to be "developed, conducted, and administered with the maximum feasible participation of residents of the areas and members of the groups served."[5] The purpose of the language was to require local communities to take the initiative in developing programs and mobilizing their resources in a concerted and coordinated manner for a broadly based, long-range attack on poverty, using the poor themselves as the subjects as well as objects of program development and administration. Without getting into a premature judgment of the impact of citizen participation in the war on poverty, it can at least be said that the effect of Title II-A, Section 202(2) (3) was to signify, once and for all, the federal government's support of citizen participation in decision making at both citywide and neighborhood levels of program planning, development, and administration.

Finally, the Demonstration Cities and Metropolitan Development Act of 1966 was a third federal program designed to encourage citizen participation in local community development programs. Conceived as an innovative neighborhood-based program, Model Cities was intended to stimulate a comprehensive and coordinated effort to solve the economic, physical, and social problems of blighted neighborhoods by facilitating the participation of residents of target areas. Although the city government retained legal responsibility for the Model Cities programs, residents of target neighborhoods were to have a significant role in planning and conducting activities and services. In fact, during the first year, participating cities were directed to prepare a five-year program and to "chronicle the methods and approaches used to achieve widespread citizen participation, and the relationship between the views of the citizens and the various elements in the model neighborhood plan." Particular stress was placed upon the involvement of local residents with the public and private agencies needed to carry out the program. About the only significant change from the language and intent of the antipoverty program to that of Model Cities was the shift from the phrase "maximum feasible participation" of the poor to "widespread citizen participation" of local residents of the target neighborhoods.

Urban renewal, the War on Poverty, and Model Cities were programs that demonstrate the federal government's commitment to citizen participation in local government decision making, whether within or outside the formal governmental structure. In any case, by the mid-sixties there was ample justification for residents of the central cities, particularly the poor and nonwhite, to demand greater participation in decision making and, ultimately, decentralization of control of public programs, services, and resources. As a result, a variety of institutional arrangements were developed and implemented to respond to the diverse and widespread demands for decentralization and community control of governmental institutions and public programs, services, and resources.

DIMENSIONS OF DECENTRALIZATION

Conceptualization and Definition

One of the major difficulties in trying to understand the impact of the community revolution on city government and urban development is the tendency to use a number of important terms interchangeably. One finds, for example, that decentralization, citizen participation, and community control are used in similar (if not identical) ways without making any effort to specify the differences among or between them. The failure to specify the meaning of such significant concepts has only compounded the problem of clarifying the relationship between local neighborhoods and centralized governmental institutions in the cities.

In the context of urban development generally and the central cities in particular, decentralization is a key term, for it serves as an umbrella under which much that is done in the name of citizen participation and community control is understood. Decentralization is an apparently simple concept, yet considerable difficulty is experienced in moving from conceptual discussions about it to analysis of experiments with it in the real world. James Felser has pointed out that part of the problem lies in the fact that the apparent simplicity is deceptive, leading to treatments which either generalize too broadly or start from doctrinaire positions that predetermine answers to concrete situations. These characteristics can be observed in the prevalent tendency to romanticize the notion of decentralization and to transfer it into an article of faith.[6]

An important source of difficulty lies in the wide assortment of experimental arrangements described as decentralization. Examples of decentralization range from district referral and information centers to neighborhood government. While decentralization implies the distribution of authority from the center to the periphery, not all decentralized arrangements confer full legal powers and autonomy to locally based institutions. In the context of urban development, decentralization involves the transfer of authority from centralized governmental institutions, commonly referred to as "city hall," to locally based territorial units, frequently referred to as neighborhoods. Unfortunately, this attempt at defining decentralization is only the tip of the iceberg, for it fails to address two key issues, namely, the nature and target of decentralization in the context of central cities and urban development.

Alan Altschuler has attempted to provide an answer to the first of these questions by distinguishing *administrative* decentralization from *political* decentralization. The former involves delegation of responsibility from superior to subordinate officials within the bureaucracy. However, the organizing principle of the bureaucracy remains hierarchical. Top officials retain authority to revoke the delegation anytime or at the very least override the decisions of lower level officials and institutions. By contrast, political decentralization involves the transfer of authority to officials whose dependence is upon a geographically delineated constituency or clientele. A requirement of political decentralization is that the officials of the locally organized unit are ultimately responsible to their constituency, i.e., a neighborhood-based electorate or clientele group.[7]

Altschuler's distinction between administrative decentralization and political decentralization leads him to define community control as "the exercise of authority by the democratically organized government of a neighborhood-sized jurisdiction."[8] This definition of community control includes no agreement on how neighborhoods should be defined, nor does it prescribe the amount of authority such a government should possess in any given domain of activity or responsibility. All it does is recognize that the key element in political decentralization is the transfer of authority from a single central institution of city government to smaller, neighborhood-based institutions. Such a transfer would not and probably could not alter the legal relationship between higher and lower levels of government, especially between states and municipalities. This and other attempts at conceptual and definitional clarification make it evident that decentralization, whether administrative or political, focuses on the status, rights, responsibilities, and powers of locally based client groups served by public programs, services, or facilities. Decentralization involves the "transference of responsibility and power to those very people who are affected by the program or innovation in question."[9]

A second aspect of decentralization is its territorial focus. The target of decentralization is client groups residing in particular areas of the central cities. These areas are frequently referred to as neighborhoods. Considerable difficulty arises from trying to conceptualize and delineate neighborhood boundaries for purposes of decentralization. The term neighborhood is used by city planners, government officials, and sociologists in at least two different ways. First, a neighborhood can be viewed as a physical entity where streets, railway lines, parks, or other artificial boundaries separate one area and its inhabitants from another. As we've already noted in a previous chapter, the intracity highway system in Chicago delineates a number of neighborhoods from each other. Second, a neighborhood can be viewed as a social or organic entity whose residents share a common life-style, values, and experiences. When viewed from this perspective, a neighborhood encompasses common loyalites and values among residents whose patterned interactions give rise to a sense of continuity and persistence over time.[10]

The problem in decentralization of governmental institutions is whether to organize local institutions around physical or social boundaries. In some instances it may be possible to draw neighborhood boundaries so that physical and social entities coincide. All too often, however, this is not possible, since patterns in social development of neighborhoods have not always followed natural landmarks or borders like streets, parks, etc. Social neighborhoods have proven useful as the territorial base of decentralization because in the central cities these have developed distinctive and often visible, ethnic, racial, and socioeconomic characteristics. One finds, for example, references to neighborhoods like Harlem and the Lower East Side in New York City, Hough in Cleveland, Watts in Los Angeles, Hyde Park-Kenwood in Chicago, and Roxbury in Boston.

Justifications for Decentralization

Additional light can be shed on the nature of decentralization by examining the justifications offered by advocates of decentralized institutional arrangements. We should begin such a discussion by recognizing that decentralization apparently is not an end in itself. Advocates of decentralization allege that it will produce benefits that centralized governmental institutions cannot (or will not) pursue.

Douglas Yates has suggested four justifications commonly found in the writings of those who advocate decentralization of the city's governmental institutions.[11] First, decentralization is justified on psychological grounds. It will bring government closer to citizens by reducing the distance between the two. Citizens will feel less removed from the institutions that affect their lives; distrust and alienation from public authority will be lessened. Second, decentralization is justified on administrative grounds. In this view, decentralization will enhance government's responsiveness to citizen needs because the information used by city officials will be more accurate and complete. The time public officials take to respond to local conditions and demands will be greatly reduced by the proximity of governmental institutions to the conditions and problems requiring action. A third and related justification is economic. Neighborhood institutions, because they respond to local problems and conditions more quickly, will make more efficient use of resources. The logic behind this justification is that decentralization will make it possible to allocate the city's resources more efficiently by enabling officials and agencies to recognize the fact that conditions and priorities differ from one neighborhood to another within the city. Resources can be targeted where they are needed and will produce the most benefit. Service levels can be varied according to neighborhood needs and priorities. Finally, there is a political justification for decentralization, based on the assumption that it is important to broaden grass-roots participation in decisions on public issues. This justification is particularly appealing and important to nonwhite groups and the poor who were typically excluded from decision making by centrally located institutions and officials. In the end, participation in public decision making will help to develop a strong, indigenous political leadership among previously quiescent groups in the city.

APPROACHES TO DECENTRALIZATION

The community revolution produced a "rush to decentralize" institutional arrangements in city government. Central cities across the nation designed and implemented governance arrangements that broadened the base of citizen participation in city government and/or enabled public service agencies and officials to be more responsive to citizens' needs and demands. Henry J. Schmandt has suggested that the variety of approaches to decentralization can be subsumed under five models, based on the degree of authority and responsibility transferred from central to local officials or participants. The five models are called exchange, bureaucratic, modified bureaucratic, developmental, and governmental.[12]

Exchange Model and Administrative Decentralization

The exchange model involves the least degree of decentralization. As such, it serves as little more than a device for improving communication between centralized city officials and neighborhood residents. Authority and responsibility for determining policies and services remain with centralized institutions and officials, but channels of communication and interaction are established to improve the information base on which decisions are made. Information and advisory processes are decentralized at the neighborhood level through such mechanisms as field offices, neighborhood information/referral centers, little city halls, or neighborhood-based multiservice centers. It is important to remember that in this model citizens are required to deal with established, centralized agencies and officials despite the existence of locally based institutions and officials.

A number of cities have established systems of administrative decentralization; neighborhood "city halls," for example, serve primarily as information and referral centers, furnishing information about municipal services and taking complaints from citizens about problems confronting neighborhood residents. In a few instances specific services are provided at a neighborhood city hall, including voter registration, issuance of licenses and building permits, tax collection, etc. Multiservice centers, on the other hand, have usually restricted their activities to social services like family counseling, vocational rehabilitation, employment referral, and health services. Often the multiservice center is also a mechanism for information referral and coordination, providing citizens with a location close to their neighborhood residence where they can find out about various services and programs provided by city, county, state, or federal governments.[13]

The city of Los Angeles was one of the first to establish and operate a network of branch city halls. Branch city halls were established to allay concerns of residents living in territories annexed to the city in 1906 and in 1909. These local city halls were essentially an attempt to bring the provision of public services closer to the neighborhood areas and citizen-consumers, and to provide citizens of the sprawling central city with more direct and convenient access to municipal service agencies.

In 1966, the city of Houston, Texas, undertook to improve relations between city government and minority groups by inaugurating a "mobile city hall" program to serve a variety of purposes. Mobile city halls provide information to neighborhood residents about city services; they receive complaints about services and refer them to appropriate city departments; they have even been used by various departments, e.g., police and fire, to recruit personnel from minority groups. Mobile city halls enable city government to enlist the cooperation of residents in support of neighborhood improvement projects. Though broadening citizen participation was not a primary purpose of the mobile city hall program, it has been used to organize neighborhood task forces for special projects.

One of the most widely studied efforts to establish neighborhood-based city halls is the program of little city halls implemented by Boston Mayor Kevin White in 1968. This program in Boston is operated by the Office of Public Service, an administrative unit in the mayor's office. Thus, the little city hall program enjoys the direct and explicit support of the mayor. The first little city hall was opened in midsummer 1968 in the heart of East Boston. By the end of the year, nine more were in operation and in 1969 three more were added. By the spring of 1972, fifteen little city halls were operational, some in mobile units, some in community centers, and still others in existing municipal buildings.

The little city hall program is an extension of the mayor's office. Each unit is headed by a manager, whose primary responsibility is to serve as the mayor's representative. Though the managers are not responsible for municipal services in the neighborhoods, their relationship with and access to the mayor's office enables them to act quickly and decisively on complaints from neighborhood residents concerning municipal services. Political scientist Eric Nordlinger studied the little city hall program in Boston during its first years and gave it generally high ratings on three of seven principal functions (direct services, complaint referral, community catalyst), moderate ratings on two other functions (service management, issue advocate), and low ratings on two others (communications, community participation).[14]

An expansion of the "little city hall" was introduced in Baltimore, Maryland, as an outgrowth of something called "mayor's stations." First proposed in 1966 by then mayoral candidate Thomas J. D'Alesandro III, the mayor's stations were supplanted by five multiservice centers, with the Model Cities program developing two more. In 1972, city voters passed a $4 million bond issue to match federal funds for the construction of nine additional multiservice centers.

While the mayor's station arrangement primarily handles information, complaints, and referrals, giving little on-site service, multiservice centers normally make on-site provisions for a full range of services needed in a particular neighborhood. In fact, some multiservice centers contain mayor's stations within the facility. The Kirk Neighborhood Center, for example, which opened in 1971, provides space for a mayor's station to operate.

The city of Chicago has operated a multiservice center program since the mid-1960s. The first such center was established in 1965 under the auspices of the Chicago Committee on Urban Opportunity. It was an attempt to identify community needs, secure cooperation from public and private social service agencies, and coordinate existing human service programs.

The largest of these centers, the Montrose Center, has a staff of more than four hundred who operate a variety of programs, including an outreach effort to canvass the target neighborhood for information, referrals for services, and recruiting participants for programs. Community service activities handle problems of housing, tenant-landlord relations, health, consumer complaints, and employment. Model Cities programs like the Neighborhood Youth Corps, Head Start, and Upward Bound are also housed in the center. Public agencies, including the Board of Education, Board of Health, the County Department of Public Aid, State Employment Service, and Legal Aid, all station personnel at the Montrose Center.

Bureaucratic Models and Functional Decentralization

The bureaucratic model involves the delegation of authority to city officials in neighborhood areas along functional and/or territorial lines. Bureaucratic decentralization along functional lines predates the community revolution in many areas. Police services, for example, frequently establish precinct stations in various parts of the city to decentralize functions. Most large public school systems delegate varying degrees of authority from central headquarters to school buildings headed by principals. When viewed from a territorial perspective, the bureaucratic model involves the delegation of authority over a combination of functions to a district or neighborhood official on assignment from central headquarters. In both the functional and territorial instances, local or district officials are ultimately responsible to their superiors in the central bureaucracy. Precinct captains and school principals, for example, follow policies developed and adopted by officials at police headquarters or the central administration of the local board of education.

It has been generally presumed that such arrangements would make the city bureaucracy more accessible to neighborhood residents and, in turn, more responsive to their needs, desires, and interests. However, the bureaucratic model is contradicted by traditional bureaucratic values of impartiality and neutrality in relationships with agency clientele and consumers of public services. This model of bureaucracy prescribes that officials approach the public in "a spirit of formalistic impersonality" in order to assure equitable treatment, and such an approach runs directly counter to the idea of decentralizing the bureaucracy to make it more responsive to the needs and desires of citizen-consumers in different neighborhoods of the city.

In the modified bureaucratic model the neighborhood or district official is made responsible not only to his superiors in central headquarters, but also the citizen-consumers he serves. This may be done through the establishment of neighborhood-based councils or advisory committees, elected by area residents, or, perhaps, appointed by elected city officials. Under either arrangement, the neighborhood-based citizens' group advises the local official on a variety of issues, including proposed renewal and development projects, major personnel appointments, neighborhood problems, service levels, etc. This gives neighborhood residents some involvement in decisions and policies made by officials in centralized institutions. It also enables central headquarters to be better informed of citizens' reactions to proposed programs and actions.

A number of cities have employed variations of the bureaucratic models to organize and improve the delivery of specific services or groups of interrelated services. San Antonio, Texas, for example, has decentralized the delivery of services by its Department of Public Works.[15] The department provides city residents with the traditional array of public works, including street maintenance, sanitary and storm sewers, street cleaning, garbage collection and disposal, sewage treatment, and maintenance of municipal buildings. To do this over a relatively large geographical area and for a substantial population, the city government has decentralized its public works delivery system to four area service centers, each serving an area of approximately two hundred thousand residents. The purpose of the San Antonio system is to improve the provision of public works services; it does not transfer or redistribute authority to make public works policy.

City police departments are a common target for bureaucratic decentralization, in part because municipal officials want to improve the delivery of police services and also because they believe that more proximity of police personnel to central city neighborhoods will improve police-community relations.[16] Though most police departments operate as paramilitary organizations, with a strict hierarchy of authority and chain of command, some attention has been given of late to the idea of neighborhood policing or police teams. One of the largest cities to experiment with neighborhood police teams is New York City. It inaugurated a pilot program in neighborhood police teams in 1971, with one team in each of four of the city's seventy-five police precincts, later extending the program to sixty-six teams in forty precincts.

In the New York City program, a neighborhood police team consists of a sergeant and approximately twenty-three patrolmen. Most teams cover two sectors, defined as the area served by a patrol car and several foot patrolmen. In all, 17 percent of the city's sectors (137 out of 808) are covered by neighborhood police teams and over two thousand police officers are involved. The sergeant in charge of each neighborhood police team has discretion in utilizing police resources, including the setting of working hours for his staff. Since the neighborhood police team is intended to improve police-community relations, team members are expected to become better acquainted with people in the neighborhood, to meet with neighborhood groups, etc. The traditional definition of the police function, investigation and apprehension, is broadened to include providing aid to those in trouble and helping neighborhood residents to avoid trouble. Departmental policies have been modified or altered to coincide with and support the broadened role of the neighborhood police team in dealing with problems in the central city neighborhoods participating in the experiment.

A third experiment with bureaucratic decentralization is found in Washington, D.C., where local government has divided the District into nine service areas. Most (but not all) municipal agencies recognize these areas as administrative subdivisions for purposes of organizing the delivery of public services. The service area system is coordinated by the Community Services Division of the Office of Planning and Management in the District government. Each service area has an advisory committee that meets regularly to review local needs, discuss common problems as they bear upon both service delivery and area (neighborhood) conditions, agree upon measures to improve services, and make recommendations to District governmental institutions and officials.

Decentralization and Community Development

The developmental model of decentralization involves institutional arrangements for citizen participation that bypass established political and administrative officials in city government. Instead, the neighborhood itself is viewed as a framework for self-generated and self-supporting action and control. The community development or neighborhood corporation chartered by state or federal authorities and controlled by neighborhood residents is an example of this approach to decentralization. The corporation undertakes both economic activities and service delivery functions. Typically it is governed by a board of directors whose members are citizens residing in the neighborhood served by the organization. It is empowered to initiate development projects, contract for services, or provide such public functions or services as the residents may need. Unlike the preceding models of decentralization, the developmental model combines policymaking and administrative control in the hands of neighborhood residents. There is no formal responsibility to municipal officials, either elected or appointed. The neighborhood corporation remains ultimately responsible to the agency that chartered it and provides funds for its projects and operations. However, that relationship tends to emphasize only periodic financial and program accountability and does not involve officials or representatives of the chartering and funding agencies in the day-to-day operations and policy decisions of the corporation.

The War on Poverty and Model Cities programs were the first to make widespread use of citizen participation in community development programs. With these programs, the federal government established the requirement that citizens, especially those affected by programs and services, must be involved in all stages of program development and implementation. Furthermore, eligibility for federal antipoverty and Model Cities funds hinged upon demonstration that citizen participation in program decision making would be substantive and consequential. For the first time, citizen participation and decentralization were broadened to include a direct role for citizen-consumers in deciding which programs and services are to be pursued, at what levels, by which agencies, etc. Antipoverty and Model Cities programs forced established governmental institutions and officials in the city to relinquish varying degrees of control and authority over public programs and resources. This in itself was the source of open dispute and hostility between city hall and antipoverty/model cities clientele groups.

The particular arrangement for organizing the poor and involving them in decision-making systems varied considerably from one city to another and one program to another. A number of modes of participation are found. First, there was almost always a citywide antipoverty governing body, some of whose members were appointed by city officials and some chosen to represent the poor. The method of selecting the latter also varied, as some representatives of the poor were appointed either by a city official, often the mayor, or by the antipoverty governing body in the target neighborhoods, while other board members were elected by the poor themselves. Also, each antipoverty target neighborhood had its own citizen governing body for the programs, services, and activities provided in its area. Members of the neighborhood-based governing body were usually elected directly by residents of the target neighborhood. In some cases the poor were represented by social service agency professionals, whose clientele were largely the poor, as members of antipoverty governing boards. This approach reflected the view that agency professionals who work with the poor on a regular basis are in the best position to know their needs and preferences.

Whichever structure of participation was used, certain issues almost always emerged. The question of identifying the poor and deciding who could properly represent them posed a difficult problem. Then, too, the distribution of authority and responsibility between citywide and target neighborhood governing bodies gave rise to substantial disagreement. Third, the nature of the participatory role was a continual source of dispute. City government viewed the role of citizens as advisory, with ultimate decisions on programs and resources being made by public officials acting in that capacity. The poor and their representatives, on the other hand, defined the participatory role of the citizen-consumer as more controlling and decisional. From this perspective, the poor and their representatives were to make decisions rather than merely provide advice on poverty programs and services. At least one analysis of community action and citizen participation efforts pursued by antipoverty programs in the San Francisco Bay Area indicates that the conflict generated by these issues consumed the attention of poverty program personnel to such an extent that substantive goals, strategies, and action received an inadequate amount of attention from citizens and program staff alike.[17]

Model Cities expanded on the notion identified with the War on Poverty, namely, that the neighborhood and its residents could be the focus for developmental decentralization. Other arrangements for decentralization and citizen participation, such as little city halls and multiservice centers, had tended to view the neighborhood as a focus for services. With the Community Action Programs the neighborhood becomes the focus of citizen-based action through federally sponsored development programs and services.

Model Cities was more limited in scope, reflected in the fact that initial planning grants were awarded to only 150 cities throughout the nation. When the Department of Housing and Urban Development awarded these grants under the Demonstration Cities and Metropolitan Development Act of 1966, it sought to encourage recipient communities to form task forces consisting of citizens and agency professionals to comply with the requirement of "widespread citizen participation" in decisions concerning programs and services. However, the lessons of the War on Poverty led Congress to assign city government and not the citizen boards with final authority over programs and services at the local level. As with the Community Action Programs, different organizational arrangements were developed in various cities.

In Seattle, Washington, for example, the Model Cities program was controlled by city government but operated in conjunction with an elaborate network of neighborhood-based citizen participation. The top citizen body was the advisory council, consisting of one hundred members representing different organizations active in the Model Cities neighborhood. Nearly 90 percent of the advisory committee members were residents of the Model Cities area and the racial composition closely approximated that of the neighborhood. In addition, there were planning task forces for each of the functional programs undertaken. The initial organizational effort resulted in the creation of task forces, one each for housing, physical environment, education, welfare, employment, and health. Later on three more task forces were added for arts and culture, youth, and citizen participation.

Another approach to organizing citizens in the Model Cities program was developed in the city of Savannah, Georgia. When Savannah was awarded a HUD planning grant, the city manager moved to appoint a Model Cities director. A technical advisory committee of agency representatives was also created. Citizen participation was initiated with the convening of a mass meeting in the model neighborhood to discuss the planning process and to establish a citizen organization. A short time later, a second mass meeting in the model neighborhood was held and residents divided into three subneighborhood groups. Within each group, nine task forces were formed. A forty-three-member Model Neighborhood Council was organized with members appointed from the neighborhood subgroups and task forces. This council was assisted by an executive committee, whose membership included council members along with other public officials.

Planning funds from the city and other poverty agencies were used by the Model Neighborhood Council to identify program priorities in the model neighborhood. Throughout the program planning and approval processes, citizens' representatives on the task forces and the Model Neighborhood Council held an advisory role to the Model Cities director, the city manager, and ultimately the city council. Though the development and approval of program plans were not without controversy, unlike the War on Poverty, the Model Neighborhood Council was able to resolve its disputes and apparently accepted its advisory role.[18]

Neighborhood Government and Community Control of Schools

The governmental model of decentralization devolves the legal powers of the state on political subunits of the city by creating neighborhood-based governmental institutions.[19] In the case of central cities, the model establishes neighborhood governments with powers and responsibilities similar to those of suburban-based towns and villages. Each neighborhood government exercises substantial authority over the functions and activities within its boundaries and under its jurisdiction. This model does not eliminate the need for an administrative structure; it simply reduces its size and scale. Neighborhood governments would be responsible to their residents for programs and services and thus would require a bureaucracy to fulfill these obligations. However, it is presumed that such an administrative structure would exist on a small scale since it would not have to operate on a citywide basis. Needless to say, the number of such small-scale bureaucracies would be large, corresponding in rough measure to the number of neighborhood governments established throughout the city.

The problems posed by this model are considerable. In addition to the proliferation of administrative structures in each neighborhood government, important issues include territorial boundaries and population size, tax base and revenues, and state-city-neighborhood relationships for each neighborhood government. Perhaps this is why no neighborhood governments exist in American cities, though there are at least two experiments involving community control of schools. However, in the case of both Detroit and New York City, the authority of the neighborhood-based school governing bodies over educational policies and operations is carefully prescribed by enabling state legislation.

Exploratory efforts leading to decentralization and community control of New York City's schools began in 1967, when Mayor John V. Lindsay was asked by the state legislature to submit a school decentralization plan to the 1968 session of the legislature as a condition of the receipt of additional state aid. Lindsay's first step in compliance with this request was to create an

Advisory Panel on Decentralization of the New York City Schools, chaired by McGeorge Bundy, president of the Ford Foundation. In November of 1967, the advisory panel submitted its report to the mayor. It recommended that a citywide system of thirty to sixty community school districts be established. Each district would be governed by an eleven-member board, six of whose members would be elected by the eligible voters residing in the district and five appointed by the mayor.

The state legislature took up the Bundy Plan for decentralization of the schools during its 1968 session. The bill supported by Mayor Lindsay, Governor Nelson Rockefeller, and the State Board of Regents granted community school boards nearly complete control of their schools. A coalition of conservative legislators, the United Federation of Teachers, the Council of Supervisory Associations, and other union groups were able to block passage of the bill in the 1968 session. Their victory was partial and short-lived, however. In 1969, after considerable debate and political maneuvering, the state legislature enacted a school decentralization plan establishing a federated system with limited community control to take effect on July 1, 1970. The plan clearly was a compromise between continuation of the existing centralized system and a completely independent, community-based system of school governance. An interim board of education, consisting of one member appointed by each of the five borough presidents, was directed to appoint a chancellor of the city's school system and divide the city into thirty-one school districts. Each district, containing at least two hundred thousand students, was to be governed by a community school board composed of nine unsalaried members elected at large for a two-year term, using a system of proportional representation. The community school boards were to have jurisdiction over public schools from prekindergarten through junior high schools; senior high schools were to remain within the jurisdiction of the central, citywide board of education. The central board of education retained authority to suspend, remove, or supersede a community board or remove any of its members. In addition, the central board retained extensive financial and personnel powers, including the preparation of the capital budget and the disciplining and licensing of teaching personnel.[20]

School decentralization in Detroit came about more gradually and with considerably less overt hostility than in New York City. The first step involved administrative decentralization in 1969, when the city's school system was divided into nine districts and a deputy superintendent of schools was appointed to head each district. In 1970, the state legislature enacted a new law mandating the creation of eight regional school districts, effective January 1, 1971. Under provisions of this law, the governor was authorized to appoint a three-member Detroit Boundary Commission to draw up boundaries of regional school districts for electoral purposes. Each region was to be governed by a five-member board with the first election to be held in November of 1970. The member of each board receiving the most votes was to serve as chairperson and also as an ex-officio member of the citywide, central board of education. The central board of education was enlarged from seven to thirteen members; five were elected at large and eight were drawn from the regional boards.

As in the New York City decentralization plan, the central board retained responsibility for allocation of capital funds, contract negotiations, preparation of guidelines for the regional boards, and other accounting and management functions. And, as in the New York City arrangement, it was apparent that authority of regional boards in the areas of personnel and curriculum was circumscribed by a system of checks and balances in which the central board of education retained ultimate and overriding authority.

IMPACT OF DECENTRALIZATION ON CITY GOVERNMENT

It would not be appropriate to conclude our examination of decentralization in American cities without considering its impact on city government and politics. The large number of cities that have experimented with decentralized institutional arrangements is evidence of the fact that the community revolution has had a long-lasting and widespread impact on the government and politics of cities. Whether decentralization and citizen participation continue to be promoted by the federal government or not, experiences with neighborhood-based institutions, programs, and services are likely to affect perceptions and expectations of city government for some time to come.

Effects on Institutional Performance

One of the most comprehensive studies of decentralization and citizen participation strategies is by Robert K. Yin and Douglas Yates. It assesses 215 cases that run the gamut from administrative to political decentralization.[21]

Two factors seemed to be particularly relevant to differences between those strategies that were associated with positive outcomes and those that were not. These are the degree of professionalism and the scope of bureaucratic control in different areas of public service. Municipal services vary considerably in the degree of professionalism of service providers. Police protection and health, for example, are dominated by a highly professionalized personnel that sets the rules for service delivery. Citizen-consumers as clients have traditionally played little role in setting policy for these services, despite the fact that at the point of delivery the individual service provider, e.g., the cop on the beat, the public health nurse or doctor, exercises considerable discretion. In other services, however, opportunities for participation in decision making by clientele groups are more numerous and the structure of policymaking is less prescribed and traditional. In multiservice programs and economic development, for example, there is no dominant group of professionals and, in fact, the thrust of these efforts has been to establish a stronger sharing of responsibility between service providers and citizen-consumers. This is particularly true in the citizen participation requirements of Community Action Programs and Model Cities. Even in education, which purports to be a highly professionalized service with elaborate licensing and requirements for service providers (teachers and administrators), parents have traditionally enjoyed relatively easy access to facilities and activities. Joint parent-teacher organizations predate community control of schools and provide an established mechanism for the exchange of ideas between service providers and consumers.

The scope of bureaucratic control bears a decided relationship to the degree of professionalism. Highly professionalized services are also usually the most bureaucratized in their organization. Bureaucratization involves the existence of a hierarchical organization of authority, a chain of command, and a specific set of rules service providers are expected to follow. Though the discretion of the cop on the beat is clearly established, police services remain among the most bureaucratized of municipal services. In fact, the bureaucratic organization of police departments bears a close resemblance to military organizations. Services, like police protection, employing a highly bureaucratized organizational arrangement are not as "penetrable" by citizen-consumers as those that are loosely structured and traditionally open to citizen participation and control. Thus, improvements in highly bureaucratized services are a result of actions adopted and pursued by the service providers rather than consumers. Furthermore, there is relatively little opportunity for effecting control by consumers in the highly bureaucratized service areas.

The strong and moderate strategies for decentralization and citizen participation that produced positive outcomes in improved services and increased client control are the ones that involved the less professionalized and bureaucratic service organizations. Strong and moderate strategies involving the creation of new neighborhood-based institutions for economic develop- ment or the employment of citizen-consumers as service providers in community control of schools, poverty programs, and the like, placed greater political and economic resources in the hands of service deliverers and clients, creating a potent instrument for reshaping policy making and the service delivery system. Weak strategies for decentralization such as community relations programs, grievance mechanisms, physical redeployment of municipal agencies, and administrative decentralization involved little or a less substantial transfer of resources and administrative authority, producing a greater flow of information between service providers and users but little improvement in services and virtually no client control over decisions and policies.

The degree of professionalism and scope of bureaucratic control are not the only factors that bear upon the relationship between decentralization and the performance of public institutions and officials. At least two additional factors appear to affect the decentralization experience, and these do not inhere in the structure of administrative organization or control. They are, in a real sense, part of the political process of the city rather than its administrative arrangements and processes.

The first is the relationship between the municipal executive and decentralization, particularly the nature and degree of support by the mayor, manager, or local executive. Mayoral support for decentralization and citizen participation is particularly important not only for what it may mean for the availability of local resources, but also for what it may signal about the degree of cooperation or resistance from city hall.[22] Though our discussion of Community Action and Model Cities programs was brief, it is apparent that much time and effort were consumed in trying to wrest control of Community Action programs away from centralized officials in city hall. The experience of the antipoverty program in cities across the nation reveals a pattern of recurring conflict between municipal officials and leaders of target groups seeking to establish control of poverty resources, activities, and policies. In fact, conflict between city hall and citizen-dominated community action agencies contributed to some important changes in the Economic Opportunity Act between its initial enactment in 1964 and reauthorization in 1966. Congressmen from areas where conflict between central and local participants was particularly bitter and intense were instrumental in clarifying and tightening the intent of "maximum feasible participation" of the poor. Furthermore, as we already noted, when Model Cities was enacted in 1966 the phrase "widespread citizen participation" was substituted for the language of the War on Poverty and, perhaps more importantly, local government was designated as the official "sign-off" authority for applications for federal funds. In doing this, Congress made an explicit attempt to reduce the ambiguity and conflict over who had ultimate authority and control over Model Cities programs and moneys.

A second factor is the nature and extent of conflict within the local community as well as governing board and agency created to channel citizen participation. Here, too, we find that Community Action and Model Cities agencies devoted a major share of community and professional resources to resolving disputes among program clientele-participants over who "really" represented the poor, how they were to be chosen, and how much authority representatives of the poor should have in decisions bearing on program priorities, activities, and services. Conflict among participants increased along with the stakes. The consequence of internal conflict on citizen boards might not be that great except that on a number of occasions it overshadowed and replaced other important activities, such as making decisions on program priorities, submitting applications to funding agencies, and hiring personnel to operate programs or provide services to the clientele group. In a real sense, the service orientation of Community Action and Model Cities took on a secondary role to resolving internal disputes and establishing "control" of the programs' citizen board and local agency.

Effects on Urban Development

It is particularly difficult to judge the effects of decentralization on urban development, largely because the evidence on which such judgments are made is partial, tentative, and even impressionistic. However, it is possible to identify aspects of the decentralization experience that are likely to impact on the way the city's governmental institutions and political processes respond to the challenges of continued urban development.

One thing that is clear, for example, is that federal promotion of citizen participation and experimentation with a variety of decentralization plans by city governments have changed the nature of institutional decision making, probably irreversibly. Simply put, the *process* by which city governments make decisions concerning priorities among competing policies and programs, as well as alternatives for allocating public resources, is now more complex and time consuming than before. The dispersion of authority and structural fragmentation characteristic of city government in the past have been compounded by a vast number of citizen boards and advisory committees. In addition to the consultation, bargaining, and accommodation normally characteristic of relations between municipal executives and legislators, citizens' groups must now be involved, even if only on an advisory basis, before final decisions are made. Oftentimes contact with these groups is made by both the municipal executive and the legislative body. Notwithstanding the advisory nature of most participatory arrangements, the symbolism and legitimacy attached to citizen participation obligates municipal officials to comply with the ritualism of citizen review and input prior to decision making. It may very well be that decentralization has broadened the process of decision making in city government while simultaneously fragmenting the structure within which it operates. On balance, city government may not be as effective and decisive as before.

Another significant result of decentralization and citizen participation is that they have mobilized a potentially large and significant constituency in the central cities. The groups introduced to city politics by urban renewal, antipoverty, and Model Cities programs were for the most part uninvolved and almost invisible prior to the decade of the sixties. They have remained a politically significant force since that time and it seems reasonable to assume that, as time goes on, their political influence will continue. Evidence of this is seen in the ability of blacks and other minorities to elect their leaders to public office in city government.

The mobilization of previous quiescent groups has produced a countertendency, namely, the mobilization of the middle class to protect their own interests. Two examples of this phenomenon are sufficient to make the point. In the mid-1960s, New York City was considering a scatter-site public housing program. Under such an arrangement, people seeking housing assistance would be scattered in traditionally stable, middle-class neighborhoods rather than concentrated in geographically separate neighborhoods. Residents of a middle-class neighborhood identified as one of the target areas for such housing objected strenuously, arguing that the introduction of public housing and low-income residents would bring instability and decline to their community. As the conflict over the location of scatter-site housing deepened, residents of neighborhoods proposed for inclusion in the program invoked demands for community control, arguing that residents of target neighborhoods should have a voice in all relevant and necessary decisions. The controversy abated when city planners and other officials agreed to reduce the number of scatter-site housing units built in any single neighborhood.

The second example draws upon New York City's experience with community control of public schools and the response of the teachers' union. Immediately after enactment of the decentralization plan, the teachers' union urged opponents of community control to resist implementation by refraining from participation in elections to community school boards. Perhaps they thought that the legitimacy and credibility of community school boards would be undermined if voter turnout in elections was very poor. In fact, elections to community school boards and boards of education in general have historically attracted a very low percentage of eligible voters in most cities and suburbs. Be that as it may, the elections went forward and by the time the second round of community school board elections was scheduled, the strategy of the teachers' union had changed. This time it selected a small number of community school districts and put forward its own slate of endorsed candidates in each one. Evidently the change in strategy was a result of the union's recognition that community control was a fact of educational life and that community school boards were going to operate with or without the involvement of the teachers' union or other special interests. Influencing the outcome of elections to community school boards enables an organized interest to affect if not dictate such things as the selection of community school superintendents, selection of curricular materials, etc.

A final observation that can be made about the effect of decentralization concerns the expectations it has raised and the permanence of citizen-based institutions created by experiments with citizen participation. After only ten or fifteen years of practicing citizen participation through decentralization of public institutions, our cities now have an identifiable constituency and demand for such arrangements. Furthermore, this constituency now expects to be consulted by municipal officials and there are substantial political risks attached to failing to meet these expectations. Even if consultation is a formality and provides only advisory opinions, city residents who were previously unorganized and quiescent expect to be consulted by municipal officials and agencies before decisions on programs and services are made. It is not likely that such expectations are going to abate. On the contrary, based on experiences thus far, it seems reasonable to assume that demands for decentralization of city governmental institutions will continue and, perhaps, accumulate over time.

DECENTRALIZATION: THE RECORD THUS FAR

In the final analysis, the experience with decentralization and citizen participation in city government must be judged on two grounds: its ability to improve services and conditions in cities and its ability to open up the institutions and processes of government. Thus far, the record is incomplete and contradictory.

There are numerous examples of decentralization experiments that produced specific, tangible results. These tend to be the ones that are targeted to locally specific problems in neighborhoods. Also, they tend to focus on problems that can be effectively addressed by administrative responses, e.g., reallocation of existing resources, better communication between service providers and service consumers, or improved communication and coordination between central and field offices of municipal agencies. Experiments with political decentralization, especially those involving the War on Poverty, Model Cities, and community control of public schools, have produced less impressive results. Problems of development requiring the mobilization and participation of citizens in city government and politics seem too remote and diffuse to be effectively addressed with decentralization strategies. Furthermore, the problems of urban development that require sustained cooperation and coordination between city, metropolitan, state, or federal governments are least amenable to strategies of decentralization.

In view of these considerations, it seems reasonable to conclude by saying that decentralization can be most effective in dealing with problems in urban development that are focused and service-oriented. The governmental model of decentralization seems to be the least useful in urban development.

NOTES

1. Daniel Bell and Virginia Held, "The Community Revolution," *The Public Interest* 16 (Summer 1969): 142-77.

2. Janice E. Perlman, "Grassrooting the System," *Social Policy* 7 (September-October 1976): 4.

3. Richard A. Watson and John H. Romani, "Metropolitan Government for Metropolitan Cleveland," *Midwest Journal of Political Science* 5 (November 1961): 365-90, examines voting patterns in a central city on metropolitan government proposals.

4. See, for example, Robert L. Lineberry, *Equality and Public Policy: The Distribution of Municipal Public Services* (Beverly Hills, Calif.: Sage, 1977).

5. Public Law 88-452.

6. James Felser, "Approaches to the Understanding of Decentralization," *Journal of Politics* 27 (August 1965): 536-66.

7. Alan Altschuler, *Community Control: The Black Demand for Participation in Large American Cities* (New York: Pegasus, 1970), esp. pp. 62-65.

8. *Ibid.*, p. 64.

9. Robert K. Yin and Douglas Yates, *Street-Level Governments: Assessing Decentralization and Urban Services* (Santa Monica, Calif.: Rand Corporation, 1974), p. 29.

10. Suzanne Keller, *The Urban Neighborhood: A Sociological Perspective* (New York: Random House, 1968), esp. chap. 2, and Gerald D. Suttles, *The Social Order of the Slum: Ethnicity and Territory in the Inner City* (Chicago: The University of Chicago Press, 1968).

11. Douglas Yates, *Neighborhood Democracy: The Politics and Impacts of Decentralization* (Lexington, Mass.: D. C. Heath, 1973), pp. 25-28.

12. Henry J. Schmandt, "Decentralization: A Structural Imperative," in *Neighborhood Control in the 1970s: Politics, Administration, and Citizen Participation*, ed. H. George Frederickson (New York: Chandler Publishing, 1973).

13. G. J. Washnis, *Little City Halls* (Washington, D.C.: Center for Governmental Studies, 1971); J. E. Grollman, *The Decentralization of*

Neighborhood Services (Washington, D.C.: International City Management Association, 1971); and C. W. Stenberg, *The Grass-Roots Government: Decentralization and Citizen Participation in Urban Areas* (Washington, D.C.: Advisory Commission on Intergovernmental Relations, 1972).

14. See Eric Nordlinger, *Decentralizing the City: A Study of Boston's Little City Halls* (Cambridge, Mass.: M.I.T. Press, 1972).

15. See G. J. Washnis, *Municipal Decentralization and Neighborhood Resources* (New York: Praeger, 1972).

16. See P. Block and D. I. Sprecht, *Evaluation of Operation Neighborhood* (Washington, D.C.: The Urban Institute, 1973).

17. Nordlinger, *Decentralizing the City*.

18. See G. J. Washnis, *Community Development Strategies: Case Studies of Major Model Cities* (New York: Praeger, 1973).

19. Milton Kotler, *Neighborhood Government: The Local Foundations of Political Life* (Indianapolis: Bobbs-Merrill, 1969).

20. For an account of the controversy surrounding the New York City decentralization experience, see Maurice R. Berube and Marilyn Gittell, eds., *Confrontation at Ocean Hill-Brownsville* (New York: Praeger, 1969).

21. Yin and Yates, p. vii. Also, chap. 3 for a comprehensive analysis of the data on outcomes of decentralization strategies.

22. Washnis, *Little City Halls*.

CHAPTER X.

Urban Development and
the Challenges of Change and Survival

Introduction

Throughout this book we have argued that the capacity of governance institutions to manage the social changes associated with urban development is shaped by four patterns of behavior that developed during the early eighteenth and nineteenth centuries. These patterns remain important as governance institutions seek ways to cope with the experience of urban development under conditions that are vastly different from those facing American cities during earlier periods of urbanization. While the early experience of urbanization has been characterized as a challenge of change, the contemporary experience is more aptly characterized as a challenge of survival. In this concluding chapter we intend to show how the patterns of behavior presented at the outset of our discussion of urban development continue to influence the role governance institutions play in responding to the challenges presented by urban development.

INSTITUTIONAL RESPONSES IN URBAN DEVELOPMENT

Unifying and Diversifying Forces

The first pattern of behavior is the presence of forces that encourage either unity or diversity in urban America. In the eighteenth century the major unifying force was the English urban tradition, especially the governance institutions established by charters of incorporation. These charters created commercial communities which were primarily concerned with economic matters. Despite the fact that the corporation was the most popular form of governance in English cities in North America, the major colonial cities offered a vast array of governance arrangements, ranging from Boston's town meeting structure to virtually no structure in Charleston, South Carolina. With the end of royal or parliamentary control a second unifying force emerged, the similarities in the relationship of cities and the newly established state governments. This relationship continued as new states were admitted to the Union and new cities were incorporated. Just as eighteenth-century colonial cities were influenced by the governance institutions of the English cities, so too were the new cities appearing across the continental United States influenced by the patterns of governance found in the older cities of the original thirteen states.

These unifying influences have given rise to a unitary conception of cities. This conception has complicated the task of coping with the challenges of urban development because it encouraged reformers in the nineteenth and twentieth centuries to advance a single, unidimensional program to apply to all cities experiencing the problems associated with urban development. In the latter part of the nineteenth century, for example, reformers had great confidence in their ability to establish governance institutions that could effectively manage urban development. They also looked upon what had occurred in Europe, and especially in England, as something to be imitated. England had established in 1835 the English Municipal Corporations Act which was applied uniformly throughout the country, except in London. While this act allowed considerable freedom in matters of specific local services, it prescribed the general form of municipal government. This example of a unitary approach to the organization of municipal government greatly excited American reformers who formed in 1894 the National Municipal League. Five years later the league adopted a model municipal charter which it hoped would become the blueprint for change in American cities.[1]

Later reformers, as they confronted the great national problems, also saw possible solutions through the adoption of a national urban policy. A major proposal for a national urban policy was the 1937 report of the National Resources Committee. This committee entitled its report, *Our Cities—Their Role in the National Economy*, and included among its recommendations the formulation of a federal policy toward cities and revision of state laws and constitutions allowing greater home rule for cities. It also recommended the elimination in metropolitan areas of "atrophied authorities like the township, and [the fostering of] consolidation and cooperation among local urban governments."[2] These proposals did not lead to the formulation of a federal policy but they set forth the goal of greater federal involvement in responding to the problems of urban development. Since the Depression there has been a growing dependence of all units of local government on the federal government. This, in turn, has reinforced the unitary conception of urban development and the problems associated with it. A few examples show the ever-increasing role of the federal government as well as the persistence of the unitary conception of urban development.

Prior to the Housing Act of 1949 there was only a modest public housing program designed to replace the slums with subsidized housing for the poor. In 1949, however, urban renewal was added to existing federal efforts. Urban renewal was not a housing-for-the-poor program, but rather an attempt to eliminate substandard and inadequate housing through clearance of slums and blighted areas. It sought to provide a stronger tax base for cities by attracting private investment capital to the cleared areas. Two decades later, in 1961, new subsidy programs were enacted to support the building and management of housing for low-income groups by private nonprofit and limited-profit corporations, and for subsidized home ownership for the poor. The federal role in housing was expanded by the Housing and Urban Development Act of 1968 and, later, by the Housing and Community Development Act of 1974. Some have argued that these programs have created as many problems as they were designed to solve, some of which were worse than the original ones.[3]

The rather substantial list of public assistance programs enacted during the New Deal of Franklin D. Roosevelt did not constitute a federal program to combat poverty. Poverty is clearly more than an urban problem, with proportionally more poverty in nonurban areas than in the central cities. However, the worst problems of the cities have been associated with poverty and its related consequences. Despite this, the first comprehensive federal program to deal with poverty is only about fifteen years old. The War on Poverty was launched under the Economic Opportunity Act of 1964 and in some respects is still being waged on a greatly reduced scale. The poverty program and the subsequent Model Cities program enacted in 1966 channeled federal dollars and activities to particular areas of the central cities, i.e., those characterized by relatively high concentrations of the poor.

Most state governments have erected virtually insuperable barriers to the capacity of city governments to expand their territorial boundaries in response to population movements within the metropolitan area. As a result, central cities find themselves surrounded by autonomous, independent suburbs whose residents use the facilities and services of the city without having to underwrite much, if any, of the costs. Particularly in the Northeast and Midwest, central cities are hemmed in by fixed boundaries, unable to annex even adjacent unincorporated areas as a means of expanding their tax base.

The federal government has sought to foster greater cooperation and coordination between central cities and suburbs. Beginning in 1949, the federal government began to provide money for the development of comprehensive plans for local communities. To obtain urban renewal and other funds, cities were obliged to present master plans. If a city didn't have a master plan, federal money was available to develop one. Local and even regional planning agencies grew at a rapid pace. Particularly in the decade of the 1960s, the federal government conditioned eligibility for categorical grants for open space (1961), mass transportation (1964), sewer and water treatment facilities (1965), and land acquisition (1965) on the presentation of a comprehensive development plan for the area. Legislation enacted in 1966 and 1968 requires review and comment by a regional planning agency of federal aid projects with regional impact. Finally, in 1966, Congress provided additional support for planning through Title II of the Demonstration Cities and Metropolitan Development Act. Subsequent endeavors by the federal government to provide grants to cities in housing, manpower development, transportation, open space, poverty, and health facilities included provisions requiring review, comment, and often approval by planning agencies at the city, regional, and state levels.[4]

The decade of the 1970s offered yet another federal program premised on the unitary conception of urban development, as the Nixon administration worked for enactment of general revenue sharing. Prior to revenue sharing, virtually all federal moneys received by urban governments were in the form of categorical grants, a not-so-simple arrangement in which over seven hundred titles existed to fund improvements in virtually all areas of physical and social development. However, there existed not a single program of federal aid for general operations despite the fact that operating costs, e.g., salaries, wages, fringe benefits, utility bills, etc., made up as much as 70 percent of municipal budgets as the decade of the 1970s unfolded. Federal revenue sharing was advanced as a "no strings attached" program that would enable local officials to allocate resources in accordance with locally determined needs. For many cities the moneys available from general revenue sharing have only postponed the most crippling aspects of the revenue-expenditure imbalance.[5]

As the federal government continues to seek a workable urban policy it finds that both the ideology of reform, calling for a national urban policy, and the practicalities of pork-barrel politics lead to a unitary view of the problems and prospects of urban development. Such a view tends to discount the diversity evident in urban America. Every city is unique; each one reflects its past, its economic and social characteristics. The diversity of urban America depends upon location, size, economic developments, and racial and ethnic characteristics. It becomes ever more apparent with the realization that there are over 2300 cities with more than 10,000 people, each city having its own past. Federal policies have failed to manage the "urban crisis" because they have failed to come to reflect this diversity.

Influence of Socioeconomic Forces on Governance Institutions

The second pattern is the influence of socioeconomic forces on governance institutions in American cities. These forces shaped the development of cities and the structure of government which cities have used to manage growth and change.

By 1920 the typical industrial city specialized in a single product with most workers employed by the same enterprise. The movement from heterogeneity to homogeneity in the economic sphere is also reflected in a lack of balance in the class structure. The cities of the twentieth century are becoming more homogeneous. Part of this is due to the end of mass immigration, which has eroded the social mosaic found in the industrial city. The older industrial cities have become increasingly black and lower class, while suburban communities and the cities of the South and West have been becoming increasingly middle class.

Socioeconomic influences have been important factors in determining whether a city government was reformed. Some cities remained unreformed because of the economy of the city. If a city's economic life was dictated by a single primary industry, structural reform usually failed. If, on the other hand, the industry was largely diversified, with a white-collar work force, the city generally adopted structural reform. Social class was a related influence. The nature of the economy determines, along with other factors, the size of the middle class. If a city had a large middle class, it was generally reformed; if not, reform most likely failed.[6]

Today, socioeconomic influences also affect the character, extent, and success of the two major structural changes proposed for improving the management of urban development. These two reforms, metropolitan reorganization and community self-determination, are beyond the scope of the traditional urban governance institutions. The few successes in metropolitan government have occurred primarily in the rapidly growing metropolitan areas of the South while the alternative to governmental reorganization, interlocal functional cooperation, has been most successful in the middle-class communities of the West. Cities of the Midwest and Northeast have been unable to implement metropolitan reorganization or cooperative agreements with the surrounding suburbs.

Socioeconomic influences have also influenced the character and the success of the community revolution. Community power tends to be more effective when a neighborhood is middle class and united on a single issue. There are exceptions to this, however. New York City's school decentralization plan gave many black communities considerable power over their neighborhood schools. Ethnic groups in the cities have also used the community revolution to their advantage, as in the case of Italian-Americans in "The Hill" neighborhood of St. Louis.[7]

Numerous problems have been encountered by cities trying to respond to the demands of the community revolution. For one thing, neighborhood boundaries delineated for purposes of decentralization and citizen participation have had little resemblance to the "real" neighborhoods of a city; the former are little more than cartographical creations. Second, minority and low-income neighborhoods lack an interested and informed citizenry. And third, central authorities, either city or federal governments, are not interested in surrendering the power to make final and binding decisions to neighborhood groups.

Failure of Governmental Institutions to Meet the Challenges of Development

The third pattern, emphasizing the failure of governmental institutions to meet the challenges of development, led urban reformers to seek changes in existing governance institutions. After the Revolutionary War, for example, reformers urged the states to grant new charters to the cities. When this resulted in the subordination of cities to state government and the intervention of the state in local affairs, the municipal reform movement sought additional changes in the form of home rule, nonpartisan and at-large elections, and council-manager government. Yet, despite these efforts, virtually all cities failed to function effectively during the Depression.

The failure of local governance institutions to manage the conditions associated with the Depression led to a call for a national urban program. While such a program has never been fully and systematically articulated, since the 1930s the partnership between the federal government and the cities has become increasingly multifaceted and complex. Though lacking the authority to effect reorganization of government in metropolitan areas, the federal government has used its considerable role in urban development to prod local governments into a more coordinated and cooperative strategy for managing the consequences and challenges of change. Such mechanisms as regional planning and development agencies have been developed to overcome the legal and traditional autonomy of local governments in metropolitan areas.

Subordination of Cities to a Higher Authority

The fourth pattern, involving the subordination of cities to a higher authority, has been part of the experience of urban development from its outset in the eighteenth century. In the contemporary experience the authority of state governments has been superseded by the expanded role and influence of the federal government. Cities, especially those in the older industrial states of the Northeast and Midwest, have looked to Washington, D.C., for assistance in meeting the challenges of survival in the 1970s. They have found not only assistance from the federal government, but fiscal and administrative subordination as well. The fiscal crisis in New York City has brought the subordination of cities to a higher authority into sharp focus.

The reasons for the crisis are many and can be found to some degree in all industrial cities. Since the 1920s the cities were expected to absorb newcomers who are poor while their middle class moved to the suburbs. The result is that the central city becomes the home of the lower classes, those most in need of public assistance in one form or another. Between 1950 and 1970 New York City's population over sixty-five increased from 8 percent to 12 percent and the percentage of families below the national median income level rose from a little over one-third to nearly one-half. Demands for services increased at the same time that revenue sources declined. In Chapter VII we documented the loss of jobs in the older industrial cities after 1960. In New York City the number of private sector jobs dropped from 3,130,000 in 1960 to 2,803,000 in 1975. New York City's problems are compounded by the fact that for a variety of reasons, including history, tradition, and state law, it has provided for its population many services not available from other city governments. These include free public higher education, operation of city hospitals to serve the lower classes, and carrying approximately one-fourth of the cost of welfare. Other pressures of the city's resources are the relatively high wages and substantial retirement benefits paid to municipal employees. These benefits are due to the tradition of strong unions and the high cost of living in New York City.[8]

New York City's financial burdens are not substantially different from those of other cities. Moreover, the fiscal crisis was not sudden, nor was it totally unexpected. The refusal in 1975 of banks to purchase the city's notes or bonds led to the prospect of bankruptcy for New York and threatened the ability of other cities to borrow.

Financial assistance from state and federal governments has been tied to a number of conditions and restrictions which substantially alter the traditional autonomy of local government. In fact, some would go so far as to say that New York City government now operates as a ward of the Emergency

Financial Control Board and the Senate Banking Committee. The board was established by the state government to oversee city hall's financial dealings; it exercises extraordinary powers, including prior approval over labor contracts, authority over all incoming city revenues, and approval of all city budgets. The board is made up of the governor as chairman, the mayor, the city controller, and three appointees of the governor; the executive director is appointed jointly by the governor and the mayor. New York State also created a Municipal Assistance Corporation empowered to sell bonds and short-term notes as well as buy municipal bonds from the city to help finance its capital budget. These measures were contingent upon receipt by New York City of federal loan guarantees, the legislation for which was recommended to the U.S. Senate by its Banking Committee. The chairman of that committee, Senator William Proxmire, has been portrayed as the viceroy of New York City.[9]

New York City government has had to pay a heavy price for assistance from state and federal governments. Local autonomy has been curtailed in the extreme and city officials have to make quarterly financial reports to the Senate Banking Committee and the Department of the Treasury to remain eligible for federally guaranteed loans. Moreover, the Control Board and MAC are regularly and decisively involved in the most important aspects of local government operation.

SCARCITY, ABUNDANCE, AND THE PUBLIC CITY

In the opening chapter we suggested that two cyclical movements have been present in urban development. These are the movement from scarcity to abundance and from "private" city to public city. Together, they shape popular attitudes about the role of governance institutions in managing the problems associated with urban development as well as the availability of resources with which governments meet the challenges of change and survival that are part of the urban development experience. In subsequent chapters we have tried to show how urban America moved from scarcity to abundance and from "private" city to public city. The challenge of change in urban development was made possible by the increasing abundance of resources and the expanding role of governance institutions in managing the development experience. Today, the challenge of survival is brought on by an increasing scarcity of resources at a time when public institutions are expected to play a substantial role in managing urban development.

The 1970s have seen a return of the threat of scarcity in urban society. How this will affect the role of governance institutions is very much an open question, but it is certain that scarcity will necessitate a change in the role of government and the expectations people have of that role. President Carter's proposed urban policy seeks in part to stimulate the economic redevelopment of central cities, reflecting the need to regulate and allocate scarce economic resources. Taxpayer revolts such as that experienced in the passage of Proposition 13 in California in 1978 are omens of a return to scarcity; citizens are becoming less willing to pay for the activities and functions of state and local governments.

The decade of the 1970s has also witnessed a movement back to the private city. The expansion of public services by governance institutions in urban areas that characterized the late nineteeth and early twentieth centuries has been curtailed, if not terminated. The number and variety of services, especially those involving public assistance for those unable to care or provide for themselves, are being reduced. At the local level, services like police protection, fire protection, and sanitation are about the only activities likely to escape severe cutbacks. Other services, including education, are experiencing cutbacks and reductions in funding levels, programs, and personnel.

URBAN DEVELOPMENT IN DETROIT AND HOUSTON

What we have been saying about the role of governance institutions in urban development is seen in the experiences of Detroit and Houston. These two cities have had different experiences in urban development, yet they both exemplify the patterns of behavior that shape the role of governance institutions as well as the two cyclical movements in the development experience. Detroit, a city of the industrial age, is typical of the aging, deteriorating, industrial cities in the Midwest and Northeast. Houston, a product of the space age, is one of the largest and fastest growing cities in the Sunbelt.[10]

One reason for the vast differences between the apparent well-being of cities in the South and West compared to the cities in the Midwest and Northeast is the ability of the former to keep their economic and legal boundaries coterminous. This is made possible by state legislation that permits central cities to annex adjacent unincorporated areas without the approval of the people residing in those areas. For example, in 1958 the Texas legislature enacted legislation permitting local governments to draw a line five miles around their perimeter exclusively for annexation purposes. This law, as well as earlier favorable legislation, has allowed Houston to increase its size from 45,950 acres to 319,040 acres between 1930 and 1973. On the other hand, the

1961-1962 constitutional convention in Michigan reaffirmed the autonomy and inviolability of rural townships by refusing to abolish township government as a separate and distinct entity. Thus Detroit's size in 1930 was 88,260 and in 1973, 88,320 acres. So, in Michigan as in many other states in the Midwest and Northeast, cities have the same boundaries they had in the 1930s, despite the fact that their "sphere of influence" and socioeconomic-political patterns are interdependent with those of the small, independent, adjacent units of government. Cities are thus unable to follow population growth to outlying areas.[11]

A second reason for the different development experiences of Detroit and Houston is the fact that one is a city of the industrial era and the other is a city of the postindustrial era. Fifty years ago Detroit was a prosperous, dynamic central city. The automobile boom combined with the diversified industrial economy to generate a population growth from 286,000 in 1900 to 1,569,000 in 1930. Industrial growth brought hundreds of thousands of dwellers from the rural South. The automobile and the overflow of industry from Detroit provided the basis for the development of outlying suburban communities and contiguous industrial cities like Dearborn and Hamtramck.

By 1973, Detroit's population had declined to 1,386,000 while the suburbs increased from 609,000 in 1930 to 2,804,000. Indicative of the acceleration of this trend is the fact that the city of Detroit has lost 300,000 people since 1960, while the suburbs have experienced a population increase of some 800,000. By way of contrast, Houston's population in 1930 was approximately what Detroit's was in 1900. By 1973, Houston had grown to 1,296,000 and the suburban population reached 856,000. Since 1960, Houston's population has increased by 360,000 while the suburban population has increased by 375,000.[12]

To understand the different circumstances and futures facing Detroit and Houston we must examine the sociohistorical development of each. Detroit's growth as a city was generated by the Industrial Revolution. The characteristics of its population, form of government, and economy reflected this. The financial, economic, and political power was in the hands of the city's industrial elite. After 1890 the industrial commercial elite had to share power both with representatives of the working class, i.e., politicians like Hazen Pingree, and later with automobile executives. Beginning in 1937, with the unionization of the automobile plants, and culminating in the postwar period, economic power in Detroit was shared by the union leadership and the auto and banking interests.

Houston on the other hand has had a different development. Its great age of expansion was in the postindustrial era. The same is true of its suburbs. Its prosperity is due to a rapid population growth during the postindustrial era, an economy and labor force reflecting this growth, a lack of a tradition of providing extensive government services to its citizens, and the ability to annex the outlying areas. Houston's economy is based on the oil and space industries. Oil is a natural resource that not only has provided an industry for Houston but also an income. Millions of dollars flow into the city treasury from oil reserves on city-owned lands. Houston lacks either a tradition of extensive public services or a population that demands such services. Texas cities, as with many of the prosperous cities of the South, do not provide money for higher education, for welfare matching, or for many other social programs that are common in the North. As a result Houston has a surplus of millions of dollars each year, as well as relatively low property taxes. These low taxes draw businesses to Houston, which in turn draw middle-class residents. The population growth of Houston does not keep up with its physical expansion. Despite the fact that Houston has the same population as Detroit, its density has decreased from 6.3 persons per acre in 1930 to 4.0 persons per acre in 1973. Detroit's density is four times that of Houston.[13]

In a comparison of Detroit and Houston one finds the four patterns that have shaped urban development experiences. The former mayor of Houston, Fred Hofheinz, saw little difference between Detroit and Houston except that the latter has been more frugal in providing services and spending taxpayers' dollars. As a result, he did not feel any special obligation toward the older cities of the North. His approach to revenue sharing was to distribute dollars according to population; every unit of government would get something whether they needed it or not. This is a common expression of those who hold the unitary conception of urban development. Mayor Young of Detroit describes Hofheinz's perspective as that of "the greedy versus the needy." Yet, Hofheinz's view is the one generally held in America and is the general approach we take to solving our urban problems. It reflects the unitary perspective.[14]

The second pattern found in Detroit and Houston is the influence of socioeconomic forces on governance institutions. Detroit is a city created by the Industrial Revolution. It is a city of single-family dwellings, blue-collar workers, and powerful unions. Its mayor in 1978, Coleman Young, is a product of the streets and of the battles of unionization. He is also black. Houston, on the other hand, is a creation of the petroleum and space industries. It has its poor, but the poor have little power and receive few services; power rests in the hands of an expanding middle class and economic interests that dominate the two major industries. Its governance institutions provide only the most basic services; other services are purchased by the middle class. Former Mayor Fred Hofheinz is white, well-educated, and wealthy.

The third pattern is the dissatisfaction with existing governance institutions. In Detroit, Young shows his dissatisfaction by demanding an increase in assistance from the federal government. On the other hand, the white middle class shows its dissatisfaction simply by moving out. The middle class of Houston is satisfied, while the lower class remains restless. Yet, the lower classes are without any real political power.

Detroit's problems are compounded by the lack of growth. Since 1960 the city has lost nearly 25 percent of its private sector jobs. Despite the investment of $330 million in the Renaissance Center real economic expansion is taking place in the outlying suburbs. Houston's problems, on the other hand, result from continued growth. The critics of Houston's success argue that it is close to beginning a long, slow slide from boom to bust. Houston lacks planning and zoning and its low taxes and commitment to laissez-faire growth could well lead to disaster within a decade. Houston's laissez-faire approach has led to increasing air and water pollution, greater racial tensions, higher crime rates, and serious problems with basic services. Thirty-seven suburban neighborhoods annexed more than twenty years ago are still without city water and sewer service. As a result parts of Houston are becoming more vulnerable to floods and outlying areas are sinking up to six inches a year as the water table drops. Also, Houston's police force is undermanned; it is less than one-half the size of Detroit's. As a result middle-class neighborhoods hire their own private security guards.[15]

The fourth pattern, the subordination of cities to a higher authority, is evident in both Houston and Detroit. Houston's growth is made possible by favorable action of the Texas state legislature. Detroit, on the other hand, has been unable to expand because of restrictive state laws. The federal government has also been involved in shaping the futures of Detroit and Houston. Houston has benefited from the very lucrative government contracts given to space industries. On the other hand Detroit has suffered from expressway building programs that have facilitated the exodus of the middle class and industry.

Houston has always had a tradition of privatism. There has never been a great deal of concern about the lower classes, and inner-city Chicano and black neighborhoods have few city services. Middle-class neighborhoods hire their own gardeners to care for nearby city parks while private security guards are hired to patrol the streets; garbage collection and other services are also turned over to private enterprise. They have little interest in supporting such services as libraries and recreational activities. Detroit is also being forced to return to privatism. Its police are unable to protect businesses and the few middle-class neighborhoods that remain. So, as in Houston, private security guard companies represent one of the fastest growing service industries. Also in Detroit, the state police have taken over patrolling the expressways within the city; garbage pickup has been greatly reduced and may be ended all together. Snow removal occurs only on the major streets and the side streets depend on the efforts of local residents.

Privatism is also seen in New York City, where, because of the fiscal crisis, it has had to enact tuition charges in the previously free city university system. At the same time thousands of public service employees have been either laid off or paid through funds provided by the Comprehensive Employment and Training Act (CETA) of 1973. Other cities of the Northeast and Midwest are also ending or reducing their support for such institutions as museums, symphony orchestras, and zoos.

A CONCLUDING NOTE

We have not attempted in this book to offer solutions for urban ills or to forecast the future of urban areas. Rather, we have provided an understanding of how governance institutions have attempted to manage the social changes associated with the urban development experience. To do this, we have suggested that four patterns of behavior have influenced the role of governance institutions. Moreover, two cyclical movements have characterized the urban development experience.

Whether cities experiencing specific problems of urban development manage those problems effectively remains open to question. Perhaps the experience of New York City provides an object lesson that other older central cities in the Midwest and Northeast might profitably draw upon. However, it will probably not be possible for the older industrial cities to copy the developmental pattern and experience of the newer Sunbelt cities like Houston or Phoenix. The most appropriate admonition we can offer at this point is to urge those responsible for managing the problems of urban development to understand the patterns of behavior that influence the role of governance institutions in the development experience. An understanding of this sort seems a logical and reasonable starting point for dealing with the problems associated with urban development.

NOTES

1. Albert Shaw, "The City in the United States—The Proper Scope of Its Activities," in *A Municipal Program*, compiled for the National Municipal League (New York: Macmillan, 1900), pp. 59-60.

2. Urbanism Committee to the National Resources Committee, *Our Cities: Their Role in the National Economy* (Washington, D.C.: United States

Government Printing Office, 1937; reprint ed., New York: Arno Press, 1974), pp. 79-81.

3. See Frank deLeeuw, Ann B. Schnare, and Raymond J. Struyk, "Housing," in *The Urban Predicament*, eds. William Gorham and Nathan Glazer (Washington, D.C.: The Urban Institute, 1976), and Marian Lief Palley and Howard Palley, *Urban America and Public Policies* (Lexington, Mass.: D. C. Heath, 1977), especially chap. 7.

4. Gorham and Glazer, chap. 1, "Introduction and Overview."

5. See George E. Peterson, "Finance," in Gorham and Glazer; also Palley and Palley, chap. 3.

6. Richard M. Bernard and Bradley R. Rice, "Political Environment and the Adoption of Progressive Reform," *Journal of Urban History* 1 (February 1975): 149-74.

7. Norton E. Long, "Have Cities a Future?" *Public Administration Review*, November/December 1973, pp. 545, 551; Maurice R. Berube and Marilyn Gittell, eds., *Confrontation at Ocean Hill-Brownsville* (New York: Praeger, 1969).

8. Palley and Palley, pp. 259-65.

9. For examples of articles on the New York City fiscal crisis, see *The New York Times*, May 21, 1978, p. E7; May 28, 1978, p. 21; March 28, 1978, p. 1; for a comparison of per capita spending among major cities see November 21, 1976, sec. E.

10. John S. Adams and Ronald Abler, *A Comparative Atlas of America's Great Cities* (Minneapolis: University of Minnesota Press, 1976), pp. 149-58, 200-18+.

11. Advisory Commission on Intergovernmental Relations, *Trends in Metropolitan Government* (Washington, D.C., 1977), pp. 17-19.

12. *Ibid.*

13. *Ibid.*, pp. 11 and 13.

14. See *The New York Times* December 1976 for articles on the U.S. Conference of Mayors; see also David C. Perry and Alfred J. Watkins, eds., *The Rise of the Sunbelt Cities* (Beverly Hills, Calif.: Sage, 1978).

15. *The New York Times*, December 16, 1977, p. B1+; Heinz Kohler, *Economics and Urban Problems* (Lexington, Mass.: D. C. Heath, 1973), p. 81.

Selected Bibliography

Chapter I. Introduction: Understanding Urban Development

The nature and consequences of urbanization in America have been the subject of a number of major studies. Many take a negative or pessimistic view, arguing that central cities may not be able to deal effectively with current problems. Included among these are Mitchell Gordon, *Sick Cities* (New York: Macmillan, 1963); Jane Jacobs, *The Death and Life of Great American Cities* (New York: Random House, 1961); Jeanne R. Lowe, *Cities in a Race with Time* (New York: Random House, 1967); and Nathan Glazer, (ed.), *Cities in Trouble* (Chicago: Quadrangle, 1970). A different and possibly a more optimistic view on the condition of American cities is presented in Edward C. Banfield, *The Unheavenly City: The Nature and Future of Our Urban Crisis* (Boston: Little, Brown, 1970) and *The Unheavenly City Revisited* (1974).

Studies examining the ability of governmental institutions in urban areas to meet the challenges of urbanization have tended to emphasize the need for new structures to provide expanded public services, functions, and activities. Representative of these studies are the Committee for Economic Development, *Modernizing Local Government* (New York, 1966) and *Reshaping Government in Metropolitan Areas* (New York, 1970); Robert O. Warren, *Government in Metropolitan Regions: A Reappraisal of Fractionated Political Organization* (Davis, California: Institute of Governmental Affairs, 1966); Milton Kotler, *Neighborhood Government: The Local Foundations of Political Life* (Indianapolis, Indiana: Bobbs-Merrill, 1969); and Alan A. Altshuler, *Community Control: The Black Demand for Participation in Large American Cities* (New York: Pegasus, 1970).

John Harrigan, *Political Change in the Metropolis* (Boston: Little, Brown, 1976) is of particular interest because of its focus on the nature of institutional changes that occur during urban development.

More recently a number of books have attempted to illuminate the relationship between the structure of a city's governmental institutions and the process of urban problem-solving. The approaches and conclusions in these books have brought them considerable acclaim, both positive and negative. One such study is Edward C. Banfield, *The Unheavenly City* (Boston: Little, Brown, 1970); others are Norton Long, *The Unwalled City: Reconstituting the Urban Community* (New York: Basic Books, 1972) and Douglas Yates, *The Ungovernable City* (Cambridge, Massachusetts: The M.I.T. Press, 1977).

Chapter II. Urban Government in the Eighteenth Century

Important studies detailing the functions of urban government in the seventeenth and eighteenth centuries include the brief but important work of Jon C. Teaford, *The Municipal Revolution in America: Origins of Modern Urban Government, 1650-1825* (Chicago: The University of Chicago Press, 1975) and the detailed, but dated, study by Ernest S. Griffith, *A History of American City Government: The Colonial Period* (New York: Oxford University Press, 1938). Other works by these two authors include Teaford's "City versus States: The Struggle for Legal Ascendancy," *The Journal of Legal History* 17 (January 1973): 51-65; Griffith's *The Modern Development of City Government in the United Kingdom and the United States*, 2 vols. (London: Oxford University Press, 1927); *A History of American City Government: The Conspicuous Failure, 1870-1900* (New York: Praeger, 1974); and *The Progressive Years and Their Aftermath, 1900-1920* (New York: Praeger, 1974). These last two works by Griffith are detailed but lack analysis. A good collection of documents on colonial municipal government is Thomas Harrison Reed and Paul Webbink, (eds.), *Documents Illustrative of American Municipal Government* (New York: The Century Company, 1926).

General works which should be consulted include Carl Bridenbaugh's two excellent studies, *Cities in the Wilderness: The First Century of Urban Life in America* (New York: Ronald Press, 1938) and *Cities in Revolt: Urban Life in America, 1743-1776* (New York: Knopf, 1955); John W. Reps, *The Making of Urban America: A History of City Planning* (Princeton: Princeton University Press, 1965); and Constance McLaughlin Green's brief survey, *The Rise of Urban America* (New York: Harper & Row, 1965).

For an extended investigation into the New England town one should begin with Charles Francis Adams, et al., *The Genesis of the Massachusetts Town* (Cambridge, Mass.: John Wilson and Son, 1892), which is a dated but interesting study. Edward M. Cook examines the diversity of urban life in "Local Leadership and the Typology of New England Towns, 1700-1785," *Political Science Quarterly* 84 (December 1971); 585-608. James A. Henretta describes the increasing class distinctions in Boston in "The Economic Development and Social Structure in Colonial Boston," *William and Mary Quarterly*, 3d ser., 22 (January 1965): 75-92. An excellent study of a New England town is Kenneth A. Lockridge, *A New England Town: The First Hundred Years* (New York: W.W. Norton, 1970).

Other relevant works include Judith Diamondstone, "Philadelphia's Municipal Corporation, 1701-1776," *Pennsylvania Magazine of History and Biography* 90 (April 1966): 183-201, which is based on her dissertation. One might also see Howard L. McBain, "The Legal Status of the American Colonial City," *Political Science Quarterly* 41 (June 1925): 177-200 and Richard G. Miller, *Philadelphia, the Federalist City: A Study of Urban Politics, 1789-1801* (Port Washington, N.Y.: Kennikat Press, 1976).

Chapter III. Urban Governance in the Nineteenth Century

General works which deal with urban government in the nineteenth century include William B. Munro, *The Government of American Cities* (New York: Macmillan, 1912); Thomas Harrison Reed, *Municipal Government in the United States* (New York: Century, 1926); John A. Fairlie, "Municipal Development in the United States" in *A Municipal Program* (New York: The National Municipal League, 1900); Ernest S. Griffith, *A History of American City Government: The Conspicuous Failure, 1870-1900* (New York: Praeger, 1974); Blake McKelvey, *The Urbanization of America, 1860-1915* (New Brunswick, N.J.: Rutgers University Press, 1974); and Kenneth Fox, *Better City Government: Innovation in American Politics 1850-1937* (Philadelphia: Temple University Press, 1977).

Adna Ferrin Weber documents the growth of cities both in the United States and the world in *The Growth of Cities in the Nineteenth Century* (New York: Macmillan, 1889). It is this growth, combined with industrialization, that generates an urban crisis in the nineteenth century. Aspects of this crisis are discussed in George R. Taylor, *The Transportation Revolution, 1815-1860* (New York: Harper & Row, 1951); Sam Bass Warner, *The Private City: Philadelphia's Three Periods of Growth* (Philadelphia: University of Pennsylvania Press, 1968); David Ward, *Cities and Immigrants* (New York: Oxford University Press, 1971); Nelson M. Blake, *Water for the Cities* (Syracuse: Syracuse University Press, 1956); William H. Bullough, *Cities and Schools in the Gilded Age: The Evolution of an Urban Institution* (Port Washington, New York: Kennikat Press, 1975); Lawrence A. Cremin, *The Transformation of the School:*

Progressivism in American Education, 1876-1957 (New York: Knopf, 1961); and James F. Richardson, *The Urban Police in the United States* (Port Washington, New York: Kennikat Press, 1975).

The transition of the American city from the "private city" to "public city" is discussed in Sam Bass Warner, *The Private City: Philadelphia in Three Periods of Its Growth* (Philadelphia; University of Pennsylvania Press, 1968); and in Bayrd Still, "Patterns of Mid-Nineteenth Century Urbanization in the Middle West," *Mississippi Valley Historical Review* 28 (September 1941): 187-206.

Chapter IV. Political Machines and Urban Development

One of the best recent studies of political machines and machine politics is found in Raymond E. Wolfinger, *The Politics of Progress* (Englewood Cliffs, N.J.: Prentice-Hall, 1974). The classic study is Harold F. Gosnell, *Machine Politics: Chicago Style* (Chicago: University of Chicago Press, 1937); the second edition of this study, published in 1968, contains an excellent Foreword by Theodore Lowi.

One of the earliest machines was the Tweed Ring. For differing interpretations of this machine see Seymour Mandelbaum, *Boss Tweed's New York* (New York: John Wiley, 1965); Alexander B. Callow, Jr., *The Tweed Ring* (New York: Oxford University Press, 1966); and Leo Hershkowitz, *Tweed's New York: Another Look* (Garden City, N.Y.: Anchor, 1977). Other case studies that have attempted to see the more positive aspects of political machines are Zane L. Miller, *Boss Cox's Cincinnati* (New York: Oxford University Press, 1968); and William D. Miller, *Mr. Crump of Memphis* (Baton Rouge, La.: Louisiana State University Press, 1964). A dated but interesting comparative study of political machines is Harold Zink, *City Bosses in the United States* (Durham, N.C.: Duke University Press, 1930).

For a romantic view of the way machine politics operated see William L. Riordon, *Plunkitt of Tammany Hall* (New York: McClure, Phillips, 1905). Descriptions of the functioning of machine politics are found in Robert K. Merton, *Social Theory and Social Structure* (New York: The Free Press, 1957), pp. 71-82; Frank R. Kent, *The Great Game of Politics* (New York: Doubleday, 1928); and the essays in *The Annals of the American Academy of Political and Social Science* (May 1964).

Chapter V. Municipal Reform and Institutional Change in the Cities

Representative of the muckrakers' exposé of political machines and bossism is Lincoln Steffens, *The Shame of the Cities* (1904; reprinted., New York: Hill and

Wang, 1957). See also the *Autobiography of Lincoln Steffens* (New York: Harcourt, Brace & World, 1931). In Melvin G. Holli, *Reform in Detroit: Hazen S. Pingree and Urban Politics* (New York: Oxford University Press, 1969), social reformers are distinguished from structural reformers. Finally, Richard Hofstadter, *The Age of Reform* (New York: Alfred A. Knopf, 1955), should be read by students interested in the intellectual and social origins of the progressive reform movement. An excellent overview of urban politics is Edward C. Banfield and James Q. Wilson, *City Politics* (Cambridge, Mass.: Harvard University Press, 1963).

The application of reform ideology to municipal governmental institutions and political processes resulted in numerous structural changes. These are treated in many studies, including John Porter East, *Council-Manager Government: The Political Thought of Its Founder, Richard S. Childs* (Chapel Hill: University of North Carolina Press, 1965); Richard S. Childs, *Civic Victories: The Story of an Unfinished Revolution* (New York: Harper & Row, 1952); Richard J. Stillman, II, *The Rise of the City Manager* (Albuquerque: University of New Mexico Press, 1974); Bradley Robert Rice, *Progressive Cities: The Commission Government Movement in America, 1901-1920* (Austin: University of Texas Press, 1977); E.S. Bradford, *Commission Government in American Cities* (New York: Macmillan, 1911).

Changes in electoral rules and systems were an integral part of the program of progressive reform. Among the more helpful studies of this dimension of reform are Marvin A. Harder, *Nonpartisan Election: A Political Illusion?* (New York: Holt, Rinehart and Winston, 1958); Willis D. Hawley, *Non-partisan Elections and the Case for Party Politics* (New York: John Wiley, 1973); Eugene C. Lee, *The Politics of Nonpartisanship: A Study of California City Elections* (Berkeley: University of California Press, 1960); William B. Munro (ed.), *The Initiative, Referendum, and Recall* (New York: Macmillan, 1913); and Ralph Straetz, *PR Politics in Cincinnati* (New York: New York University Press, 1958).

Chapter VI. Aftermath of Reform

A number of studies provide background for the aftermath of reform. Ernest S. Griffith, *A History of American City Government: The Progressive Years and Their Aftermath, 1900-1920* (New York: Praeger, 1974) is a detailed study, but reflects the bias of the National Municipal League. Bradley Robert Rice, *Progressive Cities: The Commission Government Movement in America, 1901-1920* (Austin: University of Texas, 1977) documents the origins, spread, and decline of the commission idea. Richard J. Stillman, *The Rise of the City Manager* (Albuquerque: University of New Mexico Press, 1974) is a study on the origins and the development of the city manager profession. Kenneth Fox, *Better City Government: Innovation in American Politics, 1850-1937* (Philadelphia: Temple University Press, 1977) discusses the reasons for the success or failure of reformers to improve urban government.

Recent studies of city manager government and city managers include David A. Booth, *Council-Manager Government, 1940-1964: An Annotated Bibliography* (Chicago: International City Management Association, 1965); Arthur W. Bromage, *Urban Policy Making: The Council-Manager Partnership* (Chicago: Public Administration Service, 1970); Gladys M. Kammerer, *et al.*, *The Urban Political Community: Profiles in Town Politics* (Boston: Houghton Mifflin, 1963); Ronald O. Loveridge, *City Managers in Legislative Politics* (Indianapolis: Bobbs-Merrill, 1971); Keith F. Mulrooney (ed.), "Symposium on the American City Manager," *Public Administration Review*, 31 (January-February, 1971): 6-46; Clarence E. Ridley, *The Role of the City Manager in Policy Formulation* (Chicago: International City Management Association, 1958); Frank P. Sherwood, *A City Manager Tries to Fire His Police Chief* (Indianapolis, Ind.: Bobbs-Merrill, 1963); and Richard J. Stillman, II, *The Modern City Manager: A 1971 Profile* (Washington, D.C.: International City Management Association, 1971).

A very relevant article on the aftermath of progressivism is Richard M. Bernard and Bradley Robert Rice, "Political Environment and the Adoption of Progressive Municipal Reform," *Journal of Urban History*, 2 (February 1975): 149-174. Two important works which record the history of the National Municipal League are Frank Mann Stewart, *A Half Century of Municipal Reform* (Berkeley: University of California Press, 1950); and Alfred Willoughby, "The Involved Citizen: A Short History of the National Municipal League," *National Civic Review* (December 1969): 519-564.

Two examples of studies of reformed governments are A. Theodore Brown, *The Politics of Reform: Kansas City's Municipal Government, 1925-1950* (Kansas City: Community Studies, 1958); and Kenneth Gray, *A Report of City Politics in Cincinnati* (Cambridge, Massachusetts: Joint Center for Urban Studies, 1961). Alternatives to the more traditional type of reform are discussed in John C. Bollens, *Appointed Executive Local Government: The California Experience* (Los Angeles: Haynes Foundation, 1952); Seymour Freedgood, "New Strength in City Hall," in *The Exploding Metropolis* (Garden City, New York: Doubleday, 1958); and James Q. Wilson, *The Amateur Democrat Club Politics in Three Cities* (Chicago: University of Chicago Press, 1966).

The failure of reformers to make the city more livable is described in Theodore J. Lowi, *The End of Liberalism* (New York: W.W. Norton, 1969); Edward N. Costikyan, *Behind Closed Doors* (New York: Harcourt, Brace and

World, 1966); Richard A. Cloward and Frances Fox Piven, *The Politics of Turmoil: Essays on Poverty, Race and the Urban Crisis* (New York: Pantheon, 1975); and Fred Powledge, "The Flight from City Hall," *Harper's* 239 (November 1969): 69-86. The persistence of machine politics is described in general terms in Raymond E. Wolfinger, "Why Polticial Machines Have Not Withered Away and Other Revisionist Thoughts," *Journal of Politics* 34 (May 1972): 365-398. Specific examples of the success of machines after 1920 are found in Lyle W. Dorsett, *The Pendergast Machine* (New York: Oxford University Press, 1968); Bruce Stave, *The New Deal and the Last Hurrah: Pittsburgh Machine Politics* (Pittsburgh, 1970); Lyle W. Dorsett, *Franklin D. Roosevelt and the City Bosses* (Port Washington, New York: Kennikat Press, 1977); and John M. Allswang, *Bosses, Machines, and Urban Voters* (Port Washington, New York: Kennikat Press, 1977). The success of Richard J. Daley has been chronicled, although negatively, by Mike Royko, *Boss* (New York: E.P. Dutton, 1970); Len O'Connor, *Clout: Mayor Daley and His City* (Chicago: Regnery, 1975); and Milton Rakove, *Don't Make No Waves* (Bloomington: Indiana University Press, 1975).

For a discussion of black politics see Edwin R. Lewison, *Black Politics in New York City* (New York: Twayne, 1974), William E. Nelson and Philip J. Meranto, *Electing Black Mayors: Political Action in the Black Community* (Columbus, Ohio: Ohio University Press, 1976); and Alex Poinsett, *Black Power: Gary Style* (Chicago: Johnson, 1970).

The persistence of ethnicity in politics is detailed in Raymond E. Wolfinger, *The Politics of Progress* (Englewood Cliffs, N.J.: Prentice-Hall, 1974); Michael Parenti, "Ethnic Politics and the Persistence of Ethnicity," *American Political Science Review* 61 (September 1967): 717-726; Harry A. Bailey, Jr. and Ellis Katz (eds.), *Ethnic Groups Politics* (Columbus, Ohio: Charles E. Merrill, 1969).

Chapter VII. Eclipse of the Central City

General studies of urban America since 1915 include Blake McKelvey, *The Emergence of Metropolitan America, 1915-1966* (New Brunswick, N.J.: Rutgers University Press, 1968); William H. Wilson, *Coming of Age: Urban America, 1915-1945* (New York: John Wiley, 1974); and Henry F. Bedford's topical approach, *Trouble Downtown: The Local Context of Twentieth Century America* (New York: Harcourt Brace Jovanovich, 1978).

The role of the federal government in urban America is described in Mark T. Gelfand, *A Nation of Cities: The Federal Government and Urban America, 1933-1965* (New York: Oxford University Press, 1975). The importance of the 1930s is seen in the 1937 report of the Urbanism Committee to the National

Resources Committee, *Our Cities: Their Role in the National Economy* (Washington, D.C.: U.S. Government Printing Office, 1937; reprint edition, New York: Arno, 1974). Daniel Elazer sees the involvement of the federal government as pre-dating the Depression and the New Deal. See his *Metropolitan Frontier: A Perspective on Change in American Society* (Morristown, N.J.: General Learning, 1973); "Urbanism and Federalism: Twin Revolutions of the Modern Era," *Publius: The Journal of Federalism* 5 (Spring 1975): 15-40; and "Urban Problems and the Federal Government: A Historical Inquiry," *Political Science Quarterly* 82 (December 1967): 505-525.

A discussion of the impact of annexation is found in Kenneth T. Jackson, "Metropolitan Government versus Suburban Autonomy," in Kenneth T. Jackson and Stanley K. Schultz (eds.), *Cities in American History* (New York: Knopf, 1972); John D. Kasarda and George V. Redfearn, "Different Patterns of City and Suburban Growth in the United States," *Journal of Urban History* 2 (November 1975): 43-66. The Advisory Commission on Intergovernmental Relations, *Trends in Metropolitan Government* (Washington, D.C., 1977) provides statistics showing the impact of annexation. Additional studies of interest include National League of Cities, *Adjusting Municipal Boundaries: Law and Practice* (Washington, D.C.: National League of Cities, 1966); Frank S. Sengstock, *Annexation: A Solution for the Metropolitan Area Problem* (Ann Arbor, Michigan, 1960); William G. Colman, *Cities, Suburbs, and States* (New York: Free Press, 1975); National Research Council, *Toward an Understanding of Metropolitan America* (New York: Canfield, 1975).

There are scores of studies dealing with the impact of federal programs on the city. Charles L. Leven and his co-authors in *Neighborhood Changes; Lessons in the Dynamics of Urban Decay* (New York: Praeger, 1976), examine the role of the FHA in hastening the decline of middle-class neighborhoods. Russell D. Murphy, *Political Entrepreneurs and Urban Poverty* (Lexington, Mass.: Heath Lexington Books, 1971) examines the impact of poverty programs on New Haven; Allan P. Sindler's anthology *Policy and Politics in America: Six Case Studies* (Boston: Little, Brown, 1973) includes Edward C. Banfield's critique of the Model Cities Program. A good, brief work on expressways is Richard O. Davies, *The Age of Asphalt: The Automobile, the Freeway, and the Condition of Metropolitan America* (Philadelphia: J. B. Lippincott, 1975).

Chapter VIII: Metropolitan Reform and Urban Development

The relationship between size of a governmental organization and its capacity to deal effectively with problems associated with urban development has been examined rather extensively from both theoretical and practical perspectives. On the theoretical side, students are urged to consider reading Robert L. Bish,

The Public Economy of Metropolitan Areas (Chicago: Markham Publishing, 1971) and Robert J. Kirk, *Economic Principles and Urban Problems* (Englewood Cliffs, N.J.: Prentice-Hall, 1974). Also of interest are John C. Bollens, *Special District Government in the United States* (Berkeley: University of California Press, 1957); Robert G. Smith, *Public Authorities, Special Districts and Local Government* (Washington, D.C.: National Association of Counties Research Foundation, 1964); and Roscoe C. Martin, *Metropolis in Transition* (Washington, D.C.: U.S. Housing and Home Finance Agency, 1963). Two reports issued by the Committee on Economic Development, cited in the bibliography for Chapter 1, present the argument for area-wide governmental reorganization in urban communities.

Studies of governmental reorganization are not numerous, especially since the number of successful reorganizations is quite small. However, students interested in the experience of area-wide reorganization efforts should read Chester W. Bain, *Annexation in Virginia: The Use of Judicial Process for Readjusting City-County Boundaries* (Charlottesville: University of Virginia Press, 1966); David A. Booth, *Metropolitics: The Nashville Consolidation* (East Lansing: Institute for Community Development, 1963); Scott Greer, *Metropolitics: A Study of Political Culture* (New York: John Wiley & Sons, 1963); H. Paul Friesma, *Metropolitan Political Structure: Intergovernmental Relations and Political Integration in the Quad Cities* (Iowa City: University of Iowa Press, 1971); Royce Hanson, *et al., Reform as Reorganization* (Baltimore: John Hopkins University Press, 1974); William C. Havard and Floyd Corty, *Rural-Urban Consolidation: The Merger of Governments in the Baton Rouge Area* (Baton Rouge: Louisiana State University Press, 1964); Brett W. Hawkins, *Nashville Metro: The Politics of City-County Consolidation* (Nashville: Vanderbilt University Press, 1966); Henry J. Schmandt, Paul C. Steinbicker, and George D. Wendel, *Metropolitan Reform in St. Louis: A Case Study* (New York: Holt, Rinehart and Winston, 1961); Herbert Simon, *Fiscal Aspects of Metropolitan Consolidation* (Berkeley: Bureau of Public Administration, 1943); Edward Sofen, *The Miami Metropolitan Experiment* (Bloomington: Indiana University Press, 1963); John D. Wenum, *Annexation as a Technique for Metropolitan Growth: The Case of Phoenix, Arizona* (Tempe: Institute of Public Administration, 1970); and Robert C. Wood, *1400 Governments* (Cambridge: Harvard University Press, 1961).

An alternative to reorganization of government has involved creation of cooperative systems and arrangements between units of government in metropolitan areas. This approach retains the number and autonomy of local governments and attempts to deal with problems associated with urban development in a variety of ways, all of which retain the fragmented and independent nature of the urban governmental system. One of the most recent studies to attach the theoretical assumptions of the metropolitan reorganization movement is Robert L. Bish and Vincent Ostrom, *Understanding Urban Government: Metropolitan Reform Reconsidered* (Washington, D.C.: American Enterprise Institute, 1973). See also William Anderson and Edward W. Weidner (eds.), *Research in Intergovernmental Relations* (Minneapolis: University of Minnesota Press, 1950-1960); George Blair, *Interjurisdictional Agreements in Southeastern Pennsylvania* (Philadelphia: Institute of State and Local Government, 1960); W. Brooke Graves, *Interlocal Cooperation: The History and Background of Inter-governmental Agreements* (Washington, D.C.: National Association of Counties Research Foundation, 1962); Royce Hanson, *Metropolitan Councils of Governments* (Washington, D.C.: Advisory Commission on Intergovernmental Relations, 1966); Matthew J. Holden, Jr., *Intergovernmental Agreements in the Cleveland Metropolitan Area* (Cleveland: Cleveland Metropolitan Services Commission, 1958); Roscoe E. Martin, *Cities and the Federal System* (New York: Atherton Press, 1965); Melvin B. Mogulof, *Governing Metropolitan Areas: A Critical Review of Councils of Governments and the Federal Government* (Washington, D.C.: The Urban Institute, 1971); U.S. Department of Agriculture, *Interlocal Governmental Cooperation: A Study of Five States* (Washington, D.C.: U.S. Government Printing Office, 1967); Nelson Wikstrom, *Council of Government: A Study of Political Incrementalism* (Chicago: Nelson, Hall, 1977); and Joseph F. Zimmerman, *Intergovernmental Service Agreements for Smaller Municipalities* (Washington, D.C.: International City Management Association, 1973).

Chapter IX. The Community Revolution in the Central Cities

Most materials on the community revolution and decentralization of urban governmental systems are case studies of experiences with decentralization or community control. However, an understanding of the intellectual and theoretical development of decentralization and community control can be found in both the Kotler and Altschuler citations in the bibliography in Chapter 1. In addition, students are encouraged to read Daniel P. Moynihan, *Maximum Feasible Misunderstanding* (New York: The Free Press, 1969) for a criticism of the social action theories which supported much of the public policy requiring citizen participation. Suzanne Keller, *The Urban Neighborhood: A Sociological Perspective* (New York: Random House, 1968) provides a good treatment of the role of the neighborhood in central cities. Finally, two books by Howard W. Hallman, *Neighborhood Government in a Metropolitan Setting* (Beverly Hills, California: Sage, 1974) and *Small and Large Together: Governing the Metropolis* (Beverly Hills, California: Sage, 1977), present well-developed arguments for decentralization of governmental arrangements in metropolitan areas.

Studies of experiments with decentralization or community control in specific settings include Eric A. Nordlinger, *Decentralizing the City: A Study of Boston's Little City Halls* (Cambridge, Mass.: The M.I.T. Press, 1972); George J. Washnis, *Municipal Decentralization and Neighborhood Resources Case Studies of Twelve Cities* (New York: Praeger, 1973); Joseph F. Zimmerman, *The Federated City: Community Control in Large Cities* (New York: St. Martin's Press, 1972); Ralph Kramer, *Participation of the Poor: Comparative Studies in the War on Poverty* (Englewood Cliffs, N.J.: Prentice-Hall, 1969); Dale Rogers Marshall, *The Politics of Participation in Poverty* (Berkeley: University of California Press, 1971); Hans B.C. Spiegel (ed.), *Citizen Participation in Urban Development*, 3 volumes (Washington, D.C.: NTL Institute of Advanced Behavioral Science, 1968); Douglas Yates, *Neighborhood Democracy: The Politics and Impacts of Decentralization* (Lexington, Mass.: D.C. Heath, 1973); and Douglas Yates and Robert K. Yin, *Street-Level Governments: Assessing Decentralization and Urban Services* (Lexington, Mass.: Heath Lexington Books, 1975).

Chapter X. Urban Development and the Challenges of Change and Survival

For an excellent overview of contemporary urban America see John S. Adams and Ronald Abler (eds.), *A Comparative Atlas of America's Great Cities* (Minneapolis: University of Minnesota Press, 1976); and the four companion volumes, edited by John S. Adams, *Contemporary Metropolitan America* (Cambridge, Mass.: Ballinger, 1976). See also John S. Adams (ed.), *Urban Policymaking and Metropolitan Dynamics* (Cambridge, Mass.: Ballinger, 1976). These volumes provide an up to date review of metropolitan America. Another recent study is William Gorham and Nathan Glazer (eds.), *The Urban Predicament* (Washington, D.C.: The Urban Institute, 1976). For some recent statistics on the growth of the Sunbelt, relative to the Northeast and Midwest, see Advisory Commission on Intergovernmental Relations, *Trends in Metropolitan Government* (Washington, D.C., 1977); and David C. Perry and Alfred J. Watkins (eds.), *The Rise of the Sunbelt Cities* (Beverly Hills, Calif.: Sage, 1978).

Two excellent articles have appeared in the winter 1975-1976 issue of *Urbanism Past and Present*. Philip M. Hauser's "Chicago—Urban Crisis Exemplar" was originally presented at the plenary session of the Midwest Sociological Society in April 1975 and is a stinging attack on the city government of Chicago. Zane L. Miller's "Urban History, Urban Crises, and Public Policy" looks at the role of scarcity and abundance in shaping urban institutions. Miller develops this thesis more fully in "Scarcity, Abundance, and American Urban History," *Journal of Urban History* 4 (February 1978): 131-155.

Name Index

Subject Index

234

About the authors

Peter R. Gluck was born in the Bronx, New York, and studied at Hobart College (B.A.) and the State University of New York at Buffalo (M.A., Ph.D.). He is a professor of political science and urban studies at the University of Michigan, Flint, where Richard J. Meister is a professor of history. Meister was born in Gary, Indiana, and studied at St. Joseph's College (Indiana) and the University of Notre Dame (M.A., Ph.D.).

Other New Viewpoints books
of related interest

SUBURBIA IN TRANSITION
A New York Times Book
edited by Louis H. Masotti,
Northwestern University,
and Jeffrey K. Hadden,
University of Virginia

MODERN AMERICAN CITIES
A New York Times Book
edited by Ray Ginger

METROPOLITAN COMMUNITIES:
New Forms of
Urban Sub-Communities
A New York Times Book
edited by Joseph Bensman,
City College of the
City University of New York,
and Arthur J. Vidich,
New School for Social Research

FAMILY AND KIN IN
URBAN COMMUNITIES, 1700-1930
edited by Tamara K. Hareven,
Clark University

New Viewpoints
A Division of Franklin Watts
730 Fifth Avenue
New York, New York 10019